A GRAYWOLF REDISCOVERY

The Graywolf Rediscovery Series aims to give new life
in paperback to previously out-of-print literary favorites.
We are pleased to bring these books back to a
wider readership and are grateful to all those who
have brought the titles to our attention.

Also by William Maxwell

The Outermost Dream

The Outermost Dream

ESSAYS AND REVIEWS

by William Maxwell

GRAYWOLF PRESS

"The Grand Mademoiselle," "One Creature," "Bright as a Windblown Lark," "Mr. Forster's Pageant," "The Outermost Dream of the Reverend Francis Kilvert," "Your Affectionate Son," "The Bohemian Girl," "V. S. Pritchett's Apprenticeship" (originally titled "Mr. Pritchett's Apprenticeship"), "Lord Byron's Financial Difficulties," "Mrs. Woolf" (originally published as two pieces, "Yr. V.W." and "The Habit of Recording"), "Ideas of Honor and Aristocracy," "The Duke's Child," "The Charged Imagination," "A Life," "The Whites" (originally titled "E.B.W."), "Louise Bogan's Story," and "Displaced Princes and Princesses" were originally published, in somewhat different form, in *The New Yorker*.

Grateful acknowledgment is made to the following for permission to reprint previously published material: *The New Republic:* William Maxwell's review of *A Giacometti Portrait* by James Lord, *The New Republic*, July 19, 1980. Copyright © 1980 by The New Republic, Inc. Reprinted by permission of *The New Republic*. *W. W. Norton & Company, Inc.*, and *Chatto & Windus Ltd.:* Portions of the Introduction by William Maxwell from *Four in Hand: A Quartet of Novels*, by Sylvia Townsend Warner. Introduction copyright © 1986 by William Maxwell. Copyright © 1986 by Book-of-the-Month Club. Rights outside the U.S. administered by Chatto & Windus Ltd. All rights reserved. Reprinted by permission of W. W. Norton & Company, Inc., and Chatto & Windus Ltd. *The Times Literary Supplement:* The essay "The Whites" by William Maxwell. Reprinted by permission of *The Times Literary Supplement*. *Viking Penguin Inc.* and *Chatto & Windus Ltd.:* Introduction by William Maxwell from *Letters of Sylvia Townsend Warner*, edited by William Maxwell. Copyright © 1982 by Susanna Pinney and William Maxwell, Executors of the Estate of Sylvia Townsend Warner. All rights reserved. UK rights administered by Chatto & Windus Ltd. Reprinted by permission of Viking Penguin Inc. and Chatto & Windus Ltd.

Publication of this volume is made possible in part by a grant provided by the Minnesota State Arts Board through an appropriation by the Minnesota State Legislature, and by a grant from the National Endowment for the Arts. Significant additional support has been provided by the Andrew W. Mellon Foundation, the Lila Wallace-Reader's Digest Fund, the McKnight Foundation, and other generous contributions from foundations, corporations, and individuals. To these organizations and individuals who make our work possible, we offer heartfelt thanks.

Published by Graywolf Press
2402 University Avenue, Suite 203
Saint Paul, Minnesota 55114
All rights reserved.

www.graywolfpress.org

Published in the United States of America

ISBN 1-55597-264-0

2 4 6 8 9 7 5 3 1
First Graywolf Printing, 1997

Library of Congress Catalog Card Number: 97-70220

For Edith Oliver, Alec Wilkinson,
and the Critic on the Hearth

I can never get enough of knowing about other people's lives. It is why, when I open the morning newspaper, I turn first to the obituary page, hoping for more than the end of the story. Time is no impediment to this curiosity. Or, for that matter, to feeling. Who reading Homer's account of Odysseus's homecoming is unmoved, even though it was thousands of years ago? I once saw a dramatization of Henry James's "The Sense of the Past." I don't remember the name of the playwright or what the play was called, but at the final curtain the hero was weeping at the grave of the young woman he was in love with, who died a hundred and fifty years before he was born. The fact that it was impossible did not make the situation less effective, dramatically.

I knew only four of the subjects in this book and in each instance the relationship was affectionate. Writing about the others, the ones I didn't know, I developed a fondness for them also. From time to time I feel a desire to reread the passage where Laurie Lee's mother is cooking pancakes. Or where Giacometti goes on painting when there is no longer any light for him to see by. Or Kilvert's nightmare, in which he dreamt that he dreamt that he murdered Mr. and Mrs. Venables and knocked the Holy Ghost down the stairs.

Sometimes, instead, I turn to the memoir or biography that the essay owes its being to and am interested to learn that Lord Byron, riding with Teresa Guiccioli's younger brother, was caught in a heavy rainstorm. The next day he rode again, using the same wet saddle, and that evening his gaiety gave way to chills and fever. He refused to be bled. The medical facilities of Missolonghi were inadequate, and because of the sirocco he could not be moved. He had periods of delirium, fell into a coma, and stopped breathing at six o'clock on the evening of April 14, 1824.

Samuel Butler outlived Queen Victoria by a year and died in the twentieth century, where he belonged.

Mr. Forster lived on and on to a very great age and was seen making his way along the sidewalk in London, now and then stepping aside to make room for people who weren't there. Then he too escaped into the wings. Or rather, into the bookcase, where they all are.

Books, if they don't end up on the burning pile or at the town dump, outlive those they were meant to entertain or instruct. But in time they too become superannuated. The front cover of my calf-bound 1819 fifth edition of "Childe Harold's Pilgrimage" is connected to the rest of the book by a few threads. It wasn't that way when it was given to me and I have not handled it carelessly. The damage occurred while it was sitting undisturbed on the shelf, between the Oxford edition of Byron's poems that I had in college, now also showing signs of age, and Volume One of his letters. Pasted on the inside of the loosened cover is the engraved bookplate of William Jubber Spurrier—a coat of arms, presumably his, consisting of a shield and four roweled spurs. And on one of the following blank pages, in ink that has turned brown with age, there is this note: "William Jubber Spurrier married May Oke, who was the daughter of Robert Oke, my great grandmother's brother, This book came from the library of Susan Spurrier, their daûr, who died unmarried about 1880, R.

Townsend Warner." Surely this information would not have been provided if the writer had not assumed that the book would pass from one owner to another till Kingdom Come.

In my early thirties I lived in the country with an elderly French housekeeper. When a neighbor enquired about me, she said with a shrug, "He reads, he writes. He writes, he reads." I suppose she thought it was no life for a man. Or for anybody. But it was the life for me.

With one exception, the essays in this volume are derived from books I liked very much indeed. Because half my professional life was spent in being an editor and editors work close to the page, obsessed with whether or not the writer has said what he meant to say, when I read for my own enjoyment I cannot—or mostly do not—read authors whose way of writing doesn't give me pleasure. But of course style is not in itself enough. One wants blowing through it at all times the breath, the pure astonishment of life.

The merit of the writers under consideration here has been determined. But like the dead, literary efforts live in our remembrance of them.

WILLIAM MAXWELL

June 1997

NOTE

In the summer of 1948, chance deposited my wife and me in the bleachers of a tiny one-ring circus playing under a tent on the outskirts of Florence. As the afternoon wore on, the equestrienne's little girl performed on the tightwire for the first time, while her mother and the roustabouts looked on anxiously. The roustabouts shed their grey coveralls in order to juggle hoops and ninepins or hang head-down from the flying trapeze. The lions had diarrhea. Because it was so clearly a family affair and the performers made up for the absence of numbers by the variety of their talents, it reminded me of the *New Yorker* office, where from the beginning people did more than the thing they were hired to do. John Mosher read unsolicited manuscripts and covered the movies. Philip Hamburger wrote Profiles and for a season was the music critic. Several cartoonists owed their immortality to the fact that E. B. White had recaptioned a drawing that was about to be returned to them. And there wasn't anything that Wolcott Gibbs couldn't or didn't do. Edith Oliver doubled as critic for off-Broadway theater and as book editor, and from time to time would say to me, "I have a book that I think might interest you." Looking the gift horse in the mouth (lead reviews were well paid), I would say "Can I see it?"—for I led a double life too. Three days a week I was a fiction editor and the other four days I was a novelist and worked at home. I enjoyed reading manuscripts because there was always the possibility that a first-rate story would turn up in the morning mail, but I felt no inclination to read, let alone write about, a book that didn't appeal to me. Her instinct for what I couldn't say no to was all but infallible.

Reading is rapture (or if it isn't, I put the book down meaning to go on with it later, and escape out the side door). A felicitously turned sentence can induce it. Or a description. Or unexpected behavior. Or ordinary behavior raised to the nth degree. Or intolerable suspense, as with the second half of Conrad's *Victory*. Or the forward movement of prose that is bent only on saying what the writer has to say. Or dialogue that carries with it the unconscious flowering of character. Or, sometimes, a fact.

I was never asked to deal with a work of fiction and if I had been I would have said no. Too much of a busman's holiday. Also, after you have said whether it does or does not have the breath of life, what standards are you going to invoke when confronted with a thing that, like a caterpillar, consumes whatever is at hand? A long narrative requires impersonation, hallucinating when you don't know the answer, turning water into wine, making a silk purse out of a string of colored scarves and extracting a white rabbit from a sow's ear, knowing how and when to hold the carrot in front of the donkey's nose, and sublime confidence. "The house was full of that poetic atmosphere of dullness and silence which always accompanies the presence of an engaged couple." That sort of thing will keep any reader from escaping out the side door. But diaries, memoirs, published correspondence, biography and autobiography—which are what I was asked to consider—do not spring from prestidigitation or require a long apprenticeship. They tell what happened—what people said and did and wore and ate and hoped for and were afraid of, and in detail after often unimaginable detail they refresh our idea of existence and hold oblivion at arm's length. Looked at broadly, what happened always has meaning, pattern, form, and authenticity. One can classify, analyze, arrange in the order of importance, and judge any or all of these things, or one can simply stand back and view the whole with wonder.

Contents

The Outermost Dream

The Outermost Dream of the
Reverend Francis Kilvert

In 1937, the English poet William Plomer was asked if he would look at an old diary. The diarist was a young English clergyman who spent a large part of his adult life serving as curate in a quiet but very agreeable village in the Welsh Border region. The diary was closely written, in a sloping, angular hand, and consisted of twenty-two notebooks variously shaped and bound. The period covered by them was 1870–79. Embedded in those notebooks were the following two entries. "I thought I was not going to care for anyone again. I wonder if there is any receipt for hardening the heart and making it less impressible," and "Why do I keep this voluminous journal? I can hardly tell. Partly because life appears to me such a curious and wonderful thing that it almost seems a pity that even such a humble and uneventful life as mine should pass altogether away without some such record as this." The diarist's name was Francis Kilvert, and happily for him he did not succeed in hardening his impressible heart. The day-by-day record he kept is not all of equal interest; it is not above silliness; it contains sentiments that are not now acceptable (some are even shocking) and a good many "literary" descriptions that don't come off. But these are minor flaws, no journal is without them, and so long as English diaries are read, it is unlikely that Kilvert's humble and uneventful life will pass altogether away.

There was more material than could be printed all at once, and Mr. Plomer felt, I am sure correctly, that there was no reason to print some of it at all. His selections from the diary* were published in England in three volumes between 1938 and 1940. An abridged edition, in one volume, was published in the United States and had an immediate success, but, like all abridgments, it gave a somewhat incorrect impression of the original.

Kilvert was born in 1840, of a good family. His father was the rector of a country parish in Wiltshire. The diarist was the second child, and had one brother and four sisters. He went up to Oxford, was ordained, and after serving briefly as his father's curate he became curate to Richard Lister Venables, the vicar of Clyro, in Radnorshire. Kilvert boarded comfortably with a Mrs. Chaloner, whose house was directly across the road from the village pub, and his life in Clyro went by in, roughly speaking, this fashion:

On Sunday he preached, when and where he was needed—at Clyro Church in the morning, at this or that nearby village chapel in the afternoon. He paid sick calls on elderly parishioners and read to them from the Bible. He dined rather often at the vicarage. And he seldom had time on Sunday to write in his diary.

On Monday he went to the school, where, as he taught the children reading, he was struck by the appearance of Gypsy Lizzie ("the dark soft curls parting back from the pure white transparent brow, the exquisite little mouth and pearly tiny teeth, the pure straight delicate features, the long dark fringes and white eyelids that droop over and curtain her eyes when they are cast down or bent upon her book"). In the afternoon he drove, with Mr. and Mrs. Venables, to the Hardwick Bazaar for

---

*Kilvert's Diary, edited by William Plomer. Jonathan Cape, 1941, 1960.

the Home Missions. Or, the weather being particularly beautiful and there being no invitations, he walked to Broad Meadow to see old David Price, who was in bed and weaker than when he saw him last, and poor Captain Brown, who was "lying on a sofa covered up with a rug and suffering a good deal. But he was very bright and lively and grew animated and indignant in discussing the wrongs of the Navy, the misdoings of the present Government. . . ."

On Tuesday he went to see Edward Evans, who was ill with a cold and sitting before the fire. Finding that Evans and his wife had no blankets, but only sheets and a coverlet, Kilvert was able, because of the surplus Communion Alms, to give him an order for a pair. Coming back, he made two more calls. No one was at home at Pant-y-ci, so he stuck a cowslip in the latch hole by way of leaving a card, and went on to Crowther's Pool. The red round moon was hanging over Clifford Hill. Owls were hooting in the dusk, and across the valley he heard the Volunteers band in Hay rehearsing for a concert that night.

On Wednesday he sat writing a sermon, with the windows open to the laburnum and horse chestnuts. And was interrupted when a note from David Vaughan was brought to him. Learning that Vaughan's son had delivered the note and was waiting outside, Kilvert asked him in and gave him some beer. A mistake. The cat had got the visitor's tongue, and he sat perfectly still with the tumbler of beer in his hand, looking at nothing. Kilvert could not conceive why he did not drink the beer. Then he thought his guest was ill. At last, the young man faced around in his chair and said solemnly, "My best respects to you, sir," after which he drank some beer and fell into another stony silence. At noon, Kilvert got out his old Swiss haversack, crammed night necessaries into it, made a brown-paper parcel of his dress coat, and, with the pack slung over his shoulders, went by the fields to Hay to catch the 1:50 train, for he was spending the night at Whitney Rectory. Having paid his respects to the family and watched young Elwes shoot a starling on the wing and miss a sandpiper, he went up the meadow to call on Mr. Dewing, who had recently lost his wife, and who saw Kilvert coming across the fields and left a message with a servant asking him to wait. The lilies of the valley that were planted by Miss Dew close by the front door to welcome the young bride are now, less than a year later, just coming up. Her portrait is on the dining-room mantelpiece, and Kilvert sits in that room remembering the last time he was here, the bridecake and the wine on the table, and the young woman, so early dead, not twenty-three, sitting in the window looking so well, so radiant and happy. He reflects that to her poor bereaved husband, after a short gleam of happiness, all must seem like a dream. He examines the two cases of stuffed birds, and waits and waits, and finally goes out into the garden, and presently sees Miss Dew in her black dress coming slowly up the green meadow.

On Thursday he "woke at 3 A.M. and looked out Eastwards. The sky clear as crystal and cloudless. The sun had not yet risen, yet the birds were singing loud and clear. . . . The bells ringing again at intervals today [Mrs. Venables had been brought to bed of a nice little girl two days before]. The great white clematis now in full bloom so sweet in the morning fresh air." Or it is a week later, and the falling white blossoms of the clematis drift in at the open window, and in the garden there are red roses. Or it is still Thursday, and not June but October. All the glass is smashed out of the window of the low loft in Edward Evans' cabin, there is only a cloth to keep out the rain, and it is so dark that Kilvert cannot see the old man's face or him but only hears a feeble voice proceeding out of the darkness: "Bless God, bless God." Or it is July, and instead of dire poverty we get a dinner party at Clifford Priory. Kilvert arrives before any of the other guests, and in the dark, cool drawing room he finds Mr. Allen, his brother Major Allen, and Major Allen's two bewitching pretty little girls, Geraldine and Edith.

The remaining guests arrive, and Kilvert takes Lucy Allen in to dinner but is forcibly separated from her and seated on the other side of the table, next to Louisa Wyatt, who talks of Switzerland. It is "a very nice pleasant dinner. No constraint, plenty of ice. Good Champagne and the first salmon I have tasted this year, a nice curry, and the Riflemen strawberries quite magnificent. Everybody in good spirits and tempers and full of talk." Out on the lawn, a sheepdog starts devastating the flower beds, and somebody proposes shooting him with a bow and arrow. The evening is exquisite, and they wander out into the garden, under the bright moon, which shines alone in an unclouded sky. When the party reassembles in the drawing room, there is music. Mrs. Allen asks Kilvert to a croquet party here next Tuesday, and he is invited to luncheon at Oakfield on Monday, when the Foresters are coming. In a recessed window that is flooded with moonlight, he has a long talk with Fair Helen of Troy from Hardwick Vicarage. Out in the room, the conversation is about old times, other moonlight nights, the night of the Great Meteor. And, riding home in the Allens' antiquated, most comfortable yellow chariot, they have before them, going uphill, the antiquated form of the coachman against the sky and amongst the stars.

On Friday there is a funeral—Palmer the mason's little boy Benjamin, fourteen months old. In the evening the Volunteers march past, the band playing and the drum shaking his windows.

On Saturday (now it is February) he goes out early into the dim, dark morning. The air is warm, sweet, and fragrant. There is a promise of rain, and the garden trees are all in a charm with the singing of birds. An iron east wind; bitter, piercing cold (it is now a different February). He walks to Hay and buys galoshes, calls at the Castle, and while he is there, the four Miss Llanthomases come in. He hears of Mary Bevan's misadventures in going to the Hereford Hunt Ball, and that large masses of ice, three and four inches thick, have been floating down the

Wye. Now it is June again, and he pays sick calls, and on the way home he hears the voices of wood gatherers coming up out of the ravine, and three men are dragging a long, dark punt up on the riverbank—salmon fishers, netting the river for salmon. He keeps his sitting-room windows open till very late, and is delighted to hear Teddy Evans proposing to some other children that they play the old game of fox-a-dandy. They choose dens, and begin running and catching each other, and then he hears Teddy Evans singing:

> "My mother said that I never should
> Play with the gypsies in the wood. . . ."

Sunday morning is most brilliant, and Kilvert walks to church, the road sparkles with millions of rainbows, the seven colors gleaming in every glittering point of the hoarfrost. Mr. Venables preaches, and in the afternoon Kilvert goes to Bettws.

So, for seven years, his days proceeded.

It was a rich, happy life, full of interest, full of affection, but it wasn't the life he had planned for himself. Or, rather, it was the preface to it. His real life would begin when a suitable living was conferred upon him, and he became, like Mr. Venables, the pastor of a flock. Meanwhile, he went to London, he went to Bath, he went home to stay with friends in Cornwall. He found that he had a serious attachment for Daisy Thomas, and, walking back and forth on the vicarage lawn, he had a long talk with Mr. Venables about what he should do. In the afternoon, having ascertained that Mr. Thomas had returned from Brecon by the 2:06 train, Kilvert started off for Llanthomas on foot. The whole family was at home and came into the drawing room to see him, and how was he to get Mr. Thomas away for a private talk? Daisy came into the room and Kilvert thought she colored and looked conscious. He handed her the basket she had lent him to take some grapes to Alice Davies, and gave her Alice's message of thanks. Mr. Thomas said suddenly, "Come out into the garden." When they were outside, Kilvert said, "You will be very much surprised but I hope not displeased at what I am going to say to you." Mr. Thomas guessed, and his guess was wide of the mark. Kilvert was silent a minute and frightfully nervous. Just as he said "I am attached to one of your daughters," they came suddenly round the corner upon a gardener cutting the hedge. Kilvert was much relieved to learn that the gardener was deaf. Mr. Thomas said that Kilvert had done quite right in coming to him; he also seemed a good deal taken aback. He said many complimentary things about Kilvert's honorable, high-minded conduct, asked what his prospects were, and shook his head over them. He said he could not allow an engagement under the circumstances, and that Kilvert must not destroy his daughter's peace of mind by speaking to her or showing in any way that he was attached to her, but he did not forbid Kilvert the house.

No more willing than most Victorian fathers to part with a daughter, Mr. Thomas waited ten days, and then a letter came from him, "kindly expressed and cordial, but bidding me give up all thoughts and hopes of Daisy." She was a charming girl, and perhaps in love with Kilvert. She never married. Kilvert's disappointment was great, but it did not keep him from performing his duties or from enjoying himself. He loved social occasions. The diary is full of wonderful midnight suppers, balls, skating parties, excursions, picnics, carriage rides, sea bathing. As a kind of counterweight to all this, we have those visits to the old and the sick and the dying. When there is a tragedy, he is told about it, because he is a minister. And because he is a minister, what he is told about the tragedy is everything. Though the people themselves have been dead so long, their misery— the misery of Mary Meredith, whom Juggy Price's son got with child, and who left the house in the night and was seen by people who were abroad very early in the morning, and a fortnight later a flood cast her body up near Whitney Court; of Mrs. Prosser of the Swan, a young, pretty woman dying of consumption, which she caught of her sister, Mrs. Hope of the Rose and Crown in Hay; of John Watkins, who suffered from despondency and remorse, and staggered round and round his house whirling his head about like a polar bear; of old William Jones, so sturdy and upright and independent all his life, but now helpless and infirm and put upon the parish, which he could not bear, and therefore he shut himself in the barn with a razor—is here, intact, plain to the mind's eye, and perfectly terrible.

The image of Daisy Thomas gave way to other images—in fact, to a continual succession of them. On a train journey, Kilvert was all but seduced by a beautiful young woman whom he calls Irish Mary. Meeting sweet Florence Hill as he was walking by the almshouses, he stood by the roadside holding her hand ("lost to all else and conscious only of her presence, I was in heaven already, or if still on earth in the body, the flights of golden stairs sloped to my feet and one of the angels had come down to me. Florence, Florence Hill, my darling, my darling. It was well nigh all I could say in my emotion. With one long lingering loving look and clasp of the hand we parted and I saw her no more"). Mrs. Meredith Brown had to forbid him to correspond or exchange verses with her daughter Etty.

Taking this or that or the other beautiful child on his lap, he kisses her and says, "Do you love me?" Because it is the reign of Queen Victoria, it is easy indeed for him to deceive himself about the nature of his feelings, but he only partly does so. From time to time, he lays aside his self-deception in a way that commands our respect and astonishment. Now and then, a parent is also undeceived, but generally what we have in Clyro is a condition of impenetrable innocence.

Kilvert was a tender, warmhearted man completely hedged in by his occupation, his circumstances, and the hypocritical age he lived in. He was also enough of a materialist and a snob that it seems simply not to have occurred to him that among all those beautiful young girls who followed him with their eyes as if he were a star he could choose one who had no money or who was socially beneath him. Perhaps I do him an injustice; he may not have been able to afford even this. At all events, on Sunday he preached at Bettws on the Conversion of St. Paul, with some satisfaction to himself. On Monday he met an urchin three feet high swinging on a gate, and said, "Well, and how are you?" "Pretty well," shouted the urchin, "and how's yourself?" On Tuesday the Penny Reading went off admirably; a crowded room, nearly two hundred and fifty people. On Wednesday there was a waterspout, and the brook burst its banks, and houses were flooded, and at Lower Cabalva a thick deposit of yellow mud was left upon the carpets. On Thursday he found Amy Evans in the playground after school and gave her a token, putting the blue ribbon round her neck and bidding her never part with it as long as she lived. On Friday the mountains "flushed red and purple, then faded into dark cold clear blue. The clerk who was like everyone else working in his garden this evening said he feared thunder." On Saturday "banging of guns, rabbit shooting at Wye Cliff. Then the Radnorshire postman coming from Llowes blew his horn. I set out for Pwlldwrgi to get some wild snowdrops along the river side by the Otter's Pool for Mrs. Venables." And so on and so on until, in 1872, Mr. Venables gave up the benefice, and Kilvert resigned his curacy and went back to Wiltshire to help his father, who was well along in years. Shortly after he came home, he had a dream that is so remarkable it deserves to be quoted in full:

> Last night I had a strange and horrible dream. It was one of those curious things, a dream within a dream, like a picture

within a picture. I dreamt that I dreamt that Mr. and Mrs. Venables tried to murder me. We were all together in a small room and they were both trying to poison me, but I was aware of their intention and baffled them repeatedly. At length, Mr. Venables put me off my guard, came round fondling me, and suddenly clapped his hand on my neck behind and said, "It's of no use, Mr. Kilvert. You're done for."

I felt the poison beginning to work and burn in my neck. I knew it was all over and started up in fury and despair. I flew at him savagely. The scene suddenly changed to the organ loft in Hardenhuish Church. Mr. Venables, seeing me coming at him, burst out at the door. Close outside the door was standing the Holy Ghost. He knocked him down from the top to the bottom of the stairs, rolling over head over heels, rushed downstairs himself, mounted his horse and fled away, I after him.

This dream within a dream excited me to such a state of fury, that in the outer dream I determined to murder Mr. Venables. Accordingly I lay in wait for him with a pickaxe on the Vicarage lawn at Clyro, hewed an immense and hideous hole through his head, and kicked his face till it was so horribly mutilated, crushed and disfigured as to be past recognition. Then the spirit of the dream changed. Mrs. Venables became her old natural self again. "Wasn't it enough," she said, looking at me reproachfully, "that you should have hewed that hole through his head, but you must go and kick his face so that I don't know him again?"

At this moment, Mr. Bevan, the Vicar of Hay, came in. "Well," he said to me, "you *have* done it now. You have made a pretty mess of it."

All this time I was going about visiting the sick at Clyro and preaching in Clyro Church. But I saw that people were beginning to look shy at me and suspect me of the murder which had just been discovered. I became so wretched and conscience-stricken that I could bear my remorse no longer in secret and I went to give myself up to a policeman, who immediately took me to prison where I was kept in chains. Then the full misery of my position burst upon me and the ruin and disgrace I had brought on my family. "It will kill my father," I cried in an agony of remorse and despair.

I knew it was no dream. This at last was a reality from which I should never awake. I had awakened from many evil dreams and horrors and found them unreal, but this was a reality and horror from which I should never awake. It was all true at last. I had committed a murder. I calculated the time. I knew the Autumn Assizes were over and I could not be tried until the Spring. "The Assizes," I said, "will come on in March and I shall be hung early in April." And at the words I saw Mrs. Venables give a shudder of horror.

When I woke I was so persuaded of the reality of what I had seen and felt and done in my dreams that I felt for the handcuffs on my wrists and could not believe I was in bed at home till I heard the old clock on the stairs warn and then strike five.

Nothing now seems to me so real as that dream was, and it seems to me as I might wake up at any moment and find everything shadowy, fleeting and unreal. I feel as if life is a dream from which at any moment I may awake.

Though it could well be that the double dream contains, as dreams often do, its own interpretation, and that the agonized "It will kill my father" should be taken two ways, Mr. Venables being a stand-in for the elder Kilvert, what is interesting, really, is not what the dream means but that a nightmare so Dostoyevskian should have come out of the sleeping mind of a man who was genuinely kind and good and who had, so far as we know, no impulse toward violence whatever. He seems never to have experienced anything but kindness from Mr. and Mrs. Venables, and his relations with his father and mother were equally affectionate.

The inner and the outer dream might as well all be one, but what about that strange awakening, when he felt for the handcuffs on his wrists? From this distance, more than a hundred years now, what is the sound of the clock on the stairs but still another dream that he took just a little longer to waken from?

Relations between the squire and Kilvert's father were strained, and when it began to seem not unlikely that the latter would be dispossessed, Kilvert accepted the living of St. Harmons, in Radnorshire. A year and a half later, he became the vicar of Bredwardine, in Herefordshire. Of these very quiet places he has also left an unfading picture, but the diary is much less full, because, one supposes, when he became the vicar his life was much more so. Now and again, there is a set piece that is masterly; he has not lost his hand. But also the dreaming is much nearer the surface. At times he stirs; one feels he is on the point of waking. "As I came home across Starveall Mead last night from visiting at the cottages, I had a curious attack of giddiness and weakness. My head felt dull and heavy and I could scarcely hold it up, my footsteps wavered and I could scarcely guide my feet aright. It was as if I were light in the head, or had taken too much wine. I could account for the feeling by remembering that I had been on foot all day and had not taken much food. . . . I read prayers morning and afternoon and my father preached for me in the morning from Acts on Peter and Cornelius and in the afternoon on the adoration of the Shepherds and the Wise Men. Holy Communion, 8 Guests. Alms 11/6. The church was fearfully overheated. I felt quite faint and could hardly draw breath or finish reading the Service."

But then he sinks deeper into sleep and the dream goes on as before:

> After luncheon the archers went out to shoot at a beautiful archery ground by the riverside. The ladies sat watching under the trees while the arrows flashed past with a whistling rush,

and the glorious afternoon sun shone mellow upon the beeches. . . . The ground was still wet and shining with the rain, and the gigantic shadow of the gate projected by the moonlight was cast far up the avenue in huge bars upon the shining ground. . . . The broad, shining reaches of the river winding down between rocks and woods, gentle rushing everlasting murmur of the water, the sharp clicking of the reels, the low voices of the men as they sat a little way off on the bank, the Colonel in grey standing out on the rocks like a heron fishing and Charlie standing like another heron up the next broad bend of the stream, while a stranger sat on the opposite bank watching us across the river. . . . The country was wrapped in one vast winding sheet of snow, the roads were dumb, and there was no sound but the swift sharp rustle of the driving snow in the hedges and hollies. . . . The old grey manor house and the Church Tower stood framed as in a picture by the golden elms. It was a beautiful pastoral scene, calm and peaceful. Suddenly someone began playing a beautiful air upon a horn in front of Langley House. The soft clear notes floated across the meadows exquisitely sweet till some barbarian stopped the player rudely in the midst of the lovely air. I could have cried with vexation. . . . Last night again there was a considerable fall of snow and the earth was white till noon. Amid the wastes of snow and the whistling blasts of the winter winds the blackbirds and thrushes were singing undaunted. Surely the birds must have great faith. . . . As I came down from the hill into the valley across the golden meadows and along the flower scented hedges a great wave of emotion and happiness rose up within me. . . .

In June of 1878, Kilvert was offered the chaplaincy at Cannes and refused it. The diary ends the following March; why, we do not know. It may have been—it very likely was—continued past this point. That same spring, Kilvert met in Paris an Englishwoman named Elizabeth Anne Roland. They were married in August, and went to spend their honeymoon in Scotland.

Five weeks later, quite suddenly, the threads that bound him to the outermost dream gave way.

In a preface to the 1960 edition, Mr. Plomer says that only three small fractions of Kilvert's manuscript now survive; oddly, he does not say what happened to the rest. In the manuscript as he first saw it, there were excisions. He presumes they were made by Mrs. Kilvert, and that it was she who destroyed, along with those passages that she considered too intimate, all references to herself. In any case, the moments just before Kilvert's awakening are not known to us as he experienced them. Certain facts are known: Francis Kilvert died on the twenty-third of September, 1879. The attending physician has certified that he was suffering from a perforation of the intestine, that he survived longer than he was expected to, and that he was perfectly sensible until thirty seconds before his death. He was buried in the churchyard at Bredwardine, amid universal mourning. Mr. Venables read the burial service, and while the church bells tolled, a procession of children, walking two by two, dropped bouquets of flowers into the open grave.

Mr. Forster's Pageant

E. M. Forster's *Alexandria** owes its existence partly to accident;
during the First World War Mr. Forster volunteered for service
in the Red Cross and was stationed in Alexandria, and he spent
three years visiting hospitals, collecting information, and writing
reports. He was in his late thirties, and had already published
Howards End. The city made an impression on him, and he
determined to write about it. "A guidebook suggested itself,"
he says. "I have always respected guidebooks—particularly the
earlier Baedekers and Murrays. My friends encouraged me—
English, Greek, American, French, Italian, Norwegian, Syrian,
Egyptian were then among them, for I had inserted myself a
little into Levantine life. And visions kept coming as I went
about in trams or on foot or bathed in the delicious sea. For
instance, I would multiply the height of the Fort of Kait Bey by
four and so envisage the Pharos that had once stood on the
same site. At the crossing of the two main streets I would erect
the tomb of Alexander the Great. . . ." So, writing his guidebook, he "tried to work in some history as well."

Alexandria lies on a long, narrow limestone ridge edged on
the north by the Mediterranean and on the south by a lake and

---

**Alexandria: A History and a Guide.* Anchor Books, 1961.

flat fields. Part of the city, now a peninsula, was once an island, the island of Pharos, mentioned in the *Odyssey*. Other parts were originally under the sea. Needing a seacoast capital that would link Egypt with Macedonia, Alexander saw that the site offered an excellent harbor and other advantages. He gave orders for the creation of a metropolis, was deified in the course of a visit to the temple of Zeus Ammon, in the nearby Oasis of Siwan, and hurried off to conquer Persia. After his death, Egypt fell to one of his generals, Ptolemy Soter, whose descendants ruled for nine generations, and in upper Egypt were Pharaohs and in Alexandria were Greeks.

The famous lighthouse was built in the reign of the second Ptolemy. It was at least four, and possibly five, hundred feet high. The bottom story was square and contained some three hundred rooms, where mechanics and attendants were housed, as well as the beginning of the spiral ascent. The second story was octagonal, the third was circular, the fourth contained the lantern. How this worked is not known. Mr. Forster suggests two possibilities: the "mirror" of contemporary accounts may have been a polished steel reflector, for the fire at night and heliographic signals by day, or it may have been that the Alexandrian mathematicians had discovered the lens, and their discovery was lost and forgotten when the lantern fell, about the year 700. An earthquake in the fourteenth century finished off the rest of the marvel.

Ptolemy II married his sister, in imitation of the god Osiris, and so did most of his successors. Under their patronage, art, literature, scholarship, mathematics, astronomy, geography, and medicine flourished. The artists and men of letters tended toward the decorative and the pedantic; the scientists were more serious, and their discoveries and accomplishments are of the first order. The dynasty came to an end with Cleopatra VI (see Plutarch, Shakespeare, and obelisk in Central Park), and Egypt became a Roman province. There is a tradition that Christianity was introduced into Alexandria by St. Mark. The followers of the new sect were not, in the opinion of the Emperor Hadrian, well behaved. Their refusal to worship the emperors resulted in mass martyrdom under Diocletian. With the conversion of Constantine, the Christians captured the machinery of state and promptly turned it against one another. In the fourth century, the disputations of the early Church Fathers gave way to the rule of the monks who had gathered in formidable communities outside the city and made periodic raids on it. They had, Mr. Forster says, "some knowledge of theology and of decorative craft, but they were averse to culture and incapable of thought." It was they (and not the Arabs, as is commonly believed) who burned the famous library. They believed bathing was sinful, and introduced racism into a city that had happily been free from it, but they were not against reading; the disaster was incidental. The Patriarch Theophilus led a mob against the temple of Serapis, and the books, arranged in the cloisters that surrounded the temple, were destroyed with it. Thanks to this particular moment of bigotry, we have seven out of the, roughly, hundred and twenty plays of Sophocles.

In 639 the Saracen general Amr, with an army of four thousand horsemen, crossed the border into Egypt and pursued the imperial army down the Nile to Alexandria, and after a siege of twelve months the Patriarch Cyrus signed an armistice. Protected by its superb walls and by the sea, the city ought not to have fallen to a cavalry force. "Indeed it is not easy to see why Alexandria did fall," Mr. Forster says. "There was no physical reason for it. One is almost driven to say that she fell because she had no soul. . . . The following year Amr entered in triumph through the Gate of the Sun that closed the eastern end of the Canopic Way. Little had been ruined so far. Colonnades of marble stretched before him, the Tomb of Alexander rose to his left, the Pharos to his right. His sensitive and generous soul may have been moved, but the message he sent to the Caliph in

Arabia is sufficiently prosaic. 'I have taken,' he writes, 'a City of which I can only say that it contains 4,000 palaces, 4,000 baths, 400 theatres, 1,200 greengrocers, and 40,000 Jews.' And the Caliph received the news with equal calm, merely rewarding the messenger with a meal of bread and oil and a few dates. There was nothing studied in this indifference. The Arabs could not realise the value of their prize. They knew that Allah had given them a large and strong city. They could not know that there was no other like it in the world, that the science of Greece had planned it, that it had been the intellectual birthplace of Christianity. Legends of a dim Alexander, a dimmer Cleopatra, might move in their minds, but they had not the historical sense, they could never realise what had happened on this spot nor how inevitably the city of the double harbor should have arisen between the lake and the sea. And so though they had no intention of destroying her, they destroyed her, as a child might a watch. She never functioned again for over 1,000 years."

It took another conqueror—French, this time—to bring the city back to life. The modern Alexandria dates from Napoleon's campaign in Egypt but is largely the work of Mahomet Ali, the founder of the most recent reigning house of Egypt, who was an Albanian, born in Macedonia, and began his career as a tax collector. It was he who presented us with the obelisk. His city doesn't compare favorably with the city of Alexander the Great, Mr. Forster admits. "On the other hand, it is no worse than most nineteenth-century cities. . . . Material prosperity, based on cotton, onions, and eggs, seems assured, but little progress can be discerned in other directions, and neither the Pharos of Sostratus nor the Idylls of Theocritus nor the Enneads of Plotinus are likely to be rivalled in the future. Only the climate, only the north wind and the sea remain as pure as when Menelaus, the first visitor, landed upon Ras-el-Tin, three thousand years ago; and at night the constellation of Berenice's Hair still shines as brightly as when it caught the attention of Conon the astronomer."

The first half of *Alexandria* deals with the history of that city, and covers a hundred pages. The second half is planned like any guidebook, by routes, with the chief points of interest listed, with maps of tombs and catacombs, the groundwork for visits to the Greco-Roman Museum carefully laid, and the environs of the city accounted for. "The 'sights' of Alexandria," Mr. Forster says, "are in themselves not interesting, but they fascinate when we approach them through the past, and this is what I have tried to do by the double arrangement." The history is written in short sections, with, at the end of each one, references to pertinent passages in the guide, such as "Ras-el-Tin (Homer's Pharos): p. 140," or "Departure of the God Hercules: p. 104," or "Caricature of a Roman Senator as a rat: Museum, Room 13." "*On these references,*" Mr. Forster says, and the italics are his, "*the chief utility of the book depends,* so the reader is begged to take special note of them: they may help him to link the present and the past." They do. By the time I had finished Part I, I found that, pursuing references, I had read most of Part II, and many of the passages several times. The geography of Alexandria, at first confusing in spite of the maps, had become clear to me; the history took place in a place. Conversely, in reading the guide, I found myself turning back to the history. This worked so well for an armchair tourist that in the hands of a peripatetic one the book should be a godsend.

But it is characteristic of the author that, in what he insists is a merely practical undertaking, there should also be something more: "The 'History' attempts (after the fashion of a pageant) to marshal the activities of Alexandria during the two thousand two hundred and fifty years of her existence." As in most pa-

geants, there are historical and legendary persons: Caesar and
Mark Antony, Octavian, Ptolemy Philadelphus, St. Mark, St.
Catherine of Alexandria. Carrying a short sword and a shield or
a sextant or the mystic symbol of their martyrdom, they are on
the stage long enough for a tableau to form around them, and
then the whole company passes into the wings. Here is Octavian: "He is one of the most odious of the world's successful
men and to his cold mind the career of Cleopatra could appear
as nothing but a vulgar debauch. Vice, in his opinion, should
be furtive." Here, viewed rather more kindly, is the second
Ptolemy: "The closing years of his reign were divided between
his mistresses and the gout. During a respite from the latter he
looked out of his palace window on some public holiday, and
saw beneath him the natives picnicking on the sand, as they do
at the feast of Shem-el-Nessem today. They were obscure, they
were happy. 'Why can I not be like them?' sighed the old king,
and burst into tears. His reign had been imposing rather than
beautiful and had initiated little in Alexandrian civilization beyond the somewhat equivocal item of a mystic marriage. He
could endow and patronize. But, unlike Alexander, unlike his
father, he could not create. He completed what they had laid
down, and appropriated the praise." Here is Claudius Ptolemy
the geographer: "Possibly he was a connection of the late royal
family, but nothing is known of his life. His fame has outshone
Eratosthenes', and no doubt he was more learned, for more facts
were at his disposal. Yet we can trace in him the decline of the
scientific spirit. Observe his Map of the World (p. 43). At first
sight it is superior to the Eratosthenes Map. The Caspian Sea
is corrected, new countries—e.g. China—are inserted, and there
are (in the original) many more names. But there is one significant mistake. He has prolonged Africa into an imaginary continent and joined it up to China. It was a mere flight of his
fancy: he even scattered this continent with towns and rivers.
No one corrected the mistake and for hundreds of years it was

believed that the Indian Ocean was land bound. The age of enquiry was over, and the age of authority had begun, and it is worth noting that the decline of science at Alexandria exactly coincides with the rise of Christianity.''

As in most pageants, there are changes of scenery. The Heptastadion, the dike that connected the island of Pharos with the mainland, silts up and becomes a neck of land; the great library is sacked; the lighthouse crumbles and is replaced by a fort; the Canopic mouth of the Nile fills up, and Alexandria is isolated from the rest of Egypt; where there were buildings, a palace, a temple, there is merely the base of a column down among the rocks; where there were triremes there is Lord Nelson's fleet, taking the French fleet by surprise, performing the impossible, at the Battle of the Nile; the sand advances from the east and the west, through palm groves and into streets; the ruins of the temple of Osiris stand in a field of marigolds; in the city of Alexander the Great there are minarets everywhere, and then, still later, when a building is put up in the Greek style, it is by a German, regardless of taste and expense.

The scenery of the mind also is changed, as tableau follows tableau. Paganism of a most tolerant kind, able to think of all gods as perhaps the same few deities worshiped under different names, is replaced by the rigid insistence that there is only one God, whose relation to the universe and to man poses a problem: "Was God close to man? Or was he far away? If close, how could he be infinite and eternal and omnipotent? And if far away, how could he take any interest in man, why indeed should he have troubled to create him?" The problem gives rise to three great schools of Alexandrian philosophy.

The Alexandrian Jews, Greek in spirit as well as in speech, and diverging increasingly from the conservatism of the Jews in Jerusalem, conceive of an intermediate between Jehovah and man—the Logos, or Word, the messenger, the outward expression of God's existence, who created and sustains the world.

The Neo-Platonist God has three grades. There is the One, about which nothing whatever can be said, not even that it exists, and the One, overflowing, generates the Universal Mind (that is to say, all thought of things), and, by thinking, it creates the All Soul, which is the cause of the universe we know—animals, plants, stones, all matter. And not only do all things flow from God like water from a fountain, they strive to return to him.

For the Logos of the Jews and the fountainlike, overflowing emanations of the Neo-Platonists, the Christians substituted the name and nature of Jesus Christ, and then proceeded to quarrel over it like dogs over a bone. The Gnostics said that Jesus was a man and Christ a spirit who left him at death. Orthodox Christians, in their early phase, accepted from Origen the belief that Christ had been with mankind not only at his incarnation but since the beginning of Creation, and had in all ages linked human beings with God. The Arians held that Christ was after God, of like substance but not the same substance, and made the world. The Monophysites said that Christ had one nature, that the divine in him had consumed the human. At the Council of Chalcedon, in 451, it was determined, once and for all, that he has two natures, unmixed and unchangeable, but at the same time indistinguishable and inseparable. The Monothelites said that he had two natures and one will. And the Arabs riding into the city of colonnades said, "There is no God but God, and Mohammed is the Prophet of God." They did not discuss this statement with themselves or anyone else, and neither did they attempt to bridge the gulf between the human and the divine. The whole subject was dropped.

Using Mr. Forster's phrases, I have oversimplified where he does not. The twenty-one pages he devotes to Alexandrian philosophy are one of the high points of the book, a model of compression and of clarity. They are witty and at the same time careful. The insights of Philo and of the Neo-Platonists have a certain appeal as poetry, but the fantastic controversies and the theological fantasies of Early Christianity are not very sympathetic to the twentieth-century mind. As if asked to bear more weight than they were designed to bear, words give way under the strain of such intense unreality. Every once in a while Mr. Forster says he doesn't think something *can* be explained, and then, after this initial hesitation, with the most beautiful expository virtuosity he goes on to explain it. The Ballet Russe de Monte Carlo had in its repertoire a ballet called *Union Pacific*, in which Massine, in the role of a bartender, let go with God knows how many *grandes pirouettes*. Spinning exactly like a top, he defied gravity for longer than I have ever seen it defied again. Like a top, his outlines blurred. Particular movements became a general movement. It always brought down the house. In much the same way, Mr. Forster defies the downward pull of an uncongenial incomprehensibility.

"Only through literature can the past be recovered," he says, speaking of the Fifteenth Idyll of Theocritus, "and here Theocritus, wielding the double spell of realism and of poetry, has evoked an entire city from the dead and filled its streets with men. As Praxinoe remarks of the draperies, 'Why the figures seem to stand up and to move, they're not patterns, they are alive.' " The same praise we can apply to this guidebook to Alexandria. Leaving the Murrays and Baedekers far behind, he has produced a work of literature, in the strict sense of the word. He has held back nothing. Every sentence has the particular stamp of his mind. The architecture of the book is as remarkable as the style and the content. He no doubt sweated like a dancer in producing this effortless-seeming effort, but effort is the last thing in the world one is aware of. What one *is* aware of is the rapture of reading, and it stands to reason that a book that one reads with rapture must have been written with it. How conceivably but in a state of rapture could the following sentence have got put down on paper? "Plotinus was probably born at Assiout; probably; no one could find out for certain because he was reticent about it, saying that the descent of his soul into his body had been a great misfortune, which he did not desire to discuss."

Ideas of Honor and Aristocracy

The central and quite odd thing about Karen Blixen as a writer is that she was the self-appointed representative of a social class she did not belong to and a way of life that had, in fact, ceased to exist. After the First World War the great Danish noblemen lost their land to taxes and through the new laws against the entailment of estates. The army of servants, upon which, in their great houses, their comfort and pleasure depended, was lost to the factories and the cities. The constitution was reformed, so that women and servants could vote. The political power passed to the lower and middle classes, with the Social Democrats as the ruling power. Though Karen Blixen said that being a Socialist was hardly more than fulfilling one's responsibilities to one's fellowmen, she also said, "How depressing it is to go and have tea with an old lady who has no maid to make it for her."

She was not a snob, in the ordinary sense of the word; that is to say, her snobbishness did not extend to working-class people, with whom she was always comfortable, and it was largely a dislike for the middle-class attitudes and moralizing of her mother's family. She disliked democracy not because she believed that the common people were unfit to rule but because it encouraged mediocrity, renounced all ideals that were higher than those that could be attained, and, by blurring distinctions, diminished the richness of existence. Judith Thurman says, in her solidly researched and sensible Life,* that Karen Blixen believed in a pre-industrial society, where the shared assumptions of the peasant and the aristocrat bound them together in a mutual dependence, just as the stark difference in their fates set them apart. It was a society that gave to each individual his dignity and a role to play in the divine scheme of things. The fact that this society existed almost entirely in her imagination does not make it any less compelling as a background to, and an integral part of, the narrative machinery of her tales. It must have been like a continual toothache to her that she herself, with her deeply felt and poetic concepts of aristocracy, sprang from a class that valued things according to the use they could be put to and preferred the convenient to the beautiful.

Her maternal great-grandfather was a self-made man, a shipowner who became very rich during the Napoleonic Wars. He married the daughter of a minister on the Isle of Guernsey and built a severe neoclassic mansion for her on a street in Copenhagen lined with the rococo palaces of the nobility. When his daughter Mary—Karen Blixen's grandmother—fell in love with her music teacher, he kicked the young man down the stairs and married her off to a widower almost twice her age. Regnar Westenholz, Karen Blixen's grandfather, was the son of the town clerk in Skagen. As a boy he was apprenticed to a merchant in Aalborg and worked his way up until he was a partner in a commodities firm dealing in corn. He made money hand over fist, stood for Parliament, became financial adviser to the king and, briefly, Minister of Finance.

On her father's side, Karen Blixen's ancestors were peasants until the seventeenth century, when they began accumulating land. Her grandfather Adolph Wilhelm Dinesen fought in the 1848 war between Denmark and Prussia, travelled in Italy with

*Isak Dinesen: The Life of a Storyteller. St. Martin's Press, 1982.

Hans Christian Andersen, and enlisted in the French Colonial Army. Disgusted by the fact that (the words are his, I think) "wherever the French turned up in Africa, the trees disappeared, the wells dried up, the inhabitants fled, and all that remained was the desert," he returned to Denmark, bought at public auction a run-down estate with a castle on it, and proceeded by good management to make it profitable. He married the daughter of a general, and they had two sons and six daughters. His wife's sister married Count Krag-Juel-Vind-Frijs, the greatest landowner and first nobleman of Denmark, and any firsthand knowledge Karen Blixen had of aristocratic behavior came to her through her acquaintance with this branch of the family.

Adolph Wilhelm Dinesen gave his name to his younger son, who became Karen Blixen's father. According to the Danish critic Georg Brandes, who knew him, Wilhelm Dinesen was an elusive, passionate, melancholy man—"a dreamer in broad daylight . . . whose being was a little loosely knit" and who was always in search of a more intense experience of his own nature. As a younger son in a country that held to the law of primogeniture, he was expected to make his own way in the world. He fought in the 1864 war between Denmark and Prussia, in which Denmark lost the provinces of Schleswig and Holstein, and again in the Franco-Prussian War. He was in Paris at the time of the Commune and wandered among the barricades adding a stone to each one as a symbolic gesture. In imitation of Chateaubriand, he spent three years in the wilds of Nebraska and Wisconsin, hunting and fishing and consorting with Pawnee and Chippewa Indians. Their code of honor, their bravery, their reserve, their knowledge of animals and of the wilderness around them all appealed to his romantic imagination. In Constantinople he bought a slave girl for a day, took her to a French dressmaker, and then drove around the city with her in a landau. He had an affair with a diva at the Paris Opéra. In 1879 he returned to Denmark and bought an old house, Rungstedlund,

on a large tract of coastal land fifteen miles north of Copenhagen, and, at the age of thirty-five, looked around for a wife.

What his marriage to Ingeborg Westenholz might have been
like if his mother-in-law had not interfered quite so much there
is no way of knowing. She meddled in the courtship, and as
soon as the honeymoon was over she left her house in Jutland
and settled down in a house nearby with her two unmarried
daughters and began to oversee Ingeborg's affairs. When the first
child—a girl—was born, the women of the Westenholz family
closed round the cradle. Wilhelm, feeling pushed aside, picked
up his rifle and went hunting. The next child was also a girl,
whom they named Karen, and he saw to it that she was his.
When she was still very small she became the companion of his
walks. He taught her to be observant, to recognize the wild-
flowers and the bird songs, and to delight in her senses. He told
her stories about the Indians. He gave her a feeling for masculine
pleasures.

As an adult she would not say much about her intimacy
with her father, but one of the stories in *Winter's Tales*—
"Alkmene"—has many signs of being in essence autobiography.
It is about the friendship and love of a little girl and a young
man, who is the narrator. "The chief feature of our relations,"
he remarks, "was a deep, silent understanding of which the
others could not know. We seemed, both of us, to be aware
that we were like one another, in a world different from us.
Later on I have explained the matter to myself by the assumption that we were, amongst the people of our surroundings, the
only two persons of noble blood. . . ."

The family was enlarged by a third daughter and two sons,
but Wilhelm stood by his choice. He was away from home a
great deal—at shooting parties on the great estates, or travelling.
He got himself elected to Parliament and during the week he
lived in a flat in Copenhagen. Behind the closed door of his
study he wrote two books: *From a Sojourn in the United States*

and (under the pseudonym Boganis, the Indians' name for him) *Letters from the Hunt*, now considered to be a minor classic of Danish literature. In this book, Miss Thurman says, great gestures recur over and over. Something impossible is yearned for and realized in symbolic form. A task is set involving great risk and performed as if no effort were required. A high price is demanded and a higher one casually paid. One recognizes the moral climate of Karen Blixen's stories.

She told an earlier biographer, Parmenia Migel,* that shortly before her tenth birthday something happened; something went wrong. In her father's conversations with her, "allusions to people he had known"—I am quoting from Parmenia Migel—"to an unnamed woman he had loved, reminiscences, warnings, advice, all poured out in a sort of accelerating monologue." Much of it was beyond her comprehension, and confused and frightened her. He attended a session of Parliament but left early and went home to his apartment and hanged himself from a rafter.

The children were at their grandmother's house when the news was broken to them. They were told that he was ill, then that he was dead. Later, their mother said, "You must understand, a man like Father, a soldier and an outdoorsman, could not live with the thought that he would have to continue to exist, throughout many years, as a wreck, a helpless relic of what he once was." When they were older, putting various pieces of evidence together, they concluded that the illness referred to was probably syphilis.

If orphaned children were allowed to deal with their grief in an otherwise unchanged world, they would probably, in time, extricate themselves from it naturally, because of their age. But the circumstances always *are* changed, and it is the constant

---

* *Titania*. Random House, 1967.

comparison of the way things are with the way things used to be that sometimes fixes them forever in an attitude of loss.

After the death of Wilhelm, the dominant figure in the family was old Mrs. Westenholz. Earlier in her life she had been converted to Unitarianism and she was also a passionate feminist. At her dinner table the conversation was platitudinous, the food heavy. She was widowed at thirty-four and went into permanent mourning. So wide was the black border that she decided it would be unseemly for her ever again to have a Christmas tree. In the story "Peter and Rosa"—also from *Winter's Tales*—there is a passage that could well have been written with her house in mind: "The daily life of the parsonage . . . was run with a view to the world hereafter; the idea of mortality filled the rooms. To grow up in the house was to the young people a problem and a struggle, as if fatal influences were dragging them the other way into the earth, and admonishing them to give up the vain and dangerous task of living." It was partly to escape from these deadening influences that Karen Westenholz accepted the proposal of marriage of her cousin Bror Blixen. Mrs. Westenholz was the human embodiment of one aspect of the national character; during the eighteen years that Karen Blixen lived on a coffee plantation in Africa she never went home to Denmark without falling into a depression. And as for the effect on her of her father's suicide, she once confessed to her brother Thomas that she had a frightening sense of the fragility of life, a terror of abandoning her soul to something she could lose again; that every moment of happiness she had known in Africa had been colored by a dread of its ending; that it had become a habit, an *idée fixe*, with her "to the point of calculating how much more time was left of something, even if it was only a trip to Nairobi."

Her appreciation of, and delight in, the African natives who were part of her household or who worked and camped on her farm was not unlike her father's appreciation of the American

Indians. In their complicated and indirect patterns of thought and their proud behavior she encountered the nearest approximation she was ever to find of her own ideas of honor and aristocracy.

When the First World War broke out, her husband's loyalties, like her own, were with the British. He volunteered as a noncombatant Intelligence officer and was away from the farm for considerable periods at a time. Miss Thurman says that he was, from the descriptions of his friends, "one of the most durable, congenial, promiscuous, and prodigal creatures who ever lived." By less sympathetic accounts he was totally uneducated and a boor—but a likable boor. He caught syphilis, probably from sleeping with the Masai women, and infected his wife with it. Her father's destiny had, as she herself remarked, to a great extent been repeated in her own.

She went home to Denmark for treatment. Her Danish doctor believed, mistakenly, that the disease was cured. Throughout the twenties she continued to exhibit symptoms, which were misinterpreted. When it broke out again unmistakably in the thirties, it was beyond arrest. The clinical details—I am quoting from Miss Thurman—are appalling: "The syphilitic degeneration of her spinal cord was localized in those nerves that controlled the stomach and bowels, accounting for her agonizing cramps, her gastric crises, her extreme thinness, and, at least in part, for her anorexia." Other symptoms that occurred in due time were an unsteadiness of gait, an ashen pallor, extreme facial wrinkling, and perforating ulcers. Bror had almost no syphilitic symptoms, and died in 1946 of injuries sustained in a car crash.

She went back to Africa and him. Though their relationship was not quite what it appeared to be from the outside, there was real affection on both sides. When he asked for a divorce so that he could marry a woman he had fallen in love with, she was genuinely upset and for a time put obstructions in his way. She had an eighteenth-century idea of marriage, which allowed him to go on sleeping with other women and her to take as her lover an Englishman who turned up in Nairobi in the spring of 1918—the Honourable Denys Finch Hatton, the younger son of the Earl of Winchelsea and Nottingham. Finch Hatton was tall, lean, elegant, and witty. He taught her Greek, played Stravinsky for her, and wanted her to understand modern art. Since his school days, no one had ever been immune to his charm and he was terrified of being bored, depended on, or possessed.

In 1959, during a visit to New York, she spoke at a dinner meeting of the National Institute of Arts and Letters. Her subject was "On Mottoes of My Life." In that discourse she said, "The family of Finch Hatton, of England, have on their crest the device *Je responderay*, 'I will answer.' They have had it there for a long time, I believe, since it is spelled in such antiquated French. . . . I liked this old motto so much that I asked Denys . . . if I might have it for my own. He generously made me a present of it and even had a seal cut for me, with the words carved on it. The device was meaningful and dear to me for many reasons, two in particular. The first . . . was its high evaluation of the idea of the answer in itself. For an answer is a rarer thing than is generally imagined. There are many highly intelligent people who have no answer at all in them. A conversation or a correspondence with such persons is nothing but a double monologue—you may stroke them or you may strike them, you will get no more echo from them than from a block of wood. And how, then, can you yourself go on speaking? . . . Secondly I liked the Finch Hatton device for its ethical content. I will answer *for* what I say or do; I will answer *to* the impression I make. I will be responsible."

Twice she became pregnant and miscarried. The second time she found herself pregnant she sent a cable to Finch Hatton in London in which she used a code name for the child. He cabled back, "STRONGLY URGE YOU CANCEL DANIEL'S VISIT." Her answer is missing, but he cabled again, "RECEIVED YOUR WIRE AND MY

REPLY DO AS YOU LIKE ABOUT DANIEL AS I SHOULD WELCOME HIM IF I COULD OFFER PARTNERSHIP BUT THIS IS IMPOSSIBLE STOP YOU WILL I KNOW CONSIDER YOUR MOTHER'S VIEWS DENYS." She replied, "THANKS CABLE I NEVER MEANT TO ASK ASSISTANCE CONSENT ONLY."

Not then but later, at the end of her stay in Africa, with the house dismantled and crates standing around everywhere, she and Denys Finch Hatton had a violent quarrel, possibly because he refused to marry her, possibly because he had taken up with another woman. She cut her wrists after he left the house, but managed to staunch the flow of blood. Three days later his plane crashed and he was killed.

Nothing in the second half of her life corresponded to the sweep and grandeur of her life in Africa. The crates arrived in Denmark after her and were put away in storage unopened for thirteen years. She had trouble remembering not to leave doors open: in Nairobi her house servants closed the door after her. The sea wind rattled the windows. In winter, darkness fell at three. She accused her mother, unfairly, of treating her like a child; of begrudging her money for cigarettes. She was given her father's old office on the ground floor and an attic room he had used as a study. Silence was enforced on the housemaids so that she would not be disturbed in the task she had set for herself—to write down the involuted stories that she had made up to entertain Denys Finch Hatton and that we know as *Seven Gothic Tales*.

They came within an inch of not being published at all. She offered them to the English publisher Constant Huntington. He refused to look at them and advised her to write a novel. Her brother happened to know Dorothy Canfield Fisher, who read them and found an American publisher for them, and probably was responsible for their being taken by the Book-of-the-Month

Club, since she was one of the judges. Until that moment the publisher considered that their commercial possibilities were not such as to justify an advance.

After her mother's death, in 1939, she continued to live at Rungstedlund. During the German Occupation she closed off part of the house and slept in a garret, where it was warmer and she could see from the window, on a clear day, the coast of Sweden. In the morning she came downstairs and lit the wood fires in the old ceramic or iron stoves by which the house was heated. It had no bathroom until 1960; the maids had to carry water for her bath up a flight of narrow stairs and empty it into the old tub in her dressing room. She liked to have her breakfast in the kitchen, where she could drink coffee instead of tea and listen to the conversation of the fisherwomen, the dairymaids, and the grooms.

During the early months of the war, before Denmark was occupied, a Danish newspaper agreed to send her to Berlin, Paris, and London to do articles on the warring capitals. She did get to Berlin, and had a letter of introduction to Goering. Other important Nazi officials expressed an interest in meeting her and she declined, except for Hitler; when she found he was expecting her to autograph a copy of her book for him, she avoided the interview by saying she was unwell. What she wrote about National Socialism, Miss Thurman says, was from a remote point of view that did not appear to recognize how threatening its ideas were to the rest of Europe. In the fall of 1943, the Germans, with a list of eight thousand Jews in Denmark, started to round them up, but they went into hiding and seven thousand two hundred were ferried across to Sweden by the Danish Resistance operating from houses along the Sound. She told Parmenia Migel that she gave the key to her kitchen door to two friends in the Resistance and that she "had Jews in the house and Nazis in the garden."

In 1945, at the very end of the war, Brian Urquhart, a British

Army officer who later became Under Secretary General of the United Nations, crossed the German border into Denmark. He was driving a jeep and had his batman-driver, Pvt. Mike Stannion, with him. Urquhart had an appointment on the bridge at Korsor with Halfdan Lefèvre, a senior officer of the Danish Resistance, which had already dealt with the German occupying force and was now rounding up Danes suspected of collaboration. In his autobiography* Urquhart says, "I had a list of Danes whose friends in England had lost touch with them and wanted news. When I showed this list to Dr. Lefèvre, I realized that we were on very delicate ground. . . . At the top of the list was Karen Blixen, author of *Out of Africa*, which my father-in-law, Constant Huntington, had published. Dr. Lefèvre was horrified and said she was a collaborator. I said I was convinced there was a misunderstanding. Karen Blixen was a singular and courageous woman. Her brother had been the only foreigner to win the Victoria Cross in World War I. She was an old friend of my parents-in-law. She was a remarkable writer. Dr. Lefèvre, unconvinced, strongly advised against my visiting her. I replied that I would do so anyway.

"By the time I got to Copenhagen and had seen a little of what the Danes were doing to each other, I decided that I should visit Karen Blixen right away. She lived in an old white wooden house called Rungstedlund, overlooking the Sound and across to Sweden. Stannion and I got very dirty looks when we asked the local Danes for directions, but they evidently did not wish to interfere with a British officer, and we finally drove up to the house. There was no sound of life at all. I knocked on the front door, making reassuring British sounds. Still no sign of life. We opened the door and walked through to the kitchen overlooking a lawn ringed with evergreens. There was a steaming cup of tea on the table. We went out to the lawn at the back, making

A Life at Peace and War. Harper & Row, 1987.

further encouraging British noises. Suddenly I heard Stannion give an awestruck 'Cor!', and from the evergreens stepped a figure in a black hood and cape.

"Baroness Blixen behaved as if she had just been picking mushrooms in the shrubbery, but in fact she had been hiding on the off chance that we were emissaries of the Resistance coming to get her. She was overjoyed when I explained who I was, and told us of her tribulations, which stemmed apparently from a lecture she had given in Berlin early in the war and from a misunderstanding of her latest book, *The Angelic Avengers*, which was, she said, an allegory of the German Occupation. . . . I promised to do what I could to clear things up.

"When we made ready to leave, Karen Blixen announced that she must go with us. I wasn't too happy about this. There was a strict order against taking women in military vehicles but I was mostly worried about what the Resistance might do. They had administered summary justice on lesser Danes. However, there was nothing for it but to agree, and with Stannion in the back, Sten gun at the ready, and the baroness in the front looking seigneurial, we swept into Copenhagen. We got some more dirty looks but nothing worse. That evening Karen Blixen went on Danish radio to explain all to the Danish people. In doing this she played heavily on her rescue, on higher orders, by a young British parachute officer.

"I saw her again years later in New York at the height of her fame and reminded her of this episode but she couldn't seem to recall it."

During the last fifteen years of her life, the household at Rung-stedlund consisted of the housekeeper and the housekeeper's little boy (whom she tried to appropriate), a chambermaid, a parlormaid, a gardener, the old family coachman—a survivor from her youth—and Clara Svendsen, her devoted secretary-companion, who was ill-paid and sometimes ill-treated. Karen Blixen had a bad temper, particularly when she was unwell, and if something went wrong she took it personally. Her house-keeper said, "I have never thought that she was sweet and nice all the time, or that it was always pleasant to live under her roof. She was, though, a person with stronger feelings than so many others. Therefore there were things which pained her, and when something pains you, it can well make you unreasonable. You can't blame someone for that. I know that some people criticized her for being aristocratically remote and unapproach-able, but she was in so many respects much more human than ordinary people could ever dream of being."

She was old and ill and sustained by admiration, and some-what taken in herself by what a friend who was often in her house described as a "circus act of proven witticisms and para-doxes, anecdotes and old stories," which she brought out for strangers. She could also turn her attention on a guest with such radiance that he felt he had never before been so articulate or so well understood. In general she regarded her own perfor-mance with irony.

Though another woman was now, properly speaking, the Bar-oness Blixen, she did not discourage people from addressing her by that title. Her childhood nickname, Tanne, had long since been Russianized to Tania. Intellectual young men were at-tracted to her, and she fell passionately in love with one of them—the poet Thorkild Bjornvig—and he with her. He was the third and last great love of her life. One day he read aloud to her a paragraph from Franz Werfel's *Theologumena:* "God speaks only to the oldest souls, the ones most experienced in living and suffering: 'You shall belong to no one and to nothing, to no party, to no majority, to no minority, to no society except in that it serves me at my altar. You shall not belong to your parents, not to your wife nor children, nor to your brothers and sisters, not to them who speak your language, nor those who speak any other—and least of all to thine own self. You shall belong only to *me* in this world.' " She took the book away from him, crossed out the word "God" and wrote the word "I" over it. That he did, in fact, have a wife and child was of no interest to her. When she discovered that he was having a love affair with a young woman of his own age, there was hell to pay.

Her brother Thomas loved her and had all his life been willing to do anything for her, except see her as she wished to be seen. Speaking to Miss Thurman of *Out of Africa*, he said with sardonic amusement, "Do you know the epigraph? [*"Equitare, Arcum tendere, Veritatem dicere"*: To ride, to shoot with a bow, to speak the truth.] Well, in fact, my sister couldn't ride or shoot an arrow, and she never told the truth. Her horse was unruly, and she couldn't mount it by herself. She would call her *boys* to help her, but when they couldn't hold him still, she would, on the spot, renounce riding forever, saying, 'Nobody helps me, nobody cares about me, I won't stay here. . . .' "

A friend who knew her in Africa said, "People were afraid of Tania. She was likely to do anything. You had the feeling she might suddenly shoot someone."

And *she* said, "If only people would treat me like a lunatic, it would be such a relief."

The Grand Mademoiselle

On Monday, December 15, 1670, Mme. de Sévigné wrote to her cousin Philippe-Emmanuel de Coulanges, "Now I'm going to tell you a piece of news that's most amazing, most surprising, most marvellous, most miraculous, most triumphant, most dazzling, most unheard-of, most singular, most extraordinary, most incredible, most unexpected, the biggest and the littlest, the rarest and the commonest, the most public and until today the most secret, the most brilliant, the most envy-arousing, a thing we can scarcely believe in Paris, so how could you believe it in Lyons? A thing that makes everybody cry 'Mercy!,' a thing that will take place on Sunday, when those who witness it won't believe their eyes, a thing that will take place on Sunday and will perhaps still be waiting to take place on Monday. I can't bring myself to tell it. Three guesses: do you give up? Well, then, I must tell it. Next Sunday, in the Louvre, Monsieur de Lauzun will marry—whom do you think? I'll give you four guesses, I'll give you ten, a hundred. I can hear Madame de Coulanges say: 'What's hard about that? It's Madame de La Vallière.' Not at all, Madame. 'Then it's Mademoiselle de Retz?' Not at all: you *do* live in the woods! 'Ah, how stupid of us!' you must be saying. 'It's Mademoiselle Colbert.' You're even farther from the truth. 'Then it's surely Mademoiselle de Cré-

qui.' You're still wrong. So I have no choice but to tell you:
next Sunday, in the Louvre, he is to marry, with the King's
permission, Mademoiselle, Mademoiselle de . . . Mademoiselle—guess the name! He is to marry Mademoiselle—yes, I
mean Mademoiselle, the Grand Mademoiselle, daughter of the
late Monsieur, Mademoiselle granddaughter of Henry IV,
Mademoiselle d'Eu, Mademoiselle de Dombes, Mademoiselle de
Montpensier, Mademoiselle d'Orléans, Mademoiselle the King's
first cousin, Mademoiselle destined for the throne of France,
Mademoiselle the only match worthy of Monsieur. What a subject to talk about! If you scream, if you're beside yourself, if you
say that I'm lying, that it's false, that I'm making fun of you,
that it's a joke, that it's a silly fancy, in short if you hurl insults
at me, I'll think you're right: I did the same when I heard it."

And on Friday of that same week Mme. de Sévigné wrote
again to her cousin, "What is called falling from the clouds, or
from a pinnacle, happened last night at the Tuileries. But I must
take things farther back. . . ." Louis XIV, under pressure from
the Queen, his brother, Mme. de Montespan, Condé, and various others, had broken his word, and the thing that was to have
taken place on Sunday at the Louvre perhaps took place secretly
elsewhere sometime later, as was commonly believed, or may
not have taken place at all. Mme. de Sévigné, in any case, was
not retailing second- or third-hand gossip; the woman whose
distress of mind and heart she went on to describe so vividly
was her friend, and had a few hours before called her to her,
kissed her, and showered her with her tears.

The letter is full of references that the cousins, even though
they lived in Lyons, did not need to have explained to them and
that the modern reader, unless he has a weakness for memoirs
of the French court, may. But posterity has, of course, its privileges. The princess who was referred to by her contemporaries
simply as "La Grande Mademoiselle" kept a private journal,
which it is reasonable to assume they did not know existed. A

large part of it had to be transcribed by her secretary before she could read it, so distinguished was her handwriting. The journal first appeared in print a generation after her death and three years after the first four volumes of Mme. de Sévigné's letters made their appearance. In the middle of the nineteenth century, a second version, based in part on an incomplete manuscript in the princess's own handwriting in the Bibliothèque Nationale, was published. Neither version has been translated into English. The journal adds considerably to the interest of a figure who was already, by her actions and what was known of her character, one of the most original and appealing women in French history. Around it, Francis Steegmuller has constructed a biography* that is as good on the period as it is in its treatment of its historical personages, who are, with the exception of his principal figure, nearly all of them heartless people, but also fascinating and, after three hundred years, still full of the breath of life. Among other accomplishments, he has made it possible for the reader to follow the wars of the Fronde, which were confusion incarnate. The translations of passages from Mlle. de Montpensier's journal, Mme. de Sévigné's letters, and other contemporary sources are his, and are excellent. In dealing with French material, he has managed to evoke the French attitude toward, the French manner of dealing with, human experience. In the dry, sad, haunting final section of the book, his unfortunate and very human princess reminds us of certain heroines of nineteenth-century fiction. The reader, as he follows her dignified efforts to accept what is really unacceptable, is as moved as if her life were not a matter of history but a work of art that could be put on the shelf alongside *Le Rouge et le Noir* and *Madame Bovary*.

The Grand Mademoiselle. Farrar, Straus and Cudahy, 1956.

* * *

Anne-Marie-Louise, Duchesse de Montpensier, was a Bourbon on both sides of the family. Her father was Gaston d'Orléans, the younger brother of Louis XIII and for nearly thirty years heir presumptive to the throne. When she was a few days old, she became, upon the death of her mother, whose entire dowry she inherited, the richest female in France, with an income that would be the equivalent of at least a million dollars today. Richelieu and Anne of Austria were her godparents. She was installed in her own apartments in the Tuileries, and there she grew up, under the care of an affectionate and highly permissive governess and with her own household staff, numbering about sixty ("a greater staff," she points out in her journal, "than any of my three aunts—the Queen of Spain, the Queen of England, or the Duchess of Savoy—had before marriage"). Her father was referred to simply as "Monsieur"; her mother had been "Madame," and she was "Mademoiselle." And in a self-portrait she says, "I feel that I am very bold; I am very courageous and ambitious; but since by my high birth God has limited the scope of my ambition to the very uppermost reaches, what would be overweening in another is in me mere conformity to His design." Speaking of her upbringing, again in her journal: "Children who are the object of great respect, who hear nothing spoken of except their high birth and their great wealth, usually become horribly puffed up. I myself had those things so constantly dinned into my ears that I became convinced that they were all that mattered, and the vanity I displayed at that time can scarcely have been agreeable to those around me. Eventually my reason told me that the true greatness of a highborn princess consists in going beyond such vulgar grounds for flattery. But when I was a child and anyone mentioned my grandmother Guise, I used to say: 'She's a very distant grandmother; she's not a queen.' " As for "going beyond" mere considerations of birth and wealth, Mr. Steegmuller observes that Mademoiselle never totally managed to do this; "her birth and her wealth were the underlying, if not the immediate, causes of her long spinsterhood, her exile, and her later fate. It is the extent to which she did and the extent to which, at the same time, she didn't get beyond them that make her so interesting."

To take things farther back, like Mme. de Sévigné, there was, first of all, Mademoiselle's father, whom she worshipped. Monsieur was a dangerous troublemaker. Discontented, weather-vaneish, rattlebrained, impatient to be king—the description is Mr. Steegmuller's—he was always taking part in conspiracies and the conspiracies were invariably discovered. He spent a great deal of time away from the court when Mademoiselle was a child, and she was not allowed to speak his name before the King and Queen. "He was too close to the throne," Mr. Steegmuller goes on, "to be executed for treason, too exalted ever to be punished by anything more serious than temporary banishment; but he habitually betrayed to the Cardinal [Richelieu, that is] and the Cardinal's executioners the nobles he had enlisted." And when Mademoiselle was twenty-five, he implicated her in the largest and most disastrous of these futile conspiracies, the Fronde des Princes, which in the end amounted to a civil war. She went to Orléans, then a walled city, for him, and the timid governor refused to admit her, though the duchy of Orléans belonged to her father. She then appealed for help to some of the boatmen of the Loire. They were charmed with her courage and spirit, and offered to break down one of the water gates. They made a two-boat bridge across the moat, and from the second boat raised a high ladder against the wall of a quay, which Mademoiselle climbed in the full view of hundreds. The boatmen "weakened the gate from without, loyal bourgeois helped them from within; the city guards stood by, doing nothing to help, but nothing to hinder either; and finally two planks in the Porte Brûlée gave way. There was so much dirt and debris around, and by now so much shouting and excitement, that one of Mademoiselle's footmen gathered her up in his arms and

thrust her through the breach between the iron bars." No sooner
was her head inside than the drums began to beat. In a scene
of pure grand opera, Mademoiselle took possession of the city,
and kept the governor from opening the gates to the emissaries
of the King and Cardinal Mazarin, who appeared the next day.
Later, when the war was on its last legs, she—again acting for
her father—did something that was never forgotten by the court:
she ordered the cannons on top of the Bastille, which were
turned inward toward the city to put down any insurrection
there, turned outward, instead, and loaded. At a critical moment, the cannons went off, a whole file of the royal cavalry
was mortally wounded, and the lives of a great many noble
Frondeurs were saved. She became the heroine of the hour, and
paid for it with four and a half years' exile from Paris. It may
also have cost her her one good chance of becoming Queen of
France.

When Mademoiselle was eleven years old, Anne of Austria
taught her to speak of the newly born Dauphin, her cousin, as
"mon petit mari," and Richelieu, who had other plans, gave her
a severe scolding. Though this was from her point of view the
greatest and the happiest match she could have hoped for, ex-
pectations almost as brilliant were often held out to her, and
most of her life was lived in anticipation of a suitably important
marriage—with the cardinal-infante of Spain, and, later, with
Philip IV; with Charles II of England, whose indifferent court-
ship is full of unintentional comedy; with the Holy Roman
Emperor; with the King of Hungary. For refusing to marry the
degenerate King of Portugal, she was exiled from Paris a second
time, and while she was seeking to gain Louis XIV's permission
to marry the man of her choice, she had to fend off the King's
plan to marry her to his homosexual younger brother. During
these years, Mr. Steegmuller suggests, the failure of one marriage negotiation after another disappointed only her ambitions,
never her deeper feelings, which were centered on her father.

"When she was five and a half she went to meet him at his château at Limours. He removed his distinguishing decoration, the *cordon bleu* of the order of the Saint-Esprit, to see whether without it his daughter would recognize him, for he had been in Flanders for more than a year; she picked him out at once, and flew to his arms." Five years later, after another period of banishment, she was allowed to visit him at Chambord. "Dear Papa," she wrote to him, before the visit, "I'm dying of joy at the thought of obeying the order you honor me with, and I'll leave Monday, and assure you, dear Papa, that I am your very humble daughter and servant Anne-Marie d'Orléans." Mr. Steegmuller describes their meeting: "She found him waiting for her on the famous trick staircase; when he saw her, he started down toward her; she ran up toward him; to her bewilderment, he disappeared as though by magic: the staircase was double!" It was also a symbol of their relationship, and from the moment she was old enough to inquire into his guardianship during her minority, they were at odds. His guardianship had been dishonest, and he went on to cheat and blackmail her out of a further portion of her inheritance. He repaid her tact and loyalty and devotion with unrelieved hostility and maniacal unkindness. He resented her looking after his bastard son, for whom he himself did nothing, and on his deathbed he blessed the three daughters by his second marriage but not her. She was past forty when she fell in love, for the first and only time, with the Comte de Lauzun, who was a mere nobleman, one of the four captains of the King's personal bodyguard.

That story is the center and focus of Mr. Steegmuller's book. The King gave his permission on Monday. The lovers waited, when they should have moved quickly; they allowed themselves a brief interval in which to feel their happiness, like any other engaged couple; they were diddled by Mademoiselle's lawyers. On Thursday morning, Mme. de Sévigné went to congratulate and warn her friend, who "told me word for word a conversation she had had with the King, and she seemed enraptured at the thought of making a man happy. She spoke tenderly of Lauzun's merit and gratitude. Thereupon I said, 'Heavens, Mademoiselle, I see how happy you are, but why didn't you finish the matter once and for all last Monday? Don't you know that such a great delay gives the whole kingdom time to talk, and that to prolong so extraordinary an enterprise is to tempt God and the King?' She said that I was right, but she was so full of confidence that my words made only the slightest impression."

That same evening, the King sent for her. Mr. Steegmuller continues, "On the way back to Luxembourg she gave way to hysterics; in the violence of her frenzy she shattered the windows of her coach, and although visitors waiting to see her were dismissed by tactful footmen, some of them lingered long enough to see her arrive, crying and gesticulating, her hair streaming, a tragic fury."

Lauzun did not give way to hysterics. For a time his behavior was considered exemplary, and then, little by little, it became so offensive that something had to be done about it; he spent the next nine years in a dungeon. He was an eccentric, a Gascon, like d'Artagnan, a brave and impulsive and cocky man. That he was bitterly disappointed there can be no doubt, but he did not keep a journal and we have to deduce, from his behavior during Mademoiselle's most delicate courting and afterward, what the real source of his disappointment was. It does not appear to have been love.

V. S. Pritchett's Apprenticeship

To resort to a parlor game: If Sir Victor were an instrument in a symphony orchestra, what instrument would that be? The answer is the bassoon. As a rule, it is off to one side and not in the front rows, which are hogged by the strings. It and the lyric-soprano voice seem made for each other, husband and wife, but for some reason this fact has largely gone unnoticed by composers. The bassoon cannot, even in the hands of a virtuoso, stand apart from or above what it is asked to play, like the violin, say, or the English horn, but to the ear bent on hearing it the pleasure it gives is very deep and satisfying.

The first volume of Pritchett's autobiography* begins:

> In our family, as far as we are concerned, we were born and what happened before that is myth. Go back two generations and the names and lives of our forebears vanish into the common grass. All we could get out of Mother was that her grandfather had once taken a horse to Dublin; and sometimes in my father's expansive histories, *his* grandfather had owned trawlers in Hull, but when an abashed regard for fact, uncommon in my father, touched him in his eighties, he told us that this ancestor,

*A Cab at the Door. Random House, 1968.

a decayed seaman, was last seen gutting herrings at a bench in the fish market of that city. The only certainty is that I come from a set of storytellers and moralists and that neither party cared much for the precise. The storytellers were forever changing the tale and the moralists tampering with it in order to put it in an edifying light.

What distinguishes a classic from an ordinary book is, of course, authority, and to write with *this* degree of authority you have to have a great deal to say and no hesitation about how it is to be said or about saying it.

Pritchett's mother was the daughter of a coachman and gardener and was, he says, "lively, sexy and sharp-spoken in the London way and very changeable, moody, and, in the long run, not to be trusted." His father was a Yorkshireman cut from the same cloth as Wilkins Micawber. He conned everybody in sight, including—much of the time—himself. They lived in one small, damp brick villa after another and the children learned to sit at the door and open it for him because he was affronted if he had to open it with his own key. About once a year he went bankrupt and they found themselves in a cab driving to a new house in a new part of London. Their mother would begin to cry and their father would begin to sing, in a bass voice:

> "Oh dry those tears,
>   Oh calm those fears,
>   Life will be brighter tomorrow."

He was not entirely a fraud; he had some business ability, combined with too much sense of style, and nothing less than the grandiose would satisfy him. Needless to say, his children all turned out well.

As a boy Pritchett read or read at whatever he could get his hands on. "That I understood very little of what I read did not

really matter to me. . . . I was caught by the passion for print
as an alcoholic is caught by the bottle. . . . *The Meditations of
Marcus Aurelius* in leather . . . defeated me. Wordsworth and
Milton at least wrote in short lines with wide margins. . . . I
moved to Marie Corelli and there I found a book of newspaper
articles called *Free Opinions.* The type was large. The words
were easy, rather contemptibly so. I read and then stopped in
anger. Marie Corelli had insulted me. She was against popular
education, against schools, against public libraries and said that
common people like us made the books dirty because we never
washed, and that we infected them with disease. . . . I moved
on to . . . Shakespeare's Complete Works and started at the
beginning with the *Rape of Lucrece* and the sonnets and continued slowly through the plays. . . . On the lowest shelf of my
father's bookcase were several new ornate and large volumes of
a series called *The International Library of Famous Literature.*
They were bound in red and had gold lettering. They had never
been opened and we were forbidden to touch them. I think
Father must have had the job of selling the series, on commis-
sion, at one time. I started to look at them. There were photographs of busts of Sophocles and Shakespeare. There were
photographs of Dickens, Thomas Hardy, of Sir James Barrie and
Sir Edmund Gosse in deep, starched wing collars, of Kipling
rooting like a dog at his desk and of G. K. Chesterton with his
walking stick. There was Tolstoy behind his beard. The volumes
contained long extracts from the works of these writers. I found
at once a chapter from Hardy's *Under the Greenwood Tree,* and
discovered a lasting taste for the wry and ironical. I moved on
to Longinus' *Of the Sublime* and could not understand it. I was
gripped by Tolstoy and a chapter from *Don Quixote.* In the next
two or three years I read the whole of *The International Library*
on the quiet. These volumes converted me to prose. I had never
really enjoyed poetry, for it was concerned with inner experience
and I was very much an extrovert and I fancy I have remained

so . . . but in prose I found the common experience and the solid worlds where judgments were made and in which one could firmly tread."

Midnight Oil takes up where *A Cab at the Door* left off, and suffers from the fact of being tied to it, though a very different kind of book. Unfortunately, the writer has to leave home, like everybody else; it is what is wrong with the second volume of almost every literary autobiography that has ever been written. For home—and especially a home "where manners were unknown, where everybody shouted, and no one had any notion of taste, either good or bad"—is bound to be more interesting to read about than the solitary, industrious apprenticeship of a writer. In the present instance, the reader is advised to be patient, have faith, and try to forget the raffish pleasures of *A Cab at the Door* in order to appreciate the virtues and courage of the innocent young man now occupying the center of what was until a moment ago a stage crowded with scene-stealers.

"The professional writer who spends his time becoming other people and places, real or imaginary, finds he has written his life away and has become almost nothing," Pritchett remarks at the beginning of *Midnight Oil*,* the second volume of his autobiography. "The true autobiography of this egotist is exposed in all its intimate foliage in his work. But there is a period when a writer has not yet become one, or, just having become one, is struggling to form his talent, and it is from this period that I have selected most of the scenes and people in this book. It *is* a selection, and it is neither a confession nor a volume of literary reminiscences, but as far as I am able I have put in my 'truth.' "

Thanks to all those bankruptcies and removals, his early schooling had been haphazard in the extreme. France seemed to

*Random House, 1972.

offer salvation; in France, somehow, he would make up for his lack of education. When he was pressed as to how this would come about, he said that France was different; in France a street was called a *rue*. "Is that all?" his father demanded. It was, as a matter of fact, but it was an all that he could not explain because it was too strange and immense. He got himself out of the leather trade, and he got around his father, and in the spring of 1921 arrived in Paris. He was right: France was educating. Wherever he went, he repeated to himself the names of the shops—*quincaillerie, boulangerie*—and any phrase he happened to overhear. The word that had the most significance for him was *cinquième*; his room on the *cinquième étage* of a cheap hotel near the Champ de Mars meant the liberty that had been hard to come by. The street signs were an encyclopedia of French history, and "to be alone in Paris, knowing nobody, was an intoxication: it was like being on the dizzy brink of knowing everybody."

He had been brought up a Christian Scientist ("I believed, yet did not believe, very comfortably, at the same time"), and a letter of introduction put him in touch with the little congregation in Paris. For the most part, they were American and British tourists, in whom, Pritchett says, the Divine Mind fizzed like some harmless *vin mousseux*. When his money was nearly gone, he saw an advertisement in the Paris *Daily Mail*: the Paris branch of an English manufacturer of photographic plates and supplies needed a stock clerk. An old photograph of him sitting on a counter in this shop shows "a thin youth of twenty with thick fairish hair, exclaiming eyebrows, loosely grinning mouth, and the eyes raised to the ceiling with a look of passing school-boy saintliness." The French boys in the shop could not pronounce his name, and he was the office joke until he managed to become the office humorist instead. A month after he started to work there, his awkward French had become fluent. He found a decent room in Auteuil, in the flat of a war widow who worked as a charwoman. In the evening, he went in search of a cheap restaurant and ate alone, reading or looking at the people. He lived by the appetite of the eye, and was in the simplest way happy. He made the acquaintance of a very old lady who was a friend of his landlady's priest, and on Sunday afternoons he would sit on a hard, upholstered chair and converse with her about Racine and Corneille, and submit to having his grammar and pronunciation corrected. Though it was an excruciating experience, he ended up speaking two kinds of French fairly well.

He knew that he wanted to become a writer, but he could not see that he had anything to write about except that he was alive. He sent a joke in to the Paris *Herald*, and it became his first published work. Encouraged by this, he wrote a sketch about that *cinquième-étage* hotel room—the rough blue cloth on the table, the view from the attic window, the carpet worn thin as a slice of ham by he had no way of knowing how many predecessors, the electric light flicking off at eleven, the sound of the bugle at the Champ de Mars—and sent it off to the London office of *The Christian Science Monitor*. He wrote two more pieces and sent them to English weeklies. When all three were accepted, he didn't have to go on saying, "I want to be a writer": he *was* a writer, but a writer who had taken for his models men who were no longer in fashion, and he hadn't the slightest knowledge of the writers who were in fashion.

When I read in memoirs about the Paris of the Steins, Sylvia Beach, Joyce, Hemingway, and Scott Fitzgerald, I am cast down. I was there. I may have passed them in the street; I had simply never heard of them. Nor had I any notion of what they were trying to do. I had really carried my isolation in England with me. One evening I did see a number of young people walking up the Boulevard Montparnasse with a thick, blue-covered book, like a telephone directory. They went to the Dome, the Coupole, or the Rotonde and sat there reading. I asked a young

Irishman whom I sat next to at the Dome what the book was. He was dressed in green and wore a cowboy hat. He was surprised to be asked such a question. The book, he said, was *Ulysses;* for years "everyone" had been waiting for this great moment. He allowed me to read the first page; its adjectives and images annoyed and flustered me. . . .

I did not know that I was living at the center of a literary revolution.

Because Stevenson and Borrow and Belloc walked, he walked—to Saint-Cloud, to Marly, to Chartres, to Pontoise and Poissy. Tormented by sexual longing, he tried to seduce a tall, hearty Danish girl, and was so clumsy at it that in the end she capitulated because there was no other way around his ineptitude. He left the photographic studio for a better-paying job, with a firm that dealt in shellac and glue and, briefly, ostrich feathers. After several months, the absentminded owner noticed that he had made hardly any sales whatever and gave him the sack. He decided to live by writing. For a short time he did manage to do this, and either hummed inside with the giddiness of his genius or relapsed into feeling that he was a hack:

> To write little sketches of places, how feeble! . . . A writer ought, I felt, to know about "low" society, but "low life" is as hard to discover as High Society is. The *Monitor* certainly would not publish anything about the whores prancing about the hotels of Les Halles, with their red dresses, slit up to the thigh, and their hard voices shouting at the draymen below. If I nosed my way up to a *clochard* who had kipped down on one of those iron plates on the pavement where the warmth from the central heating comes through, near the Gare d'Austerlitz, I never got much more than a grunt out of him. The paper would not like that, unless I made him a picturesque character amusing to tourists. . . . I began to get the suspicion that I was hired to leave half of life out.

Because of a lawsuit in Boston, the *Monitor's* funds were frozen. The editor in London continued to accept his sketches but could not pay for them. In order to eat, he sold his books. Boileau, Balzac, Maupassant, Vigny, Hugo went, but, significantly, not Rabelais. He sold his other suit. He fed on the menus outside restaurants and was half out of his head with hunger. He might have starved—for nothing on earth would make him give up and go home—if his landlady had not noticed that his armoire was empty and that he did not go out in the evening. She brought him a bowl of soup and a glass of wine, and then settled down to get the truth out of him. The next day, she arranged a loan, in a roundabout fashion, through the old lady who corrected his grammar and pronunciation, who knew the reader of the Christian Science church, who was an American and had money.

"I wish you'd stop gesticulating and shrugging your shoulders and raising your eyebrows all the time like a Frenchman. You've got lines on your forehead already. You look like an old man," his father said when he turned up in London. He had come over to try and collect the money that was owed him. The editor of the *Monitor* put him off with promises, but eventually paid up, and later called him in and offered him twenty-five pounds to go to Ireland and write six articles on how people were living their ordinary lives in spite of the civil war.

His first sight of the Dublin mountains "rising with beautiful false innocence in their violets, greens, and golden rust of grasses and bracken" made his breath go thin. As he walked along the Liffey, he was frisked by the patrols again and again; his green velours hat with a wide, turned-down brim, purchased in the Boulevard des Italiens so that he would pass for a Frenchman, was an item of the uniform of the I.R.A. In the foyer of the Abbey Theatre, he saw Lady Gregory talking to Lennox Robinson. There were a dozen people in the audience, watching the last act of *The Countess Cathleen*. Soot came down the chimney of his hotel room twice in the night, when a bomb went off.

The journey from Dublin to Cork took fourteen hours. Soldiers came into his room and searched his bedding and luggage but looked respectfully at his books, and one of them started to read a poem of Yeats. He travelled across Tipperary to Limerick, and on to Enniskillen, and discovered that places overwhelmed him. "Every movement of light, every turn of leaf, every person, seemed to occupy me physically, so that I had no self left." In despair, he was driven to write flatly what he saw and heard. With a conviction of failure, he sent his first four articles to the paper, and was dumbfounded to get a telegram saying that they were excellent. He settled down in an office on St. Stephen's Green, a cheerful outsider to Irish quarrels, and became the regular correspondent for a paper from whose religion he had lapsed. The weather, changing from hour to hour, excited his fancy, and so did the vivid and inventive talk. He lodged with two Protestant spinsters, who left him a supper of cold meat and pickles and a pot of very strong tea, and popped up every quarter of an hour if he brought home a young woman visitor. He walked by the sea at Blackrock or Dalkey, with a crowd of young men and girls, or over the mountains to Glendalough. He saw AE riding a bicycle and carrying a bunch of flowers. He had tea with James Stephens. One afternoon he called on Yeats:

> The exalted voice flowed over me. The tall figure, in uncommonly delicate tweed, walked up and down, the voice becoming more resonant, as if he were on a stage. At the climax of some point about the Gaelic revival, he suddenly remembered he must make tea, in fact a new pot, because he had already been drinking some. The problem was one of emptying out the old teapot. It was a beautiful pot and he walked the room with the short

steps of the aesthete, carrying it in his hand. He came toward
me. He receded to the bookcase. He swung around the sofa.
Suddenly, with Irish practicality, he went straight to one of the
two splendid Georgian windows of the room, opened it, and
out went those barren leaves with a swoosh, into Merrion
Square.

Pritchett went several times to see O'Casey, in a tenement
with a smashed fanlight above the door. The teakettle was singing over a fire of cheap coal dust, and O'Casey wore his cap in
the house. He was writing *The Plough and the Stars* and on the
wall had printed "Get on with the Bloody Play."

A passionate pleasure in the scenery did not prevent the *Monitor*'s Irish correspondent from being aware of the disheartening
villages and ruined farms of the west, or of the misery of the
Dublin slums. In his articles, he sided with the pro–Free State
faction, and there were complaints from Irish readers, who were
mostly Protestant and of the opposite faction. He was called
back to London, and expected to be fired. Instead, he was informed that nobody wanted to read about Ireland anymore, and,
shortly after his twenty-third birthday, found himself serving as
the *Monitor*'s correspondent in Madrid.

Halfway through *Midnight Oil* there is a noticeable change of
pace and focus. Events take place in time rather than at any
given moment of time. The descriptions of people tend to be
generalized: "Barefooted children ran coughing their lungs out
and poor women screamed out the names of newspapers and
sold lottery tickets in the wet." This is very good, but it is not
the same as "Mr. Shaves stuck a finger in an ear, burrowing
there, in thought." Sometimes the writing is steady ("Each light
in a window, though it might be miles away, was distinct and
itself, as if it were the signal of a person or a family"); sometimes

it is hurried, as if he felt compelled for one reason and another, including his two books on Spain, to make a long story short. And one is aware of information withheld out of delicacy. Just before he left Ireland, he married a young woman journalist who was working with him and who had also been brought up a Christian Scientist. The marriage turned out badly and Pritchett doesn't go into it, beyond saying that his father-in-law disapproved of the match and "would get up from his daylong game of patience and leave the room muttering about the 'nasty little clerk' his daughter had brought into the house," and that in Spain his wife was homesick. She must have kept returning to Ireland, for he was alone for long stretches of time.

During the lax dictatorship of Primo de Rivera, there was little in the way of news to cable home. He sat huddled over an oil stove in the freezing weather, reading about the Moorish Conquest and the Counter-Reformation. He read Miguel de Unamuno's *Del Sentimiento Trágico de la Vida* and suffered a moral shock. The "diluted transcendentalism of Mrs. Eddy" could not stand up to "the Spanish paradox: life intensely felt in the flesh and made whole by the contemplation of death." In Spain, the young man with the loose grin had stopped grinning and become thoughtful. He began to question everything he had taken for granted. When he went out to a café in the evening, it was to join a little group of liberal intellectuals, men of conscience and sensibility, who exerted an influence on his character and on his mind. In the Spanish Civil War, their reformist ideas were swept away and many of them were murdered, but all that was in the future. As in France and Ireland, he went on walking journeys, in the Guadarrama Mountains, to Ávila and Segovia. Coming into the fishing village of Llanes, he and two friends were stoned by the local youths because they were strangers. It was not uncommon. He drove, with his wife, to Córdova and Seville and Granada (where people shouted "A woman driving!" and rushed after them), and round the coast

to Barcelona, and back through Aragón, and came to the conclusion that there were as many Spains as there were provinces,
towns, villages, and, finally, individual Spaniards. Eventually, he
began to tire of his life as a newspaper correspondent; it seemed
superficial, and he was convinced that he wasn't good at it. "In
my heart I despised news and was confused by opinion." So he
sat down to write his first short story.

He was moved from Spain to North Africa when there was a
flareup of the Riff war, and then to Boston, which he disliked,
and back to Ireland. Dublin had changed, Yeats and O'Casey
were in London, and he could feel the reaction that was about
to set in, and the dullness of a growing religious domination.
Also, his writing having got too fancy, the *Monitor* at last did
fire him. He went back to London and lived in a series of
furnished rooms that stank of mice or old tea leaves or, in one
instance, cheese from the shop below. He supported himself by
various ill-paying jobs, and was subject to one nervous illness
after another, and fevers, and often sat in a crowd of outpatients
at hospitals, waiting to have his stomach X-rayed. "Are you still
doing the writing?" his mother asked, commiseratingly. In time,
his life became less precarious. He reviewed novels for *The Spectator* and wrote articles for *The New Statesman*, and had stories
published here and there. Since this did not give him enough
money to live in London, he "became a literary journalist of
highbrow tastes who lives in a country cottage because it is
cheap and who divides his time between reviewing and doing
his 'own work.' " He had to be told about the Bloomsbury
group, just as he had had to be told about *Ulysses*, and he did
not try to make their acquaintance. He and his wife, who had
been acting in repertory companies, separated for good.
  Suddenly, in his early thirties, his life changed completely.
His writing improved and his talent began to be recognized.

And, emerging from a period of emotional bankruptcy, he fell
deeply in love and married again. This second, ecstatically happy
marriage he keeps in his closed fist, like a boy with a prized
marble. "There is, I am sure," he says, "a direct connection
between passionate love and the firing of the creative power of
the mind. . . . The mind of the restrained or sexually discontented man wanders off into shallows. My mind had been abroad
too long, in a double sense: not simply in France, Ireland, or
Spain, but in a manner that had used only half of myself."

As *Midnight Oil* continues on down through the Spanish Civil
War and the Second World War (of which he says, "Looking
at the war egotistically, from a writer's point of view, it was a
feverish dispersal and waste of one's life"), the reader is aware
of ground covered too quickly, of subjects—literary friendships,
for example—not done justice to, and other subjects not done
at all. If he had allowed himself another hundred pages it still
would not have been a long book. Was he prevented by his
announced plan of writing mostly about the period when he had
not yet become a writer or, having become one, was trying to
form his talent? Plans can be altered. Was the hesitation of a
more serious kind? Could it be that the rather noticeable desire
to get on with the bloody autobiography, in the last section, is
nothing more than a fear of seeming egotistical and overblown?
He remarks that his father had taken to buying quantities of
books and storing them, unread, in his wardrobe. "We were at
the beginning of that phase so common in the lives of fathers
and sons, when the father feels *he* is the son." There is an
equally common and more lasting phase during which the son,
arriving at middle age, helplessly sees himself doing those things
that as a young man he most disliked in his father, and shudders.
That self-inflating, irresistible old poseur, going through a new
house and discovering that it had a balcony a foot wide and

three feet long, announced, "I'll have my breakfast on it," fancying himself on the Riviera. And when he was living in Uxbridge he bought himself a yachting cap, a blazer, and cream trousers suitable for the Royal Yacht Squadron and Cowes, and a monocle, in order to walk grandly among the old men fishing with worms off the towpath of the canal.

A Life

In the year 1960, Andrei Alekseyevich Amalrik submitted his dissertation to a senior history professor at Moscow State University. It dealt with the ninth-century state of Kievan Rus, and the conclusion it arrived at was that Norman traders had exerted a significant influence on early Russian civilization. He was told that his research was brilliant but that his conclusion was politically unacceptable; the official position was that Russian culture and civilization were produced by Slavs only. Amalrik refused to lop off the conclusion and was expelled from the university. He was twenty-two years old.

Sending scholarly papers abroad was not illegal but neither was it, as a rule, allowed to happen. Amalrik asked the Danish Embassy to pass his dissertation along to a Danish professor of Slavic languages whom he had been in correspondence with, and the Embassy turned it over to the Soviet Ministry of Foreign Affairs, without telling Amalrik that it was going to do this. The Ministry of Foreign Affairs referred it to the K.G.B., and Amalrik was picked up for questioning. From then on, for the rest of his not very long life, his interest was focussed on a less remote period of history and a broader subject—which he describes as "the conflict between the individual person and the system in a country where the individual is nothing and the system is everything." In the sense in which he meant it, this statement is true enough, but applied to Amalrik himself it is ludicrous. After ten years of questioning and surveillance by the police and the K.G.B., the file on him ran to six volumes, each one of which was anywhere from four hundred to six hundred pages long.

Amalrik was a slight man, of mixed ancestry. One of his forebears was French, another Swedish, and another a gypsy. The photograph of him on the dust jacket of his autobiography* suggests a lightweight boxer. He has a square head, scrub-brush hair, measuring eyes, and the mouth of a man prepared to give blow for blow. That his character comes through so consistently and understandably in his book is proof of his literary gifts. Because he is so deeply involved, he sometimes assumes a greater knowledge of the dissident movement than the ordinary non-Russian reader is likely to have, and the chronology has to be struggled over. And no index. The fact that one often feels one is listening to Amalrik talking is, of course, the work of his translator, Guy Daniels, whose language is in general so carefully considered and natural that to paraphrase Amalrik's ideas or relate a given event without using the same words is difficult.

Amalrik's father was also a historian, the author of a book called *In Search of Lost Civilizations*. While serving as a lieutenant in the Red Army he was sentenced to eight years in prison for remarking that Stalin's purges were responsible for the lack of military preparedness that made it possible for the Nazis to advance so swiftly all through the early months of the invasion. During the siege of Stalingrad, when the need for officers became acute, he was pardoned. For what offenses Amalrik does not say, one of his father's brothers was sent to prison camp. Another was shot.

As a schoolchild Amalrik upset his teacher by refusing to join

*Notes of a Revolutionary. Knopf, 1982.

the Pioneers—the Cub Scout version of the Young Communists' League. He came of age at a time when the Soviet leadership was bent on halting the process of de-Stalinization that had begun under Khrushchev. "After a quarter-century," he says, "a balance had been reached at the top between the neo Stalinists and the moderates. The top people like to feel secure, and it is better to tolerate a certain amount of opposition within the country than to be sucked again into the maelstrom of terror. The thing to do, then, is to combat the opposition by means of selective methods: by frightening some of them, by locking up others in prisons and psychiatric hospitals, by killing and beating up others, by getting others fired from their jobs, and by expelling still others from the country."

Between 1960 and 1965, he took only part-time work so that he could look after his father, who was partially paralyzed. He wrote plays that producers were interested in but backed away from producing, because of their content. And he collected "unofficial art"—that is to say, paintings with no political value. This brought him in contact with the foreign community in Moscow, which was also collecting such paintings, because they were very much cheaper than their equivalent in Western Europe. All this was, like his thesis, unacceptable. He was arrested as a "parasite" and sentenced to a period of labor on a collective farm in Siberia. In Siberia, he got a telegram saying that his father's health had given way, and he was granted permission to go home for eighteen days. His father was already dead when the telegram reached him. While he was in Moscow arranging the funeral, he married a Russian Muslim, an artist, whom he had known for some time.

Amalrik's own health suffered permanent damage from the hardships he had to endure in Siberia, and when he was allowed to live in Moscow again he was officially exempted from the decree that required every Soviet citizen to be employed. It was not the protection one might suppose, and neither was Amalrik

free to go about his life. How he appeared in the eyes of the
K.G.B. is nicely conveyed in this report:

> To the Chief of the Sixth Police Precinct:
> I hereby inform you that Andrei Amalrik, thirty years of age,
> has for a long time been leading a parasitic way of life, and has
> no job. . . . In 1964 Amalrik was sent to prison for speculation
> and parasitism. Yet since his return from there he has continued
> the same way of life, and has no job. . . . At present some
> woman, allegedly his wife, is living in his home without a resi-
> dence permit. No one knows where she came from, but one
> thing is clear: she is just as much of a parasite, and doesn't have
> a job. In her home she does paintings of some kind, and they
> are sold to private persons. I entreat you to look into this matter
> and compel these healthy young people to get work in a factory.

So that he would not be classified as unemployed, Amalrik
wrote free-lance interviews with theatre directors, actors, artists,
and composers, for a news agency designed to send propaganda
abroad, though Soviet newspapers also subscribed to it. He lived
in a large communal apartment. "From the entrance hall, where
a dim bulb burned . . . a long hallway in the shape of a capital
L led past a steamy kitchen where laundry was hung up to dry
and old ladies with weary faces stood at their tables: past the
bathroom where another neighbor—with her head bent down
over the tub and her enormous rear, swathed in blue cotton
slacks, protruding into the hallway—was doing her laundry; past
an area concealed by a curtain with suitcases and trunks sticking
out from under it; past big doors and little doors; past chests of
drawers standing along the wall; and ended up at the door of
our room." We have been here before. It is the world of *Crime
and Punishment*. ("When I wonder how the phenomenon of
dissidence could have arisen in a closed society," Amalrik says,
"and what were its roots, I think first of all of the role played
by Russian literature. . . . Although the regime did for a time

ban the books of Dostoyevsky and many works of Tolstoy, it did not totally proscribe the literature of the nineteenth century. And that may have been a mistake, since that literature is passionate in its defense of the individual against the system.") Almost blocking the doorway was a grand piano that Amalrik had inherited from an aunt who was a singer. It was completely out of tune and was seldom played. "Some people—especially foreigners—used to laugh at us, because while we didn't even have a table to eat at, half the room was occupied by a useless grand piano. But its very uselessness and beauty, together with the paintings, the old books, the grandfather clock, and the withered, spidery plants on the sideboard, made our room look like something out of a fairy tale."

With the trial of Andrei Sinyavsky and Yuri Daniel, what was later called the Democratic Movement began to make itself felt, and Amalrik became involved in it four months after his return from Siberia. The dissident Alexander Ginzburg said to him, "An English journalist recently came to Daniel's wife and left his address. You know how to socialize with foreigners. Couldn't you put that journalist in touch with me?" And Amalrik arranged this and other meetings. "In those days," he says, "all of us were a little afraid: afraid of the regime; afraid that people who feared the regime would take us for provocateurs; and afraid of provocateurs." Because he was so vulnerable, he wasn't as a general thing asked to sign petitions or take part in public demonstrations, but he didn't really want to. He had, he says, an instinctive dislike for collective actions. "I have always been repelled by the necessity of marching under one banner. All group actions based on the imitation of some people by others, be they reasonable or not, contain an element of psychosis." To the degree that the public was allowed to be present at the trials, he was present, and, knowing no language but Russian, he nevertheless continued to serve as an intermediary between the dissidents and the foreign correspondents in Moscow.

"If a person refuses the opportunity to judge the world around him and to express that judgment," Amalrik says, "he begins to destroy himself before the police can destroy him. . . . The dissidents accomplished something that was simple to the point of genius: in an unfree country, they behaved like free men, thereby changing the moral atmosphere and the nation's governing tradition." Though many of the journalists were easily intimidated and ready to take their information about the dissidents at second hand, a few were willing to run the risk of expulsion from the country. Among these was the Dutch correspondent Karel van het Reve, who was a professor at the University of Leyden. He became Amalrik's friend.

The trials followed one upon another like the tolling of a bell. In the autumn of 1967, Pavel Litvinov, Maxim Litvinov's grandson, was advised by a K.G.B. agent that he would do well to destroy a collection of documents he had put together concerning the trial of the dissidents Viktor Khaustov and Vladimir Bukovsky; instead, he wrote an account of the conversation with the K.G.B. agent, and it was circulated at home and published abroad, and the BBC went so far as to broadcast a dramatized version of it to the U.S.S.R. The broadcast made a tremendous impression on Amalrik. "It was not only the conversation itself, of course, since there had been plenty of such conversations and warnings, but the fact that Pavel had recorded it and made it public. In so doing, he had thrown out a challenge not only to the K.G.B. but to one of the most important unpublished laws of Soviet society: a kind of agreement between cat and mouse to the effect that the mouse will not squeak if the cat starts to eat him."

Amalrik had an agreement with the foreign correspondents that after a trial he would question the witnesses and relatives who were allowed in to the trial and pass on to the journalists what they said. He had developed a sixth sense about informers. And he derived amusement from his encounters with accredited foreign correspondents who had "Vasya" or "I'll never forget my dear mother" in Russian tattooed on one hand. The car that, when he emerged from a building, started up and slowly followed him, the inconspicuous gentlemen lurking behind trees, the photographer taking snapshots of him in the street outside the courthouse were by now a part of the normal background of his life. He wrote an account of his term of exile—*Involuntary Journey to Siberia*—and, by what means he does not say, managed to get this manuscript and others (including Andrei Sakharov's *Progress, Co-Existence, and Intellectual Freedom*) to Holland, where, through the efforts of van het Reve, they were published.

Pavel Litvinov and six other dissidents were arrested when they tried to stage a demonstration in Red Square against the Soviet intervention in Czechoslovakia. At the time, Litvinov was engaged in writing up the trial of Ginzburg and Yuri Galanskov. While he was in prison awaiting his own trial, Amalrik finished the job for him. He sent the manuscript to Litvinov in Siberia to look over, and arranged for it to be published abroad.

On the day that the dissident ex-General Petr Grigorenko was arrested, half a dozen agents who were hoping to find evidence bearing on his case searched Amalrik's apartment and reduced it to a shambles but failed to make off with the manuscript of a book he had just started, *Will the Soviet Union Survive Until 1984?*, in which he took a pessimistic view of the theory that the rise of an educated middle class would in time force the Soviet system to become more democratic. He knew that he would be arrested for writing it, but he figured that in any case he would be arrested sooner or later, so it was all the more urgent to get as much done as he could. This book, too, was smuggled out of the country and published abroad, and caught the attention of the foreign press. As time passed and he was not arrested, people began to feel that he must be a K.G.B. agent. "There's something amazing," he remarks, "about a country where so-

ciety decides whom the political police should arrest, and when;
and then gets nervous if the police are dilatory."

At one o'clock in the morning, on a dark and empty street,
he was picked up by a policeman. At the precinct station, he
was obliged to open his battered old suitcase, and the contents—
a portable typewriter and some documents—were confiscated.
He was questioned in the presence of four K.G.B. agents, who
wanted to know who had given him the documents. Amalrik
answered that he obtained them from friends whose names he
would not reveal; that he intended, out of curiosity, to look
them over and then destroy them. "But who *did* give them to
you?" the agent in charge said. "You'll have to tell us." "I'll
have to if you hang me up by the feet and torture me," Amalrik
said. "We don't do things like that these days," the agent said.
And Amalrik said, "Then I won't have to tell." As soon as he
was released, he filed a complaint with the City Prosecutor's
office, claiming illegal detention and the misappropriation of his
typewriter and papers; and because the agents had made no
record of the confiscation Amalrik was able to get them back.
He had come to realize that "while the powers of the K.G.B.
are great, they are not without limits; that the K.G.B. must
observe certain formalities; and that if one understands how the
bureaucratic machinery works, one can throw a monkey wrench
into the wheels."

However, the K.G.B. saw to it that the news service com-
missioned no more articles by him. It also stationed two agents
outside his door, who followed him wherever he went trying to
find work, and in every instance the chief of personnel received
a phone call telling him not to hire Amalrik. By leaving his
house very early one morning before the agents had arrived, he
managed to get a job at the local post office, delivering mail
between 6 and 8 A.M. The post office was not so easily intimidated, and he kept this job until he sensed that the pressure was
off and it was safe for him to resign.

The first time Amalrik went to the U.S.S.R. Foreign Trade Bank in response to a notice of a deposit from abroad, he was able to collect the money. The next time, it was explained to him that he must submit a document confirming that the money was in fact royalties. Armed with letters from his French and American publishers, he went back to the bank and was informed that he needed a letter from the Soviet institution through which his manuscript was sent abroad. The bank official then said "What article or book was it? What was the title?" and Amalrik said "*Will the Soviet Union Survive Until 1984?*"— after which they looked at each other attentively for quite a while before the official said, "The fact is that we're essentially a commercial enterprise and certificates are the commodity we handle." Amalrik had decided to meet danger head-on rather than flee from it. "My basic assumption was that since my status in the Soviet hierarchy was the lowly one of a 'dropout' the authorities . . . would according to their own logic have to belittle me. They had to show that a dissident of my low standing aroused nothing more than contempt in them. Naturally, there was no hope that they would ignore me. But there *was* something I *could* hope for: that they would not charge me under Article 70, which carries a penalty of up to seven years' incarceration and five years' internal exile, but under Article 190–I, which caries a penalty of no more than three years."

Though it was rash, he pursued the matter of the foreign royalties until it became clear that there was no likelihood of his getting the money, at which point he instructed the bank to return it to the publishers. Later, when he was very hard up, he asked them to send it back in his wife's name, as a gift, and it got through to them.

Some time before, knowing that if he was sent to prison he would probably not be able to get a residence permit in Moscow or the Moscow region when he got out, they made a journey deep into the country and found and bought and furnished a brick cottage that stood on the edge of a stream and was shaded by linden trees.

In April of 1970, they spent a week in Leningrad, Tallin, and Riga; he wanted his wife to see those beautiful cities before he was arrested. Toward the end of May, while he was working in the garden, a crowd of men in black suits closed in on the cottage. As he was about to be driven away, his wife came to the car, weeping, and handed him a pair of warm socks. He was charged with having published anti-Soviet writings. Before his arrest he had made up his mind that no matter what indictment was brought against him he would neither affirm nor deny incidents or the interpretation put upon them but would instead deny the right of the court and the K.G.B. to prosecute people for their views.

The trial took place in Sverdlovsk. Present in the court was a K.G.B. colonel who was wearing gold-rimmed glasses. "Brezhnev wears glasses like that," Amalrik writes, "and so do all officials down to a certain level. The colonel was at a low level for gold-rimmed glasses: one step lower and they would have been 'not in accordance with his rank.' " The judge was polite, but spoke ungrammatically and stumbled over the passages he had to read aloud. Amalrik was defended by a lawyer whom his wife had retained for him. Within the framework of the Soviet laws, Amalrik says, his trial was defective. Instead of considering whether what he had written and said was false and defamatory, the court took this for granted. It ignored the question of whether he had erred in innocence or known that what he wrote was libellous. Though his books had been circulated abroad, there was no evidence that he was responsible for this. He was allowed to read a prepared statement in court, in which he said that it was fear of his ideas that had compelled the authorities to put him on trial.

The verdict recapitulated the indictment, and he was sentenced to three years in an intensified-regimen labor camp. The police were instructed to check whether his wife had a job and whether she was engaged in anti-Soviet activity. When he emerged from the courtroom, she threw him a bouquet of flowers. The captain of the guards snatched them away and stomped on them.

From the courtroom Amalrik passed on into a nightmare world others have described before him. He was moved eastward, sometimes on trains, sometimes in police cars, to prison after prison. At Novosibirsk he was placed in an underground cell with a blocked-up toilet that overflowed. After a few days he began to feel dizzy and nauseated; then he began to vomit. The cell swayed before his eyes and he heard his cellmates pounding on the door and calling for a doctor. The supervisor standing outside said, "We didn't invite you here to get sick." The last thing he remembered was a sergeant calling out his name for transport. Unconscious and in a state of paralysis, he was dragged through the prison corridor to the train. The captain of the guards was afraid he would die on the train and refused to accept him. He was taken to the prison hospital, where (he learned afterward) he spent the night "constantly mumbling, crying out, and making delirious strange movements with my one unparalyzed hand." He was then transferred to the camp hospital, where they made a spinal puncture, which yielded only pus, and his case was diagnosed as purulent meningoencephalitis.

He was unconscious for a week and woke up in a ward for terminal cases. He couldn't move either his hands or his feet, or recall his name or what had happened to him or who he was. The next day, he remembered his first name and two or three days later his last name. His only link with the whole of his past experience was the memory of the knapsack that had his belongings in it. The doctors were of the opinion that if he did by some miracle survive he would be mentally defective for the rest of his life.

During the next two weeks he began to remember things and to walk again, holding on to the beds. Finally he made the trip to the toilet—a small room with a pail in it, for patients too enfeebled to go to the latrine. There was no bathroom in the hospital. He had lost fifty pounds. Though he gradually regained his memory, he continued to be afflicted with insomnia and quasi delirium. Printed lines of type were for a time only a blur.

As soon as he could write, he sent three letters to his wife and got no answer. One day when he was outdoors taking a short walk, a tubercular patient on the other side of a barbed-wire fence said, "Are you Amalrik? Your wife has shown up!" And then another prisoner, a man from his ward, came running and said, "They saw a woman, who from all indications is your wife, standing on the embankment and waving a handkerchief." He went to the second floor of the hospital and looked out of the window, but there was no one on the embankment. He went to the guardhouse, but nobody knew anything. Later, the barber who shaved him said that his wife had come and had not been permitted to see him, on the ground that a visit from her might upset him too much and be bad for his health.

After two months he was transferred from the camp hospital to the prison hospital, but the officer on duty at the prison said "Who needs you there?" and put him in a prison cell where there were five double bunks for forty men. Still running a fever, he was started on the five-thousand-mile trip across Siberia. From Novosibirsk to Sakhalin, then to Irkutsk, where he picked up crab lice in the bathhouse. On the train journey from Irkutsk to Khabarovsk, while he was sleeping, his compartment-mates cleaned out his knapsack; his pens and socks were traded to the escort guards for tea.

He spent three days in the prison at Khabarovsk in a crowded basement room as big as a railway station, with one bare light bulb suspended from a black ceiling and the half-naked prisoners curled up on the rough cement floor, on a table, and on the iron springs of the beds. From there he was flown to Magadan, held there for a month, and then put in a Black Maria where there was enough room to sit down but not to turn around, and taken a hundred and eighty-five miles northward along the unpaved Kolyma Road, to Talaya. He vomited all the way and by the end of the journey was unconscious. The man sitting next to him took advantage of this to steal his sugar.

"In prison," he says, "it is usually a pleasant experience to meet up with a living being who does not resemble a human. In the Sverdlovsk prison I sometimes encountered, on my way to the exercise yard, cats that hung around the kitchen; and in the Kamyshlov I got to know a pair of horses used for hauling firewood. While I was in solitary, I filed a request that I be allowed to keep a cat in my cell. But the prison commandant replied that a directive from the Minister of Internal Affairs prohibited such things." Of the thieves, con men, murderers, vagrants, rapists, and so on who were his cellmates, some were dangerous, some companionable and entertained him with the story of their lives. He was careful what he said, assuming that they were informers. In some prisons the loudspeaker shouted propaganda from behind an iron grille and was turned off only at the discretion of the prison officials. If he was lucky, it was in his cell and he could turn it off when he wanted to. He exercised, read books from the prison library, played chess and checkers, and taught himself to read English, though he had no idea how to pronounce it. As the officer in charge of political indoctrination made the rounds of the barracks tearing down magazine illustrations that the prisoners had put up on the walls, he would say, "Learn to love monotony!"

Lest he find himself accepting the way things were, Amalrik continually looked for things to complain about, demanded privileges that he knew were due the prisoners, and addressed written appeals over the heads of the prison officials.

It would be too much to expect a man as clever as Amalrik also to be what is commonly considered saintly. He enjoyed telling people off, and he had a temper. During a quarrel with a particularly irritating cellmate he exclaimed, "If you say another word, I'll throw your bread in the latrine pail," and the man foolishly kept right on talking. And it was after an exchange of insults that "Captain Shevchenko . . . dragged me off to the punishment cell, shouting: 'This is the way people like you should be dealt with!' In the cell, he and Shmykov tore off my clothes and banged my head against the wall, which of course was not pleasant for one who had recently had meningitis. I spent the night lying on a cement bag and was released the next morning by Captain Garafutdinov." To the prison officials who addressed him by the familiar—and, in the circumstances, insulting—second-person singular, he replied by calling them *"ty"* also; whereupon they instantly switched to the polite form. When he heard a key being turned in the lock of his cell, he would stand quickly so as not to have to get to his feet in the officer's presence. Once or twice he met with genuine kindness at the hands of a prison official. As a rule, a show of kindness was immediately followed by an attempt to break through his defenses.

When his wife was at last allowed to fly in to see him, she was kept waiting for two days while a microphone was installed in the visitors' room. He was so unaccustomed to regular food that he could not eat what she brought him. Because she wouldn't submit to a gynecological examination after he had been sent back to the compound, she and a prison official and a woman doctor with rubber gloves on her hands sat facing each other for five hours until the prosecutor ordered Amalrik's wife to be released. The indignities varied from visit to visit.

He developed an inflammation of the middle ear, common in

the Far North, where summer is over by the end of July and the temperature in November is sometimes sixty below. He asked for boric acid, and when that didn't help he drafted a request for a specialist to examine him, and he wrote his wife, asking her to see what she could do in Moscow. As a result of her efforts, he was examined by the chief of the medical service of the Magadan Administration of Internal Affairs, whose report began with the nervous system: "Very shattered nerves, with residual effects of meningitis. . . . Acute gastritis. Blood pressure: high. . . . Heart: defective mitral valve. Temperature: high—an aftereffect of meningitis. Ears: inflammation of middle ear. Conclusion: general condition good." The report failed to mention that he was suffering from avitaminosis, that his whole body was covered with boils, and that saliva ran from his mouth. Semi-starvation as an educational measure is, he says, the basis for the determination of prison rations. He didn't starve to death during the first year only because his wife managed to send him money for the canteen and, every month, the authorized five-kilogram parcel. "I always looked forward to the package as if it were news from her. Correspondence was prohibited, so even the list of items of food drawn up in her own hand looked like a love letter. The regulations prohibit sending food packages from Moscow, but the people in our local Moscow post office had good feelings toward me and accepted my parcels. Recently an even more remarkable regulation was introduced: food for parcels can be bought only in the town or settlement where the prison is located—perhaps so that the warders will not be irritated by the sight of some good sausage."

Though Amalrik expresses open sorrow for his wife's suffering, indignation at what was done to him never in this book bursts the confines of an habitual irony.

Eventually he found a way of getting extra food: he drafted appeals for other prisoners in exchange for a kilo of butter or a half kilo of sugar.

Four days before his term was up, he was walking in the exercise yard with a cellmate who had been a mechanic. They were talking about what car he should buy when he got out— he was planning to drive across America—when the prison guards seized him and put him in a Black Maria. He was taken from the prison to a government building, where he was charged with "disseminating information defaming the Soviet regime in places of incarceration."

Two months passed before his case came to trial. He spent most of the time in his cell lying with his face to the wall. The presiding judge this time was not polite and the testimony was either false or flimsy. Once, when the judge asked a witness why he didn't respond to a question, the reply was "They didn't tell me how to answer that one." Amalrik was sentenced to three years' more imprisonment.

"For me freedom is the highest goal of life," he writes. "I exist so long as I am free, so long as I have the right to choose." To say that he was a free man when he spent so many years in one prison or another, in cells that were often filthy, sometimes in solitary confinement, ill, barely kept alive on disgusting gruel—to say in those circumstances that he was a free man would be fatuous. His sense of what sunlight, blue sky, green grass, and the smell of the sea air were like had been sharpened on deprivation. But by refusing to acquiesce in the mistreatment that was handed out to him he remained, to a degree that is astonishing, in command of the situation. They could not make him act from fear.

He went on a hunger strike that lasted a hundred and seventeen days, for seventy of which he was force-fed through a tube up his anus. Though very weak, he went on reading— "especially Marx, whose books I could obtain from the prison library. I wanted to know if he was responsible for my being in prison. If I had read Marx in Paris instead of in Magadan, I would have got other things from him. But under the circumstances I was astounded by his antihumanism. For Marx, there was no such thing as an individual in his own right—an individual was only a part of the system. As Walt Whitman observed, people follow those who have the greatest contempt for them. And yet any human being wants to be an individual. . . . The gebists [K.G.B. agents] were not happy about what I was reading. 'You may not understand Marx correctly,' they said."

Through a series of delicate negotiations initiated by the prison doctor and carried on by officials at the K.G.B., he was promised that the sentence would be set aside and he would be allowed to return to Moscow if he made "a public disavowal of his pernicious books and actions." He made up his mind that he would get out of prison without doing this. He would pretend that he was a sick man who had given up the struggle; that he was willing to reëvaluate his books, but only after he was released.

In the end he did compose and sign an evasive petition to the Presidium of the Supreme Soviet that could have been taken for what the K.G.B. wanted. Afterward, he was afraid both that he had conceded too much and that he had not conceded enough for his petition to be granted. Given his situation, he didn't do badly: he did not get the full release he had hoped for; instead, his term in the prison camp was commuted to exile. A day of prison counted for three days of exile, so his term was already half over. He gave up his hunger strike, his wife was permitted to join him, and they spent the next year and a half in the Godforsaken prison town of Magadan.

When it came to repudiating his books, he dragged his heels. He was finally told that he must either write the repudiation, which would then be published, or request an exit visa, in which case they would get him out of the country in two weeks, or . . . The threat was left hanging in the air, but there was only one thing that it could be: sooner or later he would end up back in prison.

On May 12, 1975, his term of exile completed, he and his wife arrived at the Moscow airport. They could not stay in Moscow because they did not have residence permits. He hired a truck and they were driven to a railway station, where they picked up a crate of household possessions shipped from Siberia. Toward nightfall, at the end of the day's driving, they saw, with excitement and joy, familiar fields and trees along a stream. The driver said, "I must say, that's a strange-looking house," and they realized that the house he was pointing to was their own. "But it was no longer a house—only four brick walls. Everything else was gone: the roof, the floor, the beams and rafters and window-frames, the lean-to, and the stove. No furniture was left. There was no sign of a fire, and robbery was out of the question, since a thief wouldn't have taken the roof away with him, ripped up the half-rotten floorboards, or made off with the stove. Someone had done a long, thorough job of wrecking our home so as to make it quite uninhabitable, and it wasn't hard to guess who that someone was."

He gave the crate to the young driver and threw the house keys in the ditch, and they took a slow night train back to Moscow.

During the next year, wherever they went they were followed by two cars with four men in each. From time to time, he was picked up by the police. Once, he was dragged out of bed and taken to the precinct station in his pajamas and socks. He was frequently threatened with arrest because he had no employment. It was Amalrik's belief that the K.G.B. had actually decided to give him a residence permit for Moscow in October of that year, but by the time he submitted the required documents two things had happened that caused them to hesitate: an article of his criticizing détente was published in the *New York Times*, and he joined other dissidents in praising the awarding of the Nobel Peace Price to Andrei Sakharov.

The only solution was for him to leave Russia. "But the regime would not have been true to itself," he says, "if it had started deporting its opponents in the same way as any authoritarian regime. A regime that elects a deputy from a list of one candidate, that compels prisoners to 'thank' it for their arrest, that calls the occupation of an allied country 'brotherly aid' and, when it raises prices, rationalizes that move as a 'request' from the consumers—such a regime must necessarily package expulsion so that it appears to be voluntary departure." He and the K.G.B. reached an agreement: he would be allowed to emigrate, and also, without paying customs duties, to take along his personal belongings, paintings, and books. His wife believed that all things came from God and that it was He who was now sending them from their homeland. On July 15, 1976, she and Amalrik boarded the plane to Amsterdam with a stray cat that they had adopted. He did not know or care when they crossed the border, but as he looked down at the clouds below, suddenly, not at all expecting to, he began to weep.

Notes of a Revolutionary was written during 1977 and 1978, in Genthod, Switzerland; Utrecht; New York; Washington, D.C.; and Cambridge, Massachusetts. Amalrik lectured at Harvard on the history of the Democratic Movement. He and his wife did drive across America from coast to coast. In Indiana, they had a collision with a truck, and their car was demolished. In November, 1980, he was involved in another car accident, near Madrid. He was on his way to an international conference set up to examine compliance with the Helsinki Accords, and this time he was killed.

The Charged Imagination

Eudora Welty was asked by Harvard University to give, in the spring of 1983, a set of three lectures on how she became a writer.*

As an infant she was carried to the window and shown Halley's comet in her sleep. Her father grew up on a farm in Ohio and her mother on top of a mountain in West Virginia. When they married, Mrs. Welty, offered the choice of the Thousand Islands or Jackson, Mississippi, to live in, chose Jackson. Dream, illusion, hallucination, obsession, Eudora Welty says, "and that most wonderful interior vision which is memory, have all gone to make up my stories, to form and to project them, to impel them." It is because of this, and not because she was born in Mississippi, that she is as quintessentially Southern a writer as William Faulkner or Flannery O'Connor or Walker Percy.

Her father loved instruments that would instruct—a telescope with brass extensions, the barometer—or that, like the kaleidoscope and the magnifying glass, would fascinate. Like many American men of his period he believed in progress, in the future. The fact that he was in the insurance business may have

---

*One Writer's Beginnings. Harvard University Press, 1984.

had something to do with his habitual concern for eventualities. He taught her and her two younger brothers what to do if they were lost in a strange country and how to avoid being struck by lightning. Her mother, a romantic, scoffed at caution. ("High winds never bothered me in West Virginia! Just listen at that! I wasn't a bit afraid of a little lightning and thunder! I'd go out on the mountain and spread my arms wide and *run* in a good big storm!")

From the age of two she was read to by her mother. "She'd read to me in the big bedroom in the mornings, when we were in her rocker together. . . . She'd read to me in the diningroom on winter afternoons in front of the coal fire . . . and at night when I'd got in my own bed. I must have given her no peace." Many children have loved to be read to who didn't become writers. There has to be something else, a kind of fermentation. "In my sensory education," Miss Welty says, "I include my physical awareness of the *word*. Of a certain word, that is; the connection it has with what it stands for. At around age six, perhaps, I was standing by myself in our front yard waiting for supper, just at that hour in a late summer day when the sun is already below the horizon and the risen full moon in the visible sky stops being chalky and begins to take on light. There comes the moment, and I saw it then, when the moon goes from flat to round. For the first time it met my eyes as a globe. The word 'moon' came into my mouth as though fed to me out of a silver spoon."

Her mother wanted her to have her own library card, and, having introduced her to the librarian, said, "Eudora is nine years old and has my permission to read any book she wants from the shelves, children or adult. . . . With the exception of *Elsie Dinsmore*." On the way home she explained: "She'd made this rule because Elsie the heroine, being made by her father to practice too long and hard at the piano, fainted and fell off the piano stool. 'You're too impressionable, dear,' she told me. 'You'd read that and the very first thing you'd do, you'd fall off the piano stool.' " Mrs. Welty was not unimpressionable her own self. ("She read Dickens in the spirit in which she would have eloped with him.")

"Ever since I was first read to, then started reading to myself," Miss Welty says, "there has never been a line read that I didn't *hear*. As my eyes followed the sentence, a voice was saying it silently to me. It isn't my mother's voice, or the voice of any person I can identify, certainly not my own. It is human, but inward, and it is inwardly that I listen to it. It is to me the voice of the story or the poem itself. . . . My own words, when I am at work on a story, I hear too as they go, in the same voice that I hear when I read in books."

Long before she wrote stories, she listened for them in the anecdotal, he-said-and-then-I'm-told-she-very-plainly-said monologues of a neighbor, of the sewing woman, or whoever. "I suppose it's an early form of participation in what goes on. Listening children know stories are *there*. When their elders sit and begin, children are just waiting and hoping for one to come out, like a mouse from its hole."

She was taken out of school and put to bed for several months because of an ailment the doctor described as "fast-beating heart." She spent the day in her parents' double bed in the front upstairs bedroom, surrounded by storybooks. From there she could see what went on in the schoolyard, but young visitors were not often allowed, lest they excite her. In the evening her father and mother sat there with her. The light was partly covered by a sheet of newspaper, and in the semidarkness of her side of the room she lay enjoying the murmur of their voices until she fell asleep and was carried to her own bed. "I don't remember that any secrets were revealed to me, nor do I remember any avid curiosity on my part to learn something I wasn't supposed to—perhaps I was too young to know what to listen for. But I was present in the room with the chief secret there was—the two of them, father and mother, sitting there as one. I was conscious of this secret and of my fast-beating heart in step together, as I lay in the slant-shaded light of the room, with a brown, pear-shaped scorch in the newspaper shade where it had become overheated once. . . . I suppose I was exercising as early as then the turn of mind, the nature of temperament, of a privileged observer; and owing to the way I became so, it turned out that I became the loving kind."

It was her mother, she says, who supported her emotionally and imaginatively in her wish to become a writer. Her father gave her a portable typewriter and a Webster's Collegiate Dictionary with her name, Eudora Alice Welty, and the date, 1925, inscribed on the flyleaf, and, somewhat later on, intimated that she would not be able to support herself by writing stories. She knew that, though he liked to read, he did not read fiction, which he thought inferior to factual writing because it was not true. He died before he had a chance to discover the kind of truth that, as a mature writer, she was capable of. Since he was neither insensitive nor of limited intelligence, his idea of truth as what is known or can be demonstrated to be a fact would have had to give way before a conception of the truth that is so much more encompassing: "In writing, as in life, the connections of all sorts of relationships and kinds lie in wait of discovery, and give out their signals to the Geiger counter of the charged imagination, once it is drawn into the right field. . . . I don't write by invasion into the life of a real person: my own sense of privacy is too strong for that. . . . What I do make my stories out of is the *whole* fund of my feelings, my responses to the real experiences of my own life, to the relationships that formed and changed it, that I have given most of myself to, and so learned my way toward a dramatic counterpart. Characters take on life sometimes by luck, but I suspect it is when you can write most entirely out of yourself, inside the skin, heart, mind, and soul of a person who is not yourself, that a character becomes in his own right another human being on the page."

In these lectures, thoughtful attention is given to a great many experiences of one kind or another: ideas and attitudes she was exposed to as a child, visits to Ohio and West Virginia, family stories, old letters, train rides—whatever opened her ears and eyes and mind to the life around her and revealed to her the nature and material of what was to become her fiction. It is all wonderful. It is what she was asked to do. And she does it from a carefully calculated distance, as if she were taking pictures with a camera. But one has finally the feeling that the crucial thing was her own sensibility, which she was, of course, born with. Consider this paragraph about returning home from a visit to her grandmother: "Back on Congress Street, when my father unlocked the door of our closed-up, waiting house, I rushed ahead into the airless hall and stormed up the stairs, pounding the carpet of each step with both hands ahead of me, and putting my face right down into the cloud of the dear dust of our long absence. I was welcoming ourselves back. Doing likewise, more methodically, my father was going from room to room restarting all the clocks." Surely nothing on God's green earth could have prevented *that* child from devoting her life to a study of the connections of all sorts of relationships and kinds that lie in wait of discovery.

The parts of the book that are about her family, her immediate family and going back for two or three generations, are by turns hilarious and affecting. They are a kind of present (they could conceivably have been withheld without slighting the ostensible purpose of the lectures) from Miss Welty to her audience. The handing over of so much intimate information cannot have been easy or unconcerned. The audience was, for the most part, Harvard and Radcliffe undergraduates, many more than the hall could accommodate, with the overflow in other rooms that were wired with speakers. After the last lecture, bringing flowers, they waited in long lines for the privilege of speaking to her. Not bunches of flowers. Just one flower.

Lord Byron's Financial Difficulties

In the late eighteenth century and well into the nineteenth, it was more than could be expected of a gentleman that he should be aware of the ordinary expenses of his household. Lord Byron, when he was living in Italy, had a steward, Antonio Lega Zambelli, whose duty it was to scrutinize and satisfy tradesmen's bills, pay the servants' wages, dispense charities, and keep systematic accounts. The people who had to deal with him found him officious, but he was an honest man, and Byron trusted him with large sums of money. He kept a detailed account of all expenditures, even the most trivial, and in general looked after his noble employer's interests with a zeal that bordered on the ridiculous. At the beginning of Byron's long affair with the Countess Guiccioli, Lega's mistress, the mother of Lega's two children, had served as a go-between, but her effusive personality got on Byron's nerves, and Lega was told to keep her out of sight. Though this undoubtedly hurt his feelings, it in no way affected his loyalty.

From Byron's death, in 1824, to his own, in 1847, Lega lived in London. During that time, no sooner did the sensation created by one book about Byron begin to quiet down than another book would be announced, creating a new furor. The "most gorgeous" but socially unacceptable Countess of Blessington published her *Journal of the Conversations of Lord Byron,* based on a friendship of two months' duration in Genoa in the spring of 1823; Count Pietro Gamba, the gallant brother of Teresa Guiccioli, published *A Narrative of Lord Byron's Last Journey to Greece;* Leigh Hunt published *Lord Byron and Some of His Contemporaries,* in which both Shelley and the author are continually extolled at Byron's expense; Thomas Medwin, a half-pay lieutenant who managed to make a career out of being a cousin of Shelley and who at no time lived under the same roof with Byron, published his *Journals of the Conversations of Lord Byron Noted During a Residence with His Lordship at Pisa in the Years 1821 and 1822;* the Irish poet Thomas Moore, who was Byron's intimate friend, published the *Letters and Journals of Lord Byron with Notices of His Life;* James Kennedy, a young ship's physician, who had tried to convert Byron to Methodism, published *Conversations on Religion with Lord Byron and Others Held in Cephalonia a Short Time Previous to His Lordship's Death;* William Parry, a former firemaster—that is to say, an officer who supervised the manufacture of explosives—in the British Navy and a member of Byron's entourage in Missolonghi, published *The Last Days of Lord Byron with His Lordship's Opinions on Various Subjects.* Not a single one of these authors bothered to consult the man who had been Byron's household steward during the period they were writing about.

The amount of documentary evidence about Byron that has survived is astonishing; even when people lied about him, they failed to destroy the evidence that would eventually disprove their statements. Lega's ledgers were carefully passed down— through his daughter, who married a son of Byron's valet, Fletcher, and again through their daughter, who married a Mr. Anson Weekes, of Mattapoisett, Massachusetts, called herself Mrs. Lega-Weekes, developed a taste for genealogy, and found that she was descended from a queen of Cyprus—to, finally, *their* daughter, a Miss Ethel Lega-Weekes, who died in 1949, at the age of eighty-eight. The British Museum acquired the Zam-belli Papers from her estate, and they constitute the principal source for Doris Langley Moore's second book on Byron.* The first, *The Late Lord Byron,* published fourteen years earlier, is about the suppression, distortion, and even forgery by which the poet's already scandalous reputation was, after his death, either shored up by his friends or further blackened by his enemies and detractors.

Curiosity about Lega led Mrs. Moore to the papers in the British Museum, which had been put in order and bound but until then not looked at by any Byron scholar. It was a formi-dable task. The accounts were, of course, in Italian, and required some knowledge of Italian methods of bookkeeping, and of sev-eral currencies, all obsolete. "But after a plodding day or two, there came a moment which reminded me of one in my child-hood, when I had been gazing at views through a stereoscope not expecting them to differ in any way from views without that aid, and all of a sudden they sprang into three dimensions. Those payments for searching the coast from Leghorn to Lerici, those journeys with post-horses to places with names unfamiliar but not unheard of, the Bocca del Serchio, the Torre di Mi-gliarino, the gratuities to sanitary officers, the wine and incense bought on the way to Viareggio—these items dotted here and there about the ledger in July and August 1822 were all occa-sioned by the quest for the bodies of Shelley and Williams and their obsequies! Those five extra beds hurriedly obtained on hire from 'the Jew De Montel'—why, that was the time of Leigh Hunt's arrival with six children whom Byron had not expected him to bring from England. . . . That letter to M. Beyle, which it cost four livres and ten soldi to post in May 1823, must have been the very one he wrote to the pseudonymous Stendhal to reproach him politely for his denigration of Walter Scott. Be-

---

Lord Byron Accounts Rendered. Harper & Row, 1974.

sides the ledgers' thus turning out to be full of the most evoc-
ative information, there were notes, letters, and all manner of
bills and receipts. Thanks to Lega's capacity for saving apparently trivial memoranda, we have Byron's domestic economy so
minutely yet unconsciously reflected that there can scarcely be
anything comparable in the annals of famous men. From the
Zambelli Papers we can learn what he paid his servants, what
he spent on his table and his wine merchant, how he maintained
his animals, what people he assisted, what clothes he ordered,
and how much linen he sent to the wash. Similar records illu-
mine, though with a greyer light, his life in Greece, and, equally,
his death. The fact that struck me most curiously was that no
early biographer could have used more than a fraction of that
information even if it had been available, because, until almost
the present century, it was considered vulgar for anyone but a
clerk or professional man to go into detail about money. Large
sums could be touched upon—debts on an important scale, in-
heritances, dowries of rich brides, but not the cost of a dinner,
a suit of clothes, a pound of wax candles."

A good deal more documentary evidence was preserved in
the office of John Murray, the great-great-grandson of Byron's
publisher.

Lord Byron's financial problems began well before he was born.
The fifth Lord Byron (the poet's great-uncle, from whom he
inherited the title) by both simple and fantastic extravagance laid
waste to a very considerable patrimony. When he died, there
was hardly enough money to bury him. The bill for £11 for
black cloth for the servants' mourning was sent to Catherine
Byron, the poet's mother—Byron was ten at the time—and she,
out of her slender means, paid it.

The Court of Chancery awarded the young Lord Byron £500
a year for his education. Hampered by a solicitor who did not

answer her letters and was so slow to act that he seems almost inert, Mrs. Byron nevertheless managed to pay her son's expenses at Harrow and elsewhere and to maintain a home for him. Her account books were poorly kept ("Pd different things," "Paid sundry things," etc.), yet they give a rough idea of—I am quoting Mrs. Moore—"the careful but certainly not ungenerous management by which her son's house and Nottinghamshire lands were lifted from a state of extreme and quite deliberate depredation to one of comfort and promise of abundance." When Byron went to Cambridge, at the age of seventeen and a half, she transferred the funds from Chancery directly into his keeping. It was the equivalent of handing a small child a box of kitchen matches. He scattered the money senselessly, and, when he couldn't get his hands on more, found the moneylenders helpful, and came of age owing about £12,000.

The fifth Lord Byron had leased, for an annual rental of £60, slate quarries and coal mines on an entailed estate in Lancashire that had been in the family since the time of Edward I, and they were now producing, for someone else, an annual income of perhaps £4,000. The arrangement was illegal, and there appeared to be no reason that the quarries and coal mines should not easily be recovered, and Byron would then have been one of the richest peers in England instead of being one of the poorest, but it took years and years of litigation, during which the slate was quarried and coal mined, to Byron's disadvantage. In the continuing belief that the matter was on the point of being settled, he spent money like—well, not like a drunken sailor, because no drunken sailor could have kept up with him. Item: "An Extra Spfine Corbo Pelisse full trimmed with braid, & Sleeves body & Skirt lined with Silk £18. Rich Sable Fur collar cuffs & trimming £8.4s." Eight months later, he ordered a second, but brown instead of blue-black. And five months after that he ordered a third, exactly like the first.

Item: sixty pairs of nankeen or white jean trousers.

Item: twenty-four white quilted waistcoats £31.4s.

Item (before embarking on the Grand Tour): a fitted basket canteen, a camp table and two chairs, two four-post patent bedsteads, complete with mattresses and mosquito nets, pillows, blankets, and counterpanes, covers and straps £42.10s.

Item: eight large solid leather trunks £65.12s.

Item: a carriage (ordered and delivered in 1816 and unpaid for in 1823) requiring four to six horses and modelled on one made for Napoleon £500.

Item (as part of the refurbishing of Newstead Abbey, where he did not intend to live): "A superb LOFTY double screwed six-feet FOUR-POST BEDSTEAD, on French castors, the pillars japanned and richly gilt, with RICH CRIMSON furniture, folding VELVET and scarlet draperies and valence, with doom [sic] top, richly studded, surmounted by a Coronet, and the draperies richly fringed with scarlet and black French fringe, with tassels, &c. supported by carved Eagles, superbly gilt."

All this in the midst of acute financial distress, which was compounded by large loans to friends, who made no effort to repay them; by his vulnerability to begging letters from total strangers; by fooleries (to a certain Thomas Ashe, who had published some bogus letters from the Princess of Wales to her daughter, Byron gave a hundred and fifty guineas, remarking in explanation that no one else was likely to oblige such a charlatan); and, finally, by a highly disadvantageous marriage settlement. That he was an impossible husband nobody ever doubted, but Mrs. Moore makes a good case for thinking that this most unfortunate of all possible marriages would never have taken place at all if it had not been for the mismanagement of Byron's property by that frightful solicitor John Hanson, who so entangled himself in Byron's affairs that there was no way of removing him.

It almost doesn't bear thinking about, the muddle is so great and so hopeless. Byron did, of course, think about it a great deal. In time, he even managed to pull himself together and do something. With the help of a friend, Douglas Kinnaird, who acted as his banker and financial adviser while he was living abroad, he was able to circumvent Hanson when he could not move him to action. He also changed his mind about the impropriety of a writer with private means (i.e., a gentleman) accepting money for his work. And under the influence of Lega Zambelli he began to take an acute interest not only in where his money came from but also in where it went—with the result that he was at last freed from the anxiety of debt, and was even able to finance, out of his own pocket, the Greek struggle for independence that is forever associated with his name.

As for the information hidden away in those Italian ledgers, what the Noble Lord paid his servants, how much he gave on the fifth of March to three old men and a lame woman, exactly what he sent to the wash ("6 shirts, 10 pocket Handkerchiefs, 6 pair Silk Stockings, 2 Waistcoats, 4 Pair Trowsers, 2 Night Caps") is interesting up to a point. So is what he spent on wine and gin and brandy, since it proves that he was not a drunkard. It is more interesting to discover that at their last meeting, on July 7, 1822, Shelley borrowed £50 from Byron. The following day, sailing from Leghorn to Lerici, Shelley was, as everybody knows, overtaken by a squall in the Gulf of Spezia and drowned.

It is Mrs. Moore's particular strength (and what makes her book so continuously interesting) that, exerting the utmost patience in dealing with questions of fact, she also manages at every point to introduce questions of character. Her summing up of the relations of Byron and Shelley in three pages is masterly. "While Byron was," she says, "a man of moods, but with a fundamental steadiness in his friendships which made them durable, Shelley suffered violent oscillations of opinion."

Shelley admired Byron's poetry beyond that of any other of his contemporaries, and was highly gratified to find himself on an intimate footing with him. But he also at times couldn't bear Byron, because of his worldly habits and his skepticism about human perfectibility and his resistance to Shelley's proselytizing against religion. The "beautiful and ineffectual angel" was not at all tolerant of people who didn't think as he did. His letters are full of self-contradictory judgments, and Byron was not the only friend whose stock rose and fell. Beside "I detest all society—almost all, at least—and Lord Byron is the nucleus of all that is hateful and tiresome in it" one must place this description of a visit to Byron at Ravenna: "Lord Byron gets up at *two*. I get up, quite contrary to my usual custom, but one must sleep or die . . . at 12. After breakfast we sit talking till six. From six till eight we gallop through the pine forests which divide Ravenna from the sea; we then come home and dine, and sit up gossiping till six in the morning"—which does not suggest that Byron's company was either hateful or tiresome, though it might in the end prove exhausting. In another letter, written on the same day, he says, "The demon of mistrust & of pride lurks between two persons in our situation poisoning the freedom of their intercourse." Whose pride and whose mistrust is the question.

It has to be remembered that there was four and a half years' difference in their ages: Shelley was only twenty-nine when his boat disappeared in the fog on that hot, calm, fatal day. And a huge difference in their literary reputations during their lifetime. Though we tend to lump Byron, Shelley, and Keats together, carelessly, the age did not. To his friend John Gisborne, Shelley wrote, "I have received Hellas, which is prettily printed, & with fewer mistakes than any poem I ever published. Am I to thank you for the revision of the press? or who acted as midwife to this last of my orphans, introducing it to oblivion, & me to my accustomed failure."

In addition to everything else, the Shelleys thought that Byron was rich as Croesus (his income at this time was something under £4,000, out of which he was still paying off debts contracted before he came of age, and the immense charges of the lawsuit to recover the coal mines, which was not finally disposed of until the last year of his life), and they were shocked that a man of such wealth should check the accounts of his household steward and be so attentive to what things cost. Shelley himself was £22,500 in debt, his only financial recourse being to borrow, at one-hundred-per-cent interest, against his coming into his inheritance on the death of his father, who outlived him. A substantial part of this financial burden had been incurred for other people. Over the years, his rascally father-in-law, William Godwin, had put the touch on him for £4,500, and on one occasion alone Shelley gave Leigh Hunt £1,400.

Byron and Shelley had planned to spend the summer of 1822 on the Italian coast and to do a lot of sailing. With this in mind, Shelley took a house at Lerici, which the Shelleys shared with Edward Williams and his wife. Williams was a young officer who had retired from service in India. By the middle of June, Byron's schooner and Shelley's twenty-four-foot sailboat, built in Genoa at the same time, in the same shipyard, had arrived and were giving their owners trouble. Byron's had cost ten times more than he had anticipated. And, Shelley having decided to call his boat the Don Juan, the shipbuilder painted the name not only on the hull but on the mainsail, as if it were a coal barge. It is clear enough from an entry in Williams' journal that he and Shelley believed this had been done on instructions from Lord Byron, but the shipbuilding was handled through an intermediary, Captain Trelawny; there is no evidence that Byron gave any direct orders to the builder about anything. And whereas it is unlike Byron to have interfered in the matter of someone else's boat, it is quite in the character of the intermediary both to have thought up this tasteless idea and to have lied about it afterward. In any event, Shelley and Williams were angered by it. Did Lord Byron mean to write the Bolivar on his own mainsail? When no amount of scrubbing would obliterate the lettering, the sailmaker in Sezano cut the name from the mainsail and, taking two reefs from the scudding sail, patched it in such a way that the join was not visible. With two tons of iron ballast to bring her down to her bearings, the Don Juan was still very crank in a breeze. The two English sailors who had brought her from Genoa announced that she was a ticklish boat to manage, and cautioned the gentlemen accordingly. Shelley and Williams managed to jam the mainsheet and to put the tiller starboard instead of port.

"Hunt is not yet arrived," Shelley wrote Gisborne, "but I expect him every day. I shall see little of Lord Byron, nor shall I permit Hunt to form the intermediate link between him and me." And then Hunt arrived, with his family, though Shelley had warned him not to bring them. And expected to be fed by the ravens, as usual. And Shelley had to go and borrow £50 from Byron, there being nobody else he could get it from.

That Shelley sometimes hated him Byron had no idea. Writing to his publisher after Shelley's death, he said, "You were all brutally mistaken about Shelley who was without exception— the best and least selfish man I ever knew—I never knew one who was not a beast in comparison."

Considering the phrase "accounts rendered" as applicable beyond the confines of income and expenditure to "deeds for which a price is to be exacted," Mrs. Moore moves in and out of and around the episodes of Byron's life, stopping to fill out in detail circumstances other biographers have skimmed over, or to relate something not generally known, or to refute with persuasive new evidence some long-accepted opinion. For example, the Capucine Convent of San Giovanni, at Bagnacavallo, where Byron placed his four-year-old daughter, Allegra, and where she died of a fever and bloodletting, was not the frightful place that legend has it but a boarding school attended by the children of the best families of the district. And, furthermore, the Shelleys approved of this arrangement. During the very brief period of Allegra's illness, hardly anything was communicated directly to Byron; even letters addressed to him were filtered through Lega, who was a well-meaning but sometimes misjudging go-between. "Little dreaming that he would be likened to an executioner for placing his daughter in a well-recommended boarding-school, Byron was writing, talking, riding, shooting in Pisa, and corresponding with his men of business in England on the arbitration respecting his late mother-in-law's estate." The letter announcing Allegra's death arrived before the one announcing that the illness had become serious, which was sent by ordinary post.

No one before Mrs. Moore bothered to go at all thoroughly into the miserable life of "Mad Jack" Byron, the poet's father, or even had full access to the material that would make this possible. Peers enjoyed immunity from arrest for debt, but nephews of peers did not. Jack Byron, having gambled away the fortunes of two wives, was taken to King's Bench Prison and bailed out by his tailor and fled to France. The letters he wrote to his sister in London suggest an incestuous attachment. They also constitute a narrative of the last days of Hogarth's Rake—besieged by creditors, sponging on his social inferiors, throwing his female servant down the stairs, bragging that he never gives money to the provincial actresses he sleeps with but on the contrary accepts presents from them, robbed of seventeen pairs of silk stockings by his manservant, borrowing back from the bailiffs the forks and spoons he ate with, coughing up blood. In his will, dictated six weeks before he died, he unrealistically charged his infant son to pay his debts and funeral expenses. But at no time in his short life had he ever been realistic about anything.

Byron idealized his father, whom he last saw when he was two and a half, and could not "breathe in comfort" under the same roof with his mother. "With an exterior far from prepossessing, an understanding where nature had not been bountiful, a mind almost wholly without cultivation, and the peculiarities of northern opinions, northern habits, and northern accent"— this description of her is based on what a Scottish schoolmaster who was a snob told Thomas Moore, who was a social climber. Reinforced by Byron's early letters to his half sister, it is the picture of her that has come down through time. Mrs. Moore thinks it is extremely unfair. Catherine Byron was a short, stout, highly irritable, blundering woman, related to some of the noblest families in Scotland, and a lineal descendant, through Annabella Stuart, of James I. The woman who wrote "His Heart is good, and his Talents are *great*, and I have no doubt of his being a *great* man. God grant that he may be a prudent and happy one also" was not unintelligent. Or vulgar. But when aroused she had little, if any, control over her tongue and was (I am quoting Mrs. Moore) "outspoken beyond anything society allows—a tendency she transmitted to her descendants—and had a way of being right in the wrong manner which made her no favourite with those who had to deal with her." She had rows with schoolmasters and lawyers, and with her son's guardian, Lord Carlisle. In a fit of temper, she called Byron a lame brat. If he never forgave her for this, neither, probably, did she forgive herself. Her devotion to him was boundless. Whether she fought with him or for him, the row was always in his interest. Byron did not find her unbearable until he began to be senselessly extravagant.

"Her failure as a mother," Mrs. Moore insists, "was due as much to her virtues as to her defects and was the repetition of her failure in marriage. Even at the cost of self-immolation she could deny nothing either to her husband or her son, and such magnanimity asks to be abused. Truth speaks in every line of hers that survives, and courage never falters. Yet if she was dauntless she was also pugnacious, while her truthfulness was carried to the verge of embarrassing tactlessness. She suffered too from want of manner—but not ignorance of polite forms. All her letters are in accordance with the etiquette of the day, and if her appearance was vulgar it could only have been because it was not easy for an obese woman in neoclassical dress to look refined."

Mrs. Byron was only twenty-six when she was widowed. She brought her son up in Aberdeen, not in poverty and squalor, as is often said, but in simple respectability. Her husband's family could have helped her financially and didn't. After a time, they stopped answering her letters. They did not even bother to inform her that the fifth Lord Byron's grandson had been killed in battle, and so her son was now next in succession. She lived on £135 a year, without debt, and with a nurse and scullery maid. After her son inherited the title, she tried to live in a way that would not reflect on his position, but she was never free from financial worry, and spent less on herself, on clothes and feminine pleasures, than she gave the twelve-year-old Lord Byron for pocket money.

"The more I see of her," he wrote his half sister, "the more my dislike augments, nor can I so entirely conquer the appearance of it, as to prevent her from perceiving my opinion, this so far from calming the Gale, blows it into a *hurricane*, which threatens to destroy every thing, till, exhausted by its own violence, it is lulled into a sullen torpor, which, after a short period, is again roused into fresh and renewed phrenzy, to me most terrible, and to every other Spectator astonishing."

When provoked, she was loud and abusive. But surely Byron

meant to exasperate her when he wrote that he happened to have "a few hundreds in ready Cash lying by me" and that he found it inconvenient to remain at Cambridge and wished to spend a couple of years abroad. The letter ends, "I shall lay this Plan before Hanson & Lord C[arlisle]. I presume you will all agree, and if you do not, I will if possible get away without your consent, though I should admire it more in the Regular manner and with a Tutor of your furnishing. . . . Let me have your Answer, I intend remaining in Town a month longer, when perhaps I shall bring my Horses and myself down to your residence in that *execrable* Kennel [Newstead Abbey was let, and Mrs. Byron had taken a house nearby]. I hope you have engaged a Man Servant—else it will be impossible for me to visit you, since my Servant must attend chiefly to his horses, at the same Time you must cut an Indifferent Figure with only maids in your habitation, I remain yours, Byron."

He was past the age when she could give him a cuff. He was not even there to be shouted at. To the solicitor she wrote despairingly, "Where can he get Hundreds; has he got into the hands of Money Lenders, he has *no feeling, no Heart*. This I have long known he has behaved as ill as possible to me for years back, this bitter truth I can no longer conceal. It is wrung from me *by heart rending agony*. . . . He knows that I am doing every thing in my power to pay his Debts and he writes to me about hiring Servants and the last time he wrote to me was to desire me to send him £25.0.0. to pay his Harrow Bills which I would have done if I had had as much as he has—these hundreds. . . . God knows what is to be done with him. I much fear he is already ruined; at eighteen!"

It was not true that Byron had no heart. But he was, as Mrs. Moore says, too young to know what his interests were and too headstrong at that stage to care. When the money ran out, he came home and she forgave him. Furthermore, she managed to borrow £1,000 from relatives, using the greater part of her capital as security, and gave it to him to pay his debts. Later on, he asked her to let him have most of what was left, in the form of a loan, so he could go abroad, and she was quite willing to do this, but required security, since it would leave her without anything to live on. The correspondence with lawyers in Scotland who were taking care of her affairs dragged on so long that Byron became impatient and borrowed the money from a Cambridge drinking companion, Scrope Davies, who got it from the moneylenders, and subsequently Byron was hard put to it to prevent his ruin. Another friend had been killed in a duel after a drunken quarrel, leaving his family in want, and Mrs. Byron heard that, while standing godfather to his posthumous child, Byron had unobtrusively left £500 in a teacup. About money, at this period of his life, he was a pure and simple idiot and should have been declared legally incompetent—that is one way of looking at it. But it isn't the only way. "A mania of improvidence possessed him," Mrs. Moore says, "and yet, so capriciously is the pattern of life woven, that hardly any of these follies failed, in the long run, to justify themselves. The travel books he purchased stimulated the alert, rewarding interest he was to take in the scenes he visited; Falconer's *Shipwreck* at one guinea was among the source materials for the vivid shipwreck passages in *Don Juan*; the portrait by Sanders, now in the Royal Collection, has given posterity its best idea of Byron as a young romantic, and, as the sole illustration of the first edition of Moore's biography, was an important visual contribution to the Romantic Movement; while the greatest extravagance of all, the mounting-up of huge debts to go travelling, resulted in the writing of *Childe Harold* and the Oriental verse narratives which brought him unmeasured fame."

The loan that Mrs. Byron had arranged haunted her, and she made her son promise that he would take it over before he left

England. He went off leaving the debt still in his mother's name, and with no arrangement even for paying the interest. Hanson was supposed to take care of everything—Hanson, who never lifted a finger unless somebody threatened him, and mostly not even then. Having deposited £3,000 at Hammersley's Bank for Byron, he neglected to observe the instructions as to how and where the remittances were to reach his client, and so Byron, travelling in Asia Minor and Greece, was without cash or credit.

During the two years Byron was out of England, he wrote his mother a number of long and amusing letters, which gave her pleasure, and he also showed some solicitude for her: "Pray use my funds as far as they *go* without reserve," he wrote her. And to Hanson he wrote, "If Mrs. Byron requires any supply, pray let her have it at my expense and at all events whatever becomes of me do not allow her to suffer any unpleasant privation." When the lease on Newstead Abbey expired, Mrs. Byron moved back there, and one morning found a summons tacked on the door of the Great Hall. An upholsterer in Nottingham, to whom Byron had given a note of hand, now overdue, of £1,600, had sent two bailiffs to the Abbey. The execution, if carried out, would have meant that not only Byron's furniture, plate, books, clothing, and so on, but his mother's, too, would have been carted off. The gamekeeper's wages had gone unpaid for a year, and Mrs. Byron borrowed £10 from her maid to keep his family from starving. She also kept one of Byron's creditors out of prison by herself collecting the rents— which Hanson had expressly forbidden her to do—from four of Byron's most prosperous tenants. She wrote to the lawyer about all this, over and over, but not one word of it ever got into her letters to her son. Or of the fact that she was seriously ill. Along with the Scottish accent the schoolmaster deplored went a Scottish pride.

Byron came home with the resolution to behave better to her, and lingered in London for a fortnight, when he received, from the apothecary who had been taking care of his mother, a letter than began:

> My Lord
>   It is with concern I have to inform you that on my visit to Mrs. Byron this Morning, I found her *considerably* worse, so as to make me *most apprehensive* for the Event.—She is perfectly sensible and enquires after you—I am expecting Dr. Marsden every minute from Nottingham. . . .

Byron was completely broke and had to draw on Hanson for £40 before he could set off. On the way, he was met by a messenger with the news that his mother was dead. He wrote to a friend, from the coaching inn at Newport Pagnell, "My poor mother died yesterday! and I am on my way from town to attend her to the family vault. . . . Thank God her last moments were most tranquil. I am told she was in little pain, and not aware of her situation." In short, he took it calmly. But the night after his arrival at Newstead Abbey, Mrs. Byron's waiting woman, passing the room where the coffin was, found him sitting in the dark, in tears. On the morning of the funeral he could not bring himself to join the procession to Hucknall Torkard Church, but stood in the door of the Abbey until it passed out of sight. Then he turned to his page, the only person left in the house besides himself, and told him to get the sparring gloves, and proceeded to his usual exercise with the boy, but was silent and abstracted, and put more violence into his blows than usual, and suddenly flung the gloves away and retired to his room.

Accounts Rendered and *The Late Lord Byron* should be read together, since they are complementary. The core of the earlier book is the burning of the manuscript and only copy of Byron's uncompleted memoirs in the office of his publisher, shortly after the news of his death reached England. The person who was chiefly responsible for this appalling act was his executor, John Cam Hobhouse, who, though an honorable man and devoted to Byron, was something of a stuffed shirt. He did not himself tear up the pages and put them in the fire, but without his resolute maneuvering it could not have happened. Since he had strenuously advised the total suppression of *Don Juan*, it seems safe to say that of the literary value of Byron's manuscript he would not have been a proper judge. He had not, in fact, even read the memoirs; he did not need to, being certain that they must contain indecencies. And the result of his high-handed behavior was that the evidence that would have refuted many of the charges later brought against Byron was destroyed. What Hobhouse was afraid of was that an understanding of Byron's character would damage his reputation as a poet. The Concise O.E.D. defines "profligate" as "licentious, dissolute; recklessly extravagant," and Byron was certainly all those things, but I have never read anything about him which was trustworthy that made me dislike him. The picture of him that sticks in my mind is Thomas Moore's statement that while dining at Newstead Abbey Byron would pass a glass of wine over his shoulder to his superannuated butler, who was standing behind his chair.

Considering that Byron was as communicative and outspoken a man as probably ever lived, and a copious letter writer, both his friends and his detractors had their work cut out for them. They were more than equal to it. As one vindictive, misleading, untruthful book of conversation and recollections after another is subjected to Mrs. Moore's painstaking, ironic, informed scrutiny, the reader can hardly escape the sad conclusion that the living are nothing like so vulnerable as the dead.

Displaced Princes and Princesses

In the spring of 1919, Prince Illarion Vassiltchikov, prevented by the Revolution from having the brilliant career in the government which was predicted for him, left St. Petersburg with his wife and small children and lived abroad, mostly in France, until the early thirties, when they settled in Lithuania. The family had owned property there, but the house was burnt down by the Germans during the First World War and the land had been confiscated by the newly independent Lithuanian state. Shortly after the beginning of the Second World War, Soviet troops crossed the Lithuanian border and occupied strategically placed towns and airports, and an aristocratic family like the Vassiltchikovs could no longer feel safe there. Prince Illarion's son Alexander had died earlier that year, of tuberculosis. His eldest daughter was living in Rome. The two younger girls, Tatiana and Marie, who was called Missie, were in Germany staying in the country house of the Countess Olga Pückler, a childhood friend of their mother.

On January 1, 1940, Missie wrote in her diary, "We lit the Christmas tree and tried to read the future by dropping melted wax and lead into a bowl of water. We expect Mamma and Georgie to appear any minute from Lithuania. They have announced their arrival repeatedly. At midnight all the village bells began to ring. We hung out of the windows listening—the first New Year of this new World War."* Two days later the sisters set out for Berlin, by train, with eleven pieces of luggage, including a gramophone. They had no money of their own, and had borrowed from the Countess enough to last them for three weeks. They stayed in her Berlin flat, using only one bedroom, a bathroom, and the kitchen. The rest of the huge apartment was shrouded in dust sheets. They spent the following day blacking out the windows, and two nights later they went to a ball at the Chilean Embassy.

Both girls were beautiful. They were also highly intelligent, and humorous, and brave, and had the family independence of mind. Missie had worked for a while as a secretary in the British Legation in Kaunas. At that moment, because of the worldwide depression, a foreigner had very little chance of getting a work permit in any of the Western democracies. Only in Italy and Germany, where massive public-works programs had virtually done away with unemployment, was this possible. Their German was shaky and they hoped to find work with some firm in need of a French- or English-speaking secretary, but the war had brought international business to a halt. The consul at the American Embassy gave them a test and said he would call them as soon as there was a vacancy. On January 11th, Missie wrote in her diary, "My twenty-third birthday . . . In the evening Reinhard Spitzy took us to the cinema and then on to a night club, Ciro's, where we drank champagne and listened to the music; there is no longer any dancing in public.

"*13 January*   Mamma and Georgie arrived at crack of dawn. I had not seen Georgie for over a year. He has not changed, is full of charm and is very nice to Mamma, who looks very ill

Berlin Diaries, 1940–45, edited by George Vassiltchikov. Knopf, 1987.

and run-down. In Lithuania . . . they had been through unnerv-
ing experiences. It was high time the family left. Papa, however,
has stayed on, as he has a big business deal pending."

Mamma and Georgie had only forty dollars between them,
and were installed in the flat, so they wouldn't have to spend
money on a hotel. Georgie's appetite was alarming, and the
butter and sausage the two girls had brought with them from
the country dwindled rapidly. At I. G. Farben, only people who
could do German shorthand perfectly were wanted. The American Embassy did not call.

"*Monday, 20 January, 1941*   Supper with Bally and Bübchen
Hatzfeldt. They share a huge flat near the Tiergarten. I wandered into Bübchen's room to fix my hair, caught sight of an
open cupboard and was staggered by the quantity of suits hanging there with an equal number of shoes. I could not help thinking what Georgie and Alexander would have given to own just
a couple. Our penniless émigré life reached its peak just as they
got to the age of eighteen, when clothes for boys are often as
important as they are for girls.

"*29 January*   Today we both started work: I with the D.D.
[for Drahtloser Dienst, the news service of the Berlin equivalent
of the BBC] and Tatiana at the Foreign Ministry. . . . My office
does not seem to know who its Top Boss is, as everybody is
giving orders at the same time, although the Reich's Propaganda
Minister, Dr. Joseph Goebbels, is said to have the last word.

"*30 January*   My first job was taking down a long story about
Ronnie Cross, who is British Minister of Economic Warfare
and with whom Tatiana stayed when she was in England before
the war. My direct boss, Herr E . . . , dictates endless articles,
mostly vituperative and so involved that they become often
incomprehensible."

Missie got up at 5:30 A.M. and was at her desk by seven,
typed all day, and left at five for a long ride across town. Ta-

tiana's hours at the Foreign Ministry were from 10 A.M. until 8 P.M. and later, and so they did not see much of each other.

In February their mother and brother left Berlin to stay with the Countess before going on to Rome.

"*12 March* Mamma . . . telephoned from Vienna to say that Georgie had disappeared. When the train stopped at some small station on the way, he went to check their luggage. Without his noticing it, the luggage van was uncoupled from the main body of the train and joined onto another. He is now hurtling towards Warsaw. He has both their tickets, no passport and only five marks to his name. Mamma is waiting for him hopefully in Vienna."

Missie was a compulsive diarist, and the entries were for the most part typed openly, on office time, and tucked away in a filing cabinet between sheets of official matter. Eventually, when the pile of typed pages grew too bulky to escape notice, she would take it home and hide it there or in some country house that she happened to be visiting. The diary was written in English, which she had learned as a child, until she had something to conceal, and then she switched to a personal shorthand. Her diaries are not introspective and contain few generalizations. They record whom she saw and what she did, always with the instinct for the telling detail which is characteristic of the great diarists. Circumstances brought it about that they would also record, from ground level and at close range, the destruction of two great cities, the deterioration of the German social fabric during wartime, and the dreadful consequences of the failure of a conspiracy to assassinate Adolf Hitler. That it is a historical document of importance hardly needs saying. That it did not fall into the hands of the Gestapo—also that *she* didn't—is cause for wonder.

"*28 March* A letter from Rome telling us of Mamma's and Georgie's safe arrival, minus some things that were stolen in

Venice. These included many *objets d'art* Mamma had kept from
Russian days, Fabergé enamel frames, etc., and Georgie's suitcase
with his few clothes.

"*9 April* Today German troops occupied Denmark and invaded Norway. As a result, we worked like hell, since all these
various *coups* must be justified in the eyes of the world at large
and endless memoranda are exchanged how best to do this."

Their Lithuanian passports were invalid; there was no longer
any such country. Missie had gone to school in France, but
Russia was the country of her heart. She did not believe in the
Allied cause any more than she believed in Hitler's. She did not
belong in Germany and could not go anywhere else. If she had
tried to stop working at the news service, she might have ended
up on an assembly line in a munitions factory.

The Vassiltchikovs' world, the world of European aristocracy,
was going through the last days of its existence. Its structure was
spelled out in the *Almanach de Gotha*. It required the presence
of absolute monarchies and the belief in certain other absolutes,
Honor being one of them.

Some German aristocrats were anti-Nazi as far back as 1933;
others embraced the movement as a way of wiping out the
disgrace of the Versailles treaty, but because they could not accept Hitler's anti-Semitism and other policies, and because they
had seen their sons mowed down and the German Army half
destroyed in the disastrous Russian campaign, they turned against
him. Hitler hated them all, from the beginning.

Among the acquaintances whom the two girls saw most frequently in Berlin were Countesses Sigrid and Luisa von Welczeck, whose father was the last German Ambassador to Paris;
Prince Burchard of Prussia, a grandson of Kaiser Wilhelm II;
Count Gottfried von Bismarck-Schönhausen, a grandson of
the Iron Chancellor, and his wife, Melanie; Baroness Agathe
von Fürstenberg-Herdringen; and Princess Eleanore-Marie
Schönburg-Hartenstein. (The titles are spelled out only in the

notes and the index. In the printed text they are "Sigi Welczeck" and "Loremarie Schönburg." And in the manuscript are
simply initials, as in most private diaries.) They moved about in
a body, dining at this or that restaurant and on the spur of the
moment driving out to somebody's house in the environs of the
city. They are superficially rather like the Bright Young People
in the novels of Evelyn Waugh, who were, of course, a generation earlier. Though brought up to privilege and property, Missie's friends, when pushed to the wall, proved to have character
and nobility, were selfless when the need arose, showed great
courage and fortitude, and were, in short, aristocrats in the only
interesting sense of the word.

"*7 May* Had rather a messy supper consisting of buns, yoghurt, warmed-up tea and jam. Yoghurt is still unrationed and,
when we are at home, it constitutes our main dish, occasionally
supplemented by porridge cooked in water. We are allowed ap-
proximately one jar of jam a month per person and, butter being
so scarce, that does not go very far. Tatiana suggests our hanging
a notice over the kitchen table: 'breakfast,' 'lunch' and 'supper,'
according to the time of day, as the menu remains by and large
unchanged.

"*2 June* Yesterday we went shopping as it was pay day. We
never seem to have a cent left at the end of the month, which
is not astonishing, considering our salaries. The two of us now
earn 450 marks, of which 100 go to the family in Rome, another
100 to repay our debts and about 200 more for food, transpor-
tation, etc. This leaves us about 50 marks for our personal expenses, clothes, mail, etc. But this time I had saved and was able
to buy a dress I had spotted months ago. I had also had to put
aside enough clothing coupons, but the shop forgot to ask me
for them!

"Tonight a bath. Now that baths are rationed too, this is an
event."

At an evening party the Vassiltchikov girls heard that Russia had just annexed the whole of Lithuania. Worried about their father, they went home at once and spent all night trying to get in touch with people at the Foreign Ministry who might be helpful. Burchard of Prussia was appealed to, and alerted a Colonel Oster of the Military Intelligence.

"*17 June* Have hardly slept these last nights. It is rumored that Lithuanian President Smetona and most of his cabinet ministers escaped across the German border.

"*20 June* On returning tonight I found a telegram from Papa. Sent from Tilsit, in East Prussia, it said, 'Glücklich angekommen,' and asked for money to come and join us.

"*24 June* Dinner at Gatow on the lake with a group of Italian friends. Went home early, as the others were off to a party given by the American-born wife of one of the Italian diplomats here. It strikes me as somewhat indecent to be so jolly, considering what is happening in France.

"*25 June* On returning home, I found Papa, extraordinarily spry considering what he has just been through. His only earthly possessions now are his shaving things, two dirty handkerchiefs and a shirt. On reaching German soil he was apparently treated very well by the frontier police—thanks to Colonel Oster's intervention. He was even offered money to join us. But before that, he had had a scary time, hiding in the woods of his former estate and crossing the border at dead of night with the help of an ex-poacher.

"*4 August* After church we joined a group of friends at the Hotel Eden, where Luisa Welczeck was lunching with a boy called Paul Metternich, the famous Chancellor's great-grandson, who is half-Spanish. Afterwards, as we were all invited to the Schaumburgs' out in Cladow, we took off in different cars, with Paul Metternich in the rumble seat with Tatiana, Nagy and me. He has practically no hair on his head, poor thing, just stubble, as he is a simple soldier somewhere. Because of this unannounced intrusion, poor Burchard of Prussia had to take the train. It is obvious that Paul has fallen for Tatiana.''

Until this point, the Allies and the German High Command had both been reluctant to bomb civilian populations. On the night of August 24th, German aircraft accidentally dropped bombs on London. The British retaliated.

"*26 August* Yet another raid. We stayed in bed, although the doormen of all houses have now received orders to force everyone into the cellars. Ours came along too, rattling a saucepan to get us up.

"*27 August* Dropped in on Tatiana at her office after work. One could hear a lot of splashing from the next room, a bathroom. Her boss was evidently taking advantage of the fact that hot water is still freely available in government establishments.

"Dinner with friends, including the two Kieckebusch brothers. Both were badly wounded in France, Mäxchen was paralysed for three months. Claus's tank caught fire, he was thrown out, his face badly burnt, but he has recovered well and one does not see much.

"*2 September* Although we expected a raid, we stayed at home, hoping to get some sleep. Our cellar is rather well arranged. Small children lie in cots, sucking their thumbs. Tatiana and I usually play chess. She beats me regularly.

"*3 September* Air-raid at midnight, but as Tatiana had a slight fever, we stayed upstairs. Our beds are in different corners of the room and Tatiana fears that if the house is hit I might be hurtled into space while she would remain suspended in midair, so I got into her bed and we lay hugging each other for two full hours. The noise was ghastly. Flashes of light outside kept lighting up the room. . . . Even Papa was slightly perturbed and came in for a chat.

"*7 September*   Today we moved from the Pücklers' to Ditti Mandelsloh's *pied-à-terre*. He is at the front and does not wish it to stay vacant for fear it may be requisitioned by some party fellow. It is in the Hardenbergstrasse, near the Zoo S-Bahn station—a bad location in an air-raid—but it is tiny and therefore practical.

"*9 September*   Another raid. I slept through the whole thing, hearing neither the siren, nor the bombs, nor the all-clear."

Papa turned out to be a gifted cook, though he put too much pepper in everything—and supported himself by giving Russian lessons.

"*10 October*   In London, Aunt Katia Galitzine was killed by a bomb which hit the bus she was riding in. There was a memorial service for her here in Berlin this morning. . . . This evening I was at a party when the alarm sounded. The shooting was very loud and poor Mäxchen Kieckebusch, whose nerves have gone to pieces since he was injured in the spine in France, rolled on the floor moaning '*Ich kann das nicht mehr hören*' over and over again."

Paul Metternich was in Berlin on leave six days at the beginning of November, and Tatiana was out with him every evening. On the fourteenth, he was back. After being out with her he would ring up in the middle of the night to talk some more.

Missie was introduced to a man in the Information Department of the Foreign Ministry—Dr. Adam von Trott zu Solz. Through an American grandmother he was descended from John Hay. He had been a Rhodes Scholar, and had travelled in China and the United States. They met again by chance, and in December he suggested that she come and work for him as a sort of confidential factotum. He was an ardent patriot. In his dealings with all foreign politicians, the position he took was that they should stand up to Hitler and encourage anti-Nazi opposition but on the other hand recognize Germany's national interests. Though he was received in the highest circles in London, he was also viewed with distrust. He had joined the Nazi Party to cover his activities, and took a job in the Foreign Ministry because an active anti-Nazi group was forming there.

Missie loved the relaxed atmosphere of the Information Department. At lunchtime people faded away for an indefinite period, and to make up for this they sometimes worked until ten. "Come on, Missie," they would say, "set aside your diary and let's get a little work done!"

Missie and Adam Trott spoke English together. In dictation his German became so intellectual that she often missed half of it. If it was merely secretarial competence he was looking for, he could have done better. It is quite clear that she interested him as much as he interested her. In a letter to his wife he wrote: "Drove back with Missie and was again astonished and impressed by her. . . . She has something of a noble animal of legend about her, that one can never quite understand . . . something free that enables her to soar far above everything and everyone. This, of course, is a little tragic, indeed almost uncanny."

"*8 May* Air-raid. Am getting more nervous about them. Now my heart begins to beat whenever the siren starts.

"*24 May* People are speaking more and more of troop concentrations on the Russian border. Nearly all the men we know are being transferred from the West to the East."

With the exception of a few entries having to do mostly with the total destruction of the Metternich family castle in the Rhineland and with the elaborate festivities leading up to the marriage of H.H. Princess Maria-Adelgunde of Hohenzollern to H.R.H. Prince Konstantin of Bavaria, there is a gap in the diaries from June 23, 1941, to July 20, 1943. Some pages Missie destroyed, others were concealed in a country house in what is now Communist Eastern Europe and may be there still or may have been burnt as rubbish. The editor has been able to fill in this hiatus partly with excerpts from letters. Missie's sister Irena wrote that Hugo Windisch-Graetz, who was an officer in the Italian Air Force and whom Missie had known since childhood and seen a lot of in Venice just before the war, had been killed while trying out a new plane. At his funeral his twin brother "knelt throughout the service next to the coffin, stroking it and talking to Hugo. It is perfectly heart-rending."

Where else do you find descriptions of human behavior that, like this one, haunt the mind? The answer is, in Tolstoy, on whom the Vassiltchikov children must have been brought up. I do not mean to suggest that Marie Vassiltchikov's diaries are comparable to *War and Peace* but only that they have something in common with it.

In September of 1941, Tatiana and Paul Metternich were married in the official residence of the Spanish military attaché in Berlin, in the presence of her entire family. Irena went back to Rome immediately, Mamma and Georgie lingered and were caught by new regulations forbidding all travel by foreigners into and out of Germany. The bride and groom went to Spain, where they remained until the following spring, and in the fall of 1942 Georgie managed to get to Paris and stayed there. Mamma withdrew to the Countess Pückler's, and Missie and her father were bombed out of several apartments, and ended up as paying guests of friends, Baron and Baroness Heinz and Maria von Gersdorff, whose hospitality embraced like-minded people from every sector of German society. And it became a part of Missie's job to build up an archive of photographs of the German war effort.

"*16 November* Sadly, I and my photo-archive have been moved to the former Czech Legation in the Rauchstrasse. . . . Dined tonight at Gottfried Bismarck's in Potsdam with Adam Trott, the Hassells and Furtwängler. The latter, who is terrified of the possible arrival of the Russians, disappointed me. From a musical genius I had somehow expected more 'class.' "

During this period, Hitler's armies invaded Greece, Yugoslavia, and the U.S.S.R. Mäxchen Kieckebusch's shattered nerves were delivered from all further assault when he, like so many of Missie's friends, was killed during the first weeks of the Russian campaign. And if Bübchen Hatzfeldt's expensive suits and the shoes that went with them remained in that overstocked clothes closet, they were blown sky-high during the massive bombing of Berlin in November, 1943.

Missie's description of this is a set piece that goes on for eighteen pages. It will remind the reader of Pepys' account of the Great Fire of London and the description of the burning of Moscow in 1812, in Alexander Herzen's memoirs.

"*23 November* Last night the greater part of central Berlin was destroyed. . . . Papa was in his room, giving a language lesson to two young men. . . . We all hurried down to the half-basement behind the kitchen, where we usually sit out air-raids. We had hardly got there when we heard the first approaching planes."

Exploding bombs shook the house. "The air pressure was dreadful. . . . At one point there was a shower of broken glass and all three doors of the basement flew into the room, torn off their hinges. We pressed them back into place and leant against them to try to keep them shut. . . . In the middle of it all the cook produced my soup. I thought that if I ate it I would throw up. I found it even impossible to sit quietly and kept jumping to my feet at every crash." The pupils cowered in a corner. A house next door collapsed, and Papa muttered in Russian, "Let God's will be done!" When the all-clear sounded, they discovered they no longer had any electricity, gas, or water. With flashlights and candles they groped their way through the house and saw it was intact. "We could see a steady shower of sparks raining down on our and the neighboring houses and all the time the air was getting thicker and hotter, while the smoke billowed in through the gaping window frames. . . . Towards 2 A.M. I decided to sleep for a while. Papa came and held his torch over me as I took off my shoes and tried to wash. Towards three, Maria also lay down. Presently I heard the telephone ring and then her ecstatic 'Liebling!,' which meant that Heinz was all right. Soon she, too, fell asleep. Every now and then a crashing building or a delayed time bomb would tear one awake and I would sit up with a pounding heart. By now the firestorm had reached its peak and the roar outside was like a train going through a tunnel.''

In the morning, Maria Gersdorff went out to buy some bread and returned with an old woman on her arm. "She had stumbled into her at the street corner and, peering into her grimy face, had recognized her own eighty-year-old mother, who had been trying to reach her, walking through the burning town all night. Her own flat had been completely burnt out.''

Missie decided to try to get to her office, in the hope of a hot bath. "Clad in slacks, my head muffled in a scarf and wearing a pair of Heinz's fur-lined military goggles, I started off. The instant I left the house I was enveloped in smoke and ashes rained down on my head. . . . Many buildings were still burning. . . . There were many people in the streets, most of them muffled in scarves and coughing. . . . At the end of Lützowstrasse, about four blocks away from the office, the houses on both sides of the street had collapsed and I had to climb over mounds of smoking rubble, leaking water pipes and other wreckage. . . . Cars were weaving their way cautiously through the ruins, blowing their horns wildly. . . . Somehow I could still not imagine that our office too was gone, but on reaching the corner I saw that the porter's lodge and the fine marble entrance were burning merrily.''

Missie spent that night with the Gottfried Bismarcks in Potsdam, and once more the Allied planes bombed Berlin. When she went into town the next morning, she found that a mine had come down behind the Gersdorffs' house and the roof and some of the walls had caved in. She spent the greater part of the afternoon nailing cardboard and carpets over all the windows to keep out the cold and smoke. People kept dropping in from other parts of town to find out how they were. Her father had not slept for two nights and was totally exhausted, and she took him back to Potsdam with her.

The next morning and again the morning after that, she and Loremarie Schönburg went into the city in search of lost friends. "Wherever we looked, firemen and prisoners-of-war . . . were busy pumping air into the ruins, which meant that some people were still alive in the collapsed cellars. . . . In some places one could not even tell where the streets had been and we no longer knew where we were."

On the blackened walls of wrecked houses were inscriptions in chalk: "Dearest Frau B., where are you? I have been looking for you everywhere. Come and stay with me. I have room for you," and "Everyone from this cellar has been saved," and "My little angel. Where are you? I worry greatly." Sometimes answers were chalked underneath. The two girls discovered the whereabouts of several of their friends this way, and when they came to their own office they picked up a piece of chalk from the rubble and wrote in large square letters next to the entrance, "Missie and Loremarie are well, staying in Potsdam at the Bismarcks."

None of this would have been of any interest to military strategists at the time (or, for that matter, would be now), but, as the editor, George Vassiltchikov, points out, Air Marshal Arthur Harris, the head of the R.A.F.'s Bomber Command, made a miscalculation. Berlin was bombed twenty-four times between the middle of November and the middle of March, and each attack involved a thousand planes. No major military advantage was gained by the massive bombing. The railroad lines were repaired within hours, and by this time the munitions plants were either dispersed or underground, and the morale of the civilian population was not broken.

As for the straining of the social fabric, one entry will dispose of the subject:

"On 26 December, our old postman, whom she [Maria Gersdorff] had allowed to use my wrecked room under the eaves, fell ill with pneumonia. His family had been evacuated, so Maria and Heinz brought the old man downstairs and fixed up an improvised bed in the kitchen. No doctor could be reached and he died on the 28th. For three days nobody came for the body and he lay in state on the kitchen table, surrounded by candles. Finally Professor Gehrbrandt dropped in to see Maria and, appalled by the sight, alerted the authorities. Still nobody came for the body. On the 30th bombs again rained down on our square and the surrounding houses caught fire. Ours did too but was saved thanks to the efforts of Kicker Stumm and several of his friends. As they fetched water to douse the roof, the rescue party kept bumping the body, while Maria sat at its feet making sandwiches for the hungry men. Some neighbors volunteered to throw the body into the ruins of a burning house; Maria favored the idea of digging a hole in the so-called garden, which is now a mere strip of debris. The poor postman remained another two days in the house and only then was at last removed."

The photo-archive that Missie had spent months acquiring went up in flames along with that marble entrance. The Department of Information, with the rest of the Foreign Ministry, was transferred to the charming but remote village of Krummhübel, which was in no way prepared to receive the five hundred people who were evacuated to it. They used every excuse to get back to Berlin, though it meant that they, too, might end up under a pile of rubble. And Missie set to work to replace the photographs that had been destroyed.

How she came to know about what she referred to as the *Kon-spiration* may have been recorded in some missing part of her diary. Very likely the evidence accumulated under her nose until it dawned on her what Adam Trott and his friends were up to. The attempt on the part of a group of aristocratic Army officers and government officials to assassinate Hitler, seize the government, and sue for peace has the melancholy fascination of those high-minded and courageous enterprises that have everything going for them but luck. As people who are of a certain age will remember, Count Claus Schenck von Stauffenberg, a colonel on the General Staff, placed a briefcase with a bomb in it at Hitler's feet during a conference at Rastenburg, in East Prussia, on July 20, 1944. He then left the room in order to answer a prearranged telephone call. A staff officer, finding the briefcase in his way, shoved it to the other side of a heavy wooden trestle. As a rule, Hitler's briefings were held in an underground bunker, but because of the heat this one was held aboveground in a wooden hut, and when the bomb went off the walls caved outward and much of the explosive force was lost. Seeing the cloud of smoke and flames, Stauffenberg assumed that the deed was done. He and another conspirator jumped in a car and drove to a nearby airstrip, where they took off for Berlin to set further plans in motion. The arrangements for taking over the government succeeded briefly in Berlin, Paris, and Vienna—that is to say, everywhere except where it mattered. The sound of Hitler's voice over the radio put an end to the uprising.

At some point Adam Trott confided to Missie the exact nature of his activities. His trips abroad, undertaken under some official pretext, were all efforts to create a platform for peace talks with the Allies after Hitler had been killed. Loremarie

Schönburg, who knew about the conspiracy also, was so indiscreet as to be a problem to the conspirators, and blamed Missie for not taking an active part in it. "The truth is," Missie wrote in her diary, "that there is a fundamental difference in outlook between all of *them* and me: not being German, I am concerned only with the elimination of the Devil. I have never attached much importance to what happens afterwards. Being patriots *they* want to save their country from complete destruction by setting up some interim government. I have never believed that even such an interim government would be acceptable to the Allies, who refuse to distinguish between 'good' Germans and 'bad.' " But when Loremarie Schönburg told her that Hitler was dead, Missie grabbed her by the shoulders and they went waltzing around the room.

In making plans for the future government, the conspirators had drawn up lists, which were soon found, and proved fatally incriminating. Neither the civilian population nor the rank and file of the Army was sympathetic toward the attempt to kill Hitler, and the churches formally condemned it. One by one, the conspirators were rounded up, brought to trial, and executed. Several, knowing they were about to be arrested and would undoubtedly be tortured, committed suicide. According to an editorial note, "not only Stauffenberg's wife and children, but his mother, mother-in-law, brothers, cousins, uncles, aunts (and all their wives, husbands and children) were arrested." They were first sent to Dachau and then moved from camp to camp. The children were separated from their parents and put in a different camp, under the name of Meister. All of them more than once came close to being executed. Among Missie's friends was Count Friedrich-Werner von der Schulenburg, who had been Ambassador to Moscow and was a highly cultivated, charming, kind old man. His name was found on a list of people who would head the new government, and even though he had not taken any part in the conspiracy, he was tried and hanged. It was Missie's belief that the conspirators "are not simply hanged, but are slowly strangulated with piano wire on butchers' hooks and, to prolong their agony, are given heart booster injections. It is rumored that the killings are being filmed and that Hitler regularly gloats over these films at his headquarters."

An editorial note says, "According to official Nazi sources those arrested after the *coup* numbered some 7,000. A total of 5,764 were executed in 1944 and a further 5,684 in the five remaining months of Nazi rule in 1945. Of these, some 160 to 200 were directly implicated in the plot. They included 21 generals, 33 colonels and lieutenant-colonels, 2 ambassadors, 7 senior diplomats, one minister of state, 3 secretaries of state, the head of the Criminal Police and numbers of high officials, provincial governors and top police chiefs." George Vassiltchikov's notes supplying the historical background and biographical information are so comprehensive that they could only have been a labor of love, and so interesting that they amount almost to a collaboration.

Missie's diary is the only firsthand eyewitness account of the abortive attempt and the arrests and executions that followed it which is known to exist. On the night of July 22nd, she sat up talking with Adam Trott at his house until four in the morning. He told her that if he was arrested he would deny everything in order to get out and try again. She saw him once more outside the office, at the Gersdorffs', and gave him an icon of St. Serafim of Sarov, and he said they must not see each other again, for they were all being watched. He was arrested the next day, at his office.

In their efforts to find out where Adam Trott, Gottfried Bismarck, Count Schulenburg, and other friends were being held, and to take food and messages to them, Missie and Loremarie Schönburg risked their lives repeatedly.

"*3 August* On one of her visits to the Gestapo, Loremarie ran in a corridor into Adam himself. His hands were manacled, he was evidently being led to interrogation; he recognized her but looked straight through her. The expression on his face, she said, was that of somebody already in another world."

He was hanged in the Plötzensee Prison on August 26th.

In the fall of 1942, the Countess Pückler's husband, busy working his way up through the S.S., denounced Mamma to the Gestapo. She had criticized the treatment of Russian prisoners of war. His letter might easily have landed her in a concentration camp, but all that happened was that the Foreign Ministry was told to deny her an exit visa if she asked for one. And in March, 1944, Missie learned that letters from Papa to Georgie in Paris expressing concern over his "activities" had aroused the interest of the Censor. Georgie was able to convince the Gestapo that it referred to the black market, but in actual fact it was his involvement with the French Resistance that his father was alarmed about.

In September of that same year, Missie was given four months' sick leave and spent it with her mother and father at Königswart, another Metternich castle, in what until the war had been Czechoslovakia. She was suffering from an enlarged thyroid gland and was extremely thin. At the end of that time, the local manpower board suggested that she go to work as a nurse— which was what she and Tatiana had wanted to do when the war started, but they had been rejected because of their Lithuanian passports. Through her friend Sita Wrede, Missie was taken on as a Red Cross nurse at the Luftwaffe hospital in Vienna. Once more she had to sit out air raids and, wandering through the rubble, see a great city destroyed. What in Berlin was pure horror in Vienna had a touch of the macabre, as in this entry about a shortage of coffins during the air raids of the spring of 1945.

"*12 March*   It appears that at first people made them out of the cardboard panels that in many buildings have replaced smashed windowpanes, but now there is a shortage even of that. . . . Friends and relatives must dig the graves themselves, as all the gravediggers have been called up. . . . In many places there are piles of improvised coffins awaiting burial. . . . The other day a solemn funeral of a defunct colonel took place. There was even a military band. Just as the coffin was being lowered into the grave, the lid slipped and the face of a grey-haired old woman appeared. The ceremony continued!

"*19 March* Things have become particularly uncomfortable because the town has been virtually without water for several weeks now. How they can still cook our meals I do not understand. None of us trust ourselves to drink tea or coffee anymore. There is still no light and I am rapidly using up the Xmas candles Sisi gave me. In the evenings I sit in my room in the dark and practise the accordion."

The Red Army was drawing closer and closer to Vienna, and how serious the danger would be if she were found there by the Russians when they came was perfectly clear to her, but she remained passive and in the end was saved largely through the ingenuity of a Hungarian diplomat, Count Geza Pejacsevich, who against all odds rounded up a car, permits, gas, and a handful of people and escaped to the West.

She resumed her nursing at a hospital in Gmunden, in Upper Austria. There she came down with scarlet fever—caught, she suspected, from delousing the soldiers who were coming through in great numbers. It was aggravated by lack of proper nourishment and exhaustion. She was on the point of death by starvation when the Americans arrived. They were greatly to be preferred to the Russians, but, even so, their behavior was not always ingratiating. She heard that while billeted at the Mumms' castle, next door to the ruined Schloss Johannisberg, they threw china and furniture out of the windows and distributed to the village girls the clothes they found in closets.

"*3 September* I have now learnt that two days after the Americans arrived at Königswart, Tatiana, Paul, Mamma and Papa left with a cart drawn by two horses and escorted by seven French ex-P.O.W.s, who had been working on Paul's estate. The local American Commandant, who happened to be a friend of cousins of ours in the U.S.A., had warned them that the Americans would be relinquishing that part of Czechoslovakia to the Soviets shortly, and had advised them to leave instantly. They had taken twenty-eight days to cross Germany, spending the nights in farmhouses or barns or, occasionally, at friends'. . . . They had left most of their possessions behind and are very unhappy."

In 1946, Marie Vassiltchikov married a United States Army Intelligence officer on the staff of the military government in Bavaria. After he was demobilized, they settled in Paris, and he started an architectural firm that became internationally recognized. Her mother was run over by a car and killed there, in 1948. Her father died in Baden-Baden twenty-one years later. Missie died in London, of leukemia, in 1978. Her diaries were, for me, one long astonishment.

Louise Bogan's Story

Louise Bogan seldom talked about her life, Elizabeth Frank says in her biography* of that poet. "To those correspondents who committed the blunder of asking for biographical information, Bogan would reply—when she bothered to reply at all—that there were certain details, possessing 'tragic interest alone, and these I never describe or explain.' . . . Self-revelation she equated with confession; and . . . in her view, to confess was to ask for pardon, an act she considered as useless as it was ignoble." What was it she didn't care to go into? Her childhood, probably. Her forlorn first marriage. Her emotional dependence on a man she could not trust and unwillingly loved. Her struggle to forgive her own failures and those of the people who had failed her. Her periods of severe depression. The withdrawal, for years at a time, of her poetic gift.

As a schoolgirl she used to go home in the afternoon and write poems in the manner of Swinburne and William Morris and the Rossettis. The headmaster, noticing that her verse or prose compositions appeared in almost every issue of the school magazine, sent for her mother and told her to warn Louise that

*Louise Bogan: A Portrait. Knopf, 1985.

no Irish girl could expect to be editor of *The Jabberwock*. ("It
was borne in upon me, all during my adolescence, that I was a
'Mick,' no matter what my other faults or virtues might be. It
took me a long time to take this fact easily, and to understand
the situation which gave rise to the minor persecutions I endured
at the hands of supposedly educated and humane people.")

Her paternal grandfather emigrated from Londonderry as a
boy, before the Potato Famine, and settled in Maine, became a
captain of sailing vessels, and built a big house in Portland. He
had twelve children. The oldest, Daniel, Miss Bogan's father,
went with him as cabin boy on a voyage to South America that
lasted several years. The ship was called the Golden Sheaf. His
father kept a parrot in a cage in the saloon, and at the end of
the voyage the boy discovered that cigars, rum, and Panama
hats were hidden under the floorboards.

Miss Bogan's maternal grandfather was a schoolteacher whose
last name was Murphy. He married a Dublin woman. Louise
Bogan said, in a letter to a friend, "My maternal grandmother
once picked up her mother-in-law, and was restrained only with
some difficulty from dropping her down a stair-well." When
and why they came to New England Miss Frank was unable to
learn. He enlisted or was conscripted into the Union Army and
was killed in battle. Either because his wife died or because she
was destitute, their only child, named Mary Helen and called
May, was adopted and raised by a Mr. and Mrs. Shields, who
ran a saloon in Portland and were fairly prosperous. Miss Frank
thinks that Louise Bogan never knew them. The adopted child
was much loved and fussed over, and a great deal of attention
was paid to the way she was dressed. She was sent to a convent
school, and taught to sing and play the piano and other accomplishments expected of a young lady. At seventeen she married
Daniel Bogan. He was twenty-one, and his copperplate handwriting had got him a job as a clerk in a paper mill. They were

both the same height—five feet four inches—but he had finished his growing and she grew another five inches and towered over her husband. She was impulsive, high-spirited, and a beauty. She loved clothes, especially large hats with veils. When she was nineteen she gave birth to a son and thirteen years later, in 1897, to Louise. Between them there was another child, a boy, who only lived four or five months.

Like the heroine of *Madame Bovary* May Bogan was a romantic, married to a man who bored her, and trapped in a world of the commonplace. As he worked his way up from clerk to superintendent, they lived in one ugly New England mill town after another—sometimes in a house of their own, sometimes in a hotel or a boarding house. "At some point," Miss Frank says, "Louise became aware of . . . whisperings and intrigues at whose center her mother occupied some dread-inspiring role; conversations excluded her; secret signals were exchanged in her presence." The waitresses in the hotel dining room knew. And a woman who used to come to see her mother, one of her confidantes, who had the angry face of the queen of spades. The child went blind and then two days later suddenly saw the gas light in its etched glass shade, and knew that her sight had come back. Her father threatened to kill her mother, and her brother fought with him. On at least one occasion May Bogan took her small daughter with her to an assignation. As a grown woman Louise Bogan wrote, "As I remember my bewilderment, my judgment even now can do nothing to make things clear. The child has nothing to which it can compare the situation. And everything that then was strange is even stranger in retrospect. . . . The door is open, and I see the ringed hand on the pillow; I weep by the hotel window as she goes down the street with *another*; I stare at the dots which make up the newspaper photograph (which makes me realize that I then had not yet learned to read). The chambermaid tells me to stop crying.

How do we survive such things? But it is long over. And forgiven . . ."

Erratically, during a good part of her life, Miss Bogan kept a journal. In it she wrote, "The poet represses the outright narrative of his life. He absorbs it, along with life itself. The repressed becomes the poem. Actually, I have written down my experience in the closest detail. But the rough and vulgar facts are not there. At the same time, the desire (and need) remains to write of a time which has disappeared, and cannot be seen again, except in memory. . . . A few old stories . . . But not egoistic or *minor* ones." She referred to the journal as her "long prose thing" and thought of publishing it as fiction, with the title *Laura Daly's Story*. At the time of her death, in 1970, it amounted to about seventy handwritten pages. It is in the main about remembered details of her childhood—sights and sounds, impressions, memories: the mill flume; her mother's character; a moment of illumination brought on by seeing a bouquet of French marigolds in a hospital room; a boarding house where for the first time she experienced true order; her brother's crippling attachment to her mother; and so on. Without it, no really adequate biography would have been possible. Again and again in these fragments she approaches the hurdle that she clearly intended to take, and at the last minute turns aside, and it is this turning aside that, finally, says all there is to say: What was unbearable once is unbearable still.

The journal was published in the January 30, 1978, issue of *The New Yorker*, under the heading "From the Journals of a Poet." In 1973, Ruth Limmer, Miss Bogan's literary executor, brought out a volume of her selected correspondence (*What the Woman Lived*) and, in 1980, a book of excerpts from the journal and from Miss Bogan's stories, poems, letters, and literary criticism. The title, *Journey Around My Room*, was borrowed from the title of her best short story. The subtitle, "The Autobiography of Louise Bogan," is a misnomer. My copy of Webster's New Collegiate Dictionary defines "autobiography" as "a biography written by the subject of it; memoirs of one's life written by oneself." This was a paste-up job, with a biographical end in view. It contained information at the time not generally known and of considerable interest, but until now Louise Bogan's life and work had not been subjected to the careful and intelligent scrutiny of a dispassionate mind.

"The innermost secrets of a proud and dignified spirit have a way of retreating when too strenuously pursued," Miss Frank says. "Nevertheless, something stopped Louise Bogan dead in her tracks, not once, but many times. Until we discover this principle of arrest, even the most copious supply of documentation and the most perceptive psychological guesswork will be of little advantage in our attempt to enter the sanctuaries of either the life or the work. What we must do, instead, is to look at them long and hard, until, as Bogan herself learned from Hopkins and Rilke, they begin to look back at us."

The biography is divided into alternating sections of narrative and literary analysis. Miss Frank is equally well equipped for both.

When Louise Bogan was eight years old she was sent for two years to the same convent school her mother had gone to. For reasons Miss Frank could not discover, she was kept out of school for a year. Then the family moved to Boston, and her mother placed her for the next five years in the Girls' Latin School, in Roxbury, where, Miss Frank says, she received "the best classical education then available to girls in this country." The local branch of the Boston Public Library subscribed to *Poetry* and she read it closely. She had, she says, "the double vision of the born reader, from the beginning." By the age of eighteen she had "learned every essential of my trade. . . . I had no relations whatever with the world about me: I lived in a dream, populated by figures out of Maeterlinck and Pater and Arthur Symons and Compton Mackenzie . . . and H. G. Wells and Francis Thompson and Alice Meynell and Swinburne and John Masefield and other oddly assorted authors."

In her freshman year at Boston University she fell in love with Curt Alexander, a corporal in the Army. He was born in Breslau and trained as an architectural draftsman, and he became a soldier because he couldn't find a job in his chosen profession. He was nine years older than she was, tall and blond and handsome in a proud way. Her mother did not want her to repeat the mistake she herself had made, and Alexander struck her father as "very German and 'Achtung!' " She was nineteen when she married him, in 1916. He was transferred from New York City to Panama when the United States entered the First World War, and, four months pregnant, she followed him there on a troopship. She was so seasick that she had to be carried from the ship on a stretcher. She hated Panama. Her shoes were always moldy and her dresses stuck to her. She could not talk to the other Army wives. Or to her husband; they played cards, being unable to think of anything to say. "It had become clear to her," Miss Frank says, "that she and Alexander had nothing in common, a fact that was all the more apparent after the baby's birth, when Alexander inexplicably ceased to desire sexual relations."

She stuck it out for a year, and during that time two of her poems were published in a little magazine edited by Alfred Kreymborg. Then she took her daughter and went home to her parents. Her brother, fighting with the American Army in France, was killed a few weeks before the Armistice. After the war, she and Alexander lived together in various Army posts. Alexander was promoted to lieutenant, then captain. Once when they were living in an Army base off Portland, she telephoned from the mainland during a bad storm to say that she thought it would be better to spend the night where she was, and he told her to come right home with the baby and cook his dinner. His wants came before all other considerations. She said long afterward to Ruth Limmer, "What could I do. One must break free. One must burst forth." She left him again, this time for good. Alexander died of pneumonia after an operation for a gastric ulcer, at the age of thirty-two.

Her parents looked after the baby for her, so that she could support herself. She worked first as a clerk in Brentano's and then in various branches of the New York Public Library.

In a species of questionnaire that the mature Louise Bogan put to herself she wrote:

> *Did you ever seek God?*
> No.
> *What is it that you sought?*
> I sought love.
> *And you sought love for what reason?*
> Those about me, from childhood on, had sought love. I heard and saw them. I saw them rise and fall on that wave. I closely overheard and sharply overlooked their joy and grief. I worked from memory and example.

At a fund-raising party in a bookstore, the poet Raymond Holden saw her, was struck by her beauty, and went up to speak to her. He had a wife and children but was living apart from them, in his Washington Square house. After a few weeks he and Louise Bogan began living together. "Holden quickly learned," Miss Frank says, "that there were at least two Louises: one a tender, passionate, intensely sexual being, and the other a violent, cruel, and deeply suspicious fiend, who couldn't stand

being loved and did everything possible to test and invalidate
Raymond's feelings for her." She was twenty-five and he was
twenty-nine. Two years later, when his wife divorced him, they
were married.

He was witty and charming and the physical attraction between them was very strong. He was a loving father to her child.
He came of a well-to-do family, but little by little his inheritance
slipped through his fingers. He also had a tendency toward what
he called "passionate renewing delight" and Louise Bogan called
"Shelleyism." "By whatever name," Miss Frank says, "this was
an addiction to romantic love. Raymond had grown up reading
The Idylls of the King . . . and his hunger to do and risk all for
love, to be perpetually scaling its heights and plunging into its
depths, was insatiable." That he was by no means as good a
poet as his wife he apparently failed to recognize.

During the period of the greatest happiness of their marriage
they were living in the country, in an old farmhouse they had
bought and fixed up, in Hillsdale, New York. Such times of
happiness, Miss Frank observes, "seem so certain to go on forever, since nothing about them even hints at a built-in flaw in
their design." The house caught on fire and burned to the
ground. They moved back into the city. He went to work as
managing editor of *The New Yorker*. She published short stories,
reviews, a Profile of Willa Cather. She and Holden led a fairly
social life. It was still Prohibition, and the gin was homemade.
She was intensely jealous and accused him of having designs on
other women, was sure that they had designs on him, and would
not believe anything he said in his own defense. Her paranoid
suspicions were not totally without foundation. Sometimes on
the way home from a party they would engage in shouting
matches in the street. Once in a moment of anger she threw a
pot of hot coffee at him. On another occasion he knocked her
down a flight of steps and injured her eye. "She was caught,"

Miss Frank says, "in a fatal paradox of simultaneously desiring and fearing the emotional violence she had always known." Without pushing things or asking the reader to accept suppositions that are unsupported by any real evidence, Miss Frank shows the effect of childhood shock working its way up through and ultimately destroying the marriage.

In the critical part of the book Miss Frank moves from poem to poem, right straight through the published work, identifying the voice, decoding the symbols, making the connection between a given poem and the same or similar ideas in poems that have come before, establishing the literary influence when there is one. It suggests many years of thoughtful reading, but in any case for the first time the whole run of the poems, so moving and beautiful even when one only partly understands them, opens out and becomes clear. A single example—part of Miss Frank's consideration of "The Sleeping Fury"—will perhaps give some idea of how secure her exegesis is. Having explained that in the spring of 1933 Louise Bogan saw in Rome, in the Museo Nazionale delle Terme, a head of one of the Erinyes, Miss Frank goes on to say, "While she gazed at the sculptured head in Rome and then [that is to say, months later] at the postcard with its image, and then at the image which her memory preserved, the figure became detached from all the occasions of viewing, turning from an object into a symbol that she consciously placed within a geography familiar from her earlier work. In her 1935–36 journal she wrote, 'To trace the dream-landscape that has grown inside me every night, all my life, along with daylight reality, and which has mountains, ruins, islands, shores, cities, and even *suburbs* and summer "resorts" *of its own,* related to one another and, many times, recurrent (almost in the sense of revisited).' The setting of 'The Sleeping Fury' is this region fused with details picked up from the *Encyclopaedia Britannica* entry about the Furies. Thus the New England of Bogan's childhood becomes transposed to a land in which the most primitive cruelty and the most serene tenderness coexist."

In her journal Louise Bogan wrote, "The continuous turmoil in a disastrous childhood makes one so tired that 'Rest' becomes the word forever said by the self to the self. The incidents are so vivid and so terrible that to remember them is inadequate: they must be forgotten." When it is not done effortlessly, without the person's knowledge, the act of forgetting can be, of course, as difficult as the act of remembering. In 1931, a year and three months after the fire, she committed herself to a psychiatric hospital for treatment of depression. From the Neurological Institute she wrote to John Hall Wheelock, who was her editor at Scribners and her friend, "I refused to fall apart, so I have been taken apart, like a watch." Two years later she went to Europe for five months on a Guggenheim fellowship, and when she got home she discovered that Holden had been living with a woman in their apartment. And again had to put herself under treatment.

For thirty-eight years she covered the poetry scene for *The New Yorker.* She looked down her nose at Surrealism, thought T. S. Eliot's *Four Quartets* as beautiful as anything he had ever written and that they showed what he could do "in the province of pure emotion when all irony has been eliminated." She loathed the New Criticism, and saw in the poetry of John Berryman and Robert Lowell an exploitation of personal trauma that was relentless and theatrical. She was a pacifist, and during the time that Communism was stylish was never drawn to it. Her own identification with the working class was nonideological; she had lived through the nightmare of being dis-possessed and seeing her furniture on the street.

Sometimes poets took offense at her chiselled opinions, but it is also true that many of the people she thought of as her ene-mies were not. With certain younger writers whose talent she believed in—Theodore Roethke was one of them—her patience and generosity were extraordinary.

After her mother's death, in 1936, she made a sentimental pilgrimage to Ireland. It was not a success. The faces in Dublin were, she wrote to her daughter, the faces of conspirators. She grew frightened. Afterward she wrote to the critic Morton Za-bel, who was perhaps her closest friend, "There must be a God, Morton, for on the Southampton boat-train, there appeared a tall thin man who proceeded to take care of me like a baby. (No, Morton: it's not another of those things. This was proba-bly, is,—the Angel Gabriel in disguise!) . . . He says *Nuttin* when he means *Nothing;* his parents came from Sligo. . . . I told him the whole story the second day out, and he nursed me along even more tenderly, thereafter. He laughed me out of it; he tricked me into deck chairs; he brought me lots of rye when the panic became too bad. But for that touch of human understand-ing, I should certainly have started gibbering." The relationship lasted for eight years. Though she mentioned him to her friends, she did not allow any of them to meet him.

She was devoted to her daughter, and her friendships were important to her, but as she grew older she felt less and less need for human company. People who wanted to see her for one reason or another—because they loved her or admired her or in some important way felt forever indebted to her—were usually put off with postponements or "visits to the dentist" too consistent to be plausible.

She had a third breakdown in her middle sixties. It was brought on by a brief period of living in Boston, when she was teaching at Brandeis University. Old experiences long laid to rest now rose to haunt her, and she saw herself living out her days in some shabby Boston boarding house. The therapy, which included a brief series of electroshock treatments, was only partly successful. She had weeping spells in the morning.

In her journal she wrote:

> Surely I have acted in a consistently *optimistic* fashion, ever since the 1933 breakdown.—I have surmounted one difficulty after another; I have *worked* for life and "creativity"; I have cast off all the anxieties and fears I could; I have helped others to work and hold on. Why this collapse of psychic energy? . . .
>
> *Who* have I become? *What* has me in hand? . . .
>
> What am I afraid of?
>
> *Death*—for one thing. Yes, that is part of it.—These deaths that are reported in the newspapers seem to be all my age—or younger.
>
> But people keep hopeful and warm and *loving* right to the end—with much more to endure than I endure.—I see the old constantly, on these uptown streets—and they are not "depressed." Their eyes are bright; they have bought themselves groceries; they gossip and laugh—with, often, crippling handicaps evident among them.
>
> Where has this power gone, in my case?

Miss Frank says that for twenty years she "had not permitted herself to feel (as far as anyone can know) new or rekindled love, for anyone or anything. Her carefully erected, thoroughly adult maturity had at last engendered its own defeat by refusing to countenance its opposite: the eternal, hungry, clamoring, yearning, angry, weeping child. . . . She could not feel, she could not give. Since the last depression she could not even listen to music."

But more poems did come. A few. And very beautiful and strange they are. Consider "Masked Woman's Song," which she placed at the end of her final collection, *The Blue Estuaries*:

Before I saw the tall man
Few women should see
Beautiful and imposing
Was marble to me.

And virtue had its place
And evil its alarms,
But not for that worn face,
And not in those roped arms.

"Darkness was her fate," Miss Frank says, "what she knew best."

She died alone in her apartment on West 169th Street, of a coronary occlusion, at the age of seventy-two. In a commemorative tribute delivered before the American Academy of Arts and Letters, W. H. Auden said, "By temperament she was not a euphoric character and in her life she had much to endure. What, aside from their technical excellence, is most impressive about her poems is the unflinching courage with which she faced her problems, her determination never to surrender to self-pity, but to wrest beauty and joy out of dark places. . . . It was a privilege to have known her."

The Duke's Child

That Frank O'Connor belongs among the great short-story writers of the twentieth century few people, I think, would deny. Frank O'Connor was a pseudonym, which he adopted as a very young man so that he would not get in trouble over things he published and lose his job as a librarian in Wicklow. His real name was Michael O'Donovan, and he was called by both names. He was born in Cork, on September 17, 1903. The first twenty years of his life are covered in a volume of autobiography, *An Only Child*, published in 1961. His father had been a drummer in an Irish regiment of the British Army, was mustered out with a pension of a guinea a month, and found work when he could as a laborer. He was given to periodic benders, during which he was a terror to his family. Only when everything of value had been pawned and the landlord was threatening eviction would he stop drinking and the family pull back from the brink of disaster. When O'Connor's paternal grandfather died, his grandmother, an irritating old woman who ate with her fingers and was overfond of porter, came to live with them. His grandmother on his mother's side was widowed and driven out of her mind by poverty and bereavement, and died in the workhouse. His mother was raised in a Catholic orphanage. As a child she walked in her sleep and was once found pacing a corridor in her nightdress, reciting Wolsey's speech from *Henry VIII* "Farewell! a long farewell, to all my greatness." When she was old enough, the nuns placed her in domestic service, and she was so starved and mistreated that she came close to drowning herself. She was thirty-six when she married. Because there was never enough money she went out to work as a charwoman.

"For kids like myself," O'Connor says in *An Only Child*, "social life was represented by the shop-front and the gas-lamp. This was mainly because we could rarely bring other kids home in the evenings; the houses were too small, and after the fathers came home from work, children became a nuisance. Besides, most families had something to hide; if it wasn't an old grandmother like mine or a father who drank, it was how little they had to eat. . . . The shop-fronts and gas-lamps were quite as exclusive as city clubs. The boys from our neighborhood usually gathered outside Miss Murphy's shop at the foot of the Square, while the respectable boys of the Ballyhooley Road—the children of policemen, minor officials, and small shopkeepers—gathered outside Miss Long's by the Quarry. I lived in a sort of social vacuum between the two, for though custom summoned me to Miss Murphy's with boys of my own class who sometimes went without boots and had no ambition to be educated, my instinct summoned me to Miss Long's and the boys who wore boots and got educated whether they liked it or not. . . . I was always very sympathetic with children in the story-books I read who had been kidnapped by tramps and gipsies, and for a lot of the time I was inclined to think that something like that must have happened to myself. Apart from any natural liking I may have had for education, I knew it was the only way of escaping from the situation in which I found myself."

In his story "The Duke's Children" a boy very like what he must have been observes that in "those moments of blinding illumination when I was alone in the station yard on a spring morning with sunlight striking the cliffs above the tunnel, and, picking my way between the rails and the trucks, I realized that it was not for long, that I was a duke or earl, lost, stolen, or strayed from my proper home, and that I had only to be discovered for everything to fall into its place."

One day at school, when he was nine years old, an assistant teacher, a man with a lame leg and a vile temper, wrote on the blackboard in a mysterious script the words *"Muscail do mbisneail, a Banba,"* which he then paid no attention to as he went on to give the class their first lesson in Gaelic. O'Connor lingered after class to ask what the words on the blackboard meant, and the teacher smiled and said, "Waken your courage, Ireland." The teacher was Daniel Corkery, who left his mark, in the form of plays, a novel, and stories, on Irish literature. The boy had at last found someone to direct his insatiable enthusiasm for learning. He discovered that Gaelic, not English, was his grandmother's native language, and she set out to teach it to him. He also used his mother's card to get into the adult section of the public library and memorized anything that appealed to him.

At fourteen he dropped out of school. With his head stuffed full of poetry, he failed to give satisfaction in a wholesale drapery shop, a chemist's, and a job printer's, in succession. He was working as a messenger for the Great Southern & Western Railway when his first published writing appeared, in a children's newspaper.

During the Troubles he became a political activist, and at the age of nineteen was picked up by Free State soldiers and put in prison, where for the most part he was not unhappy. The prison camp had been built as an American aerodrome during the First World War, and what with one thing and another, including the American plumbing, he led a healthier life than he could have at home. He taught German and Gaelic to the other prisoners, and immersed himself in an enthusiastic study of grammar. *An Only Child* ends with his release from prison after nearly a year.

A second volume, *My Father's Son*, put together after his death in 1966, from unfinished drafts and separate pieces, deals with his work as a librarian in Cork and Dublin, his friendships with AE and Yeats, and the at this late date not very interesting feuds among the directors of the Abbey Theatre. It leaves his periods of living in England and his ten years in the United States, his two marriages, a liaison with an English girl that resulted in a child born out of wedlock, and his writing all undisposed of.

This an American, James Matthews, attempted to rectify. The dust jacket of his biography* reads, "James Matthews was born and raised near Seattle, Washington, graduated from Seattle Pacific College in 1964, and received a Ph.D. from Vanderbilt University in 1968. He taught for two years at the University of Tulsa, where his interest in Irish literature began, and then for eleven years at Eckerd College in St. Petersburg, Florida. Now a lapsed academic, he has returned to the Pacific Northwest, and lives on a farm outside Stanwood, Washington, with his wife and three children."

In fairness to Mr. Matthews and to the reader of this review I think I ought to explain that of the material O'Connor published in *The New Yorker*—fifty-one stories and autobiographical pieces in all—a considerable part passed over my desk, and as a result of the hours we spent going over manuscripts and galleys together we became friends.

The absence of any genuine sympathy on Mr. Matthews' part becomes apparent very early in his book. In dealing with the events of O'Connor's seventeenth year he says, "So when in the spring of 1920 Corkery handed him the opportunity to go to Dublin for a special course in Irish, he jumped at the offer. It

---

Voices: A Life of Frank O'Connor. Atheneum, 1983.

was a Gaelic League school 'formed to train teachers of Irish, who would later cycle about the country from village to village, teaching in schools and parish halls.' Actually, he spent more time around the bookstalls on the quays than he did in the study of Irish. Although at the end of the summer he was granted a certificate qualifying him to teach Irish, he was probably not qualified at all."

Mr. Matthews cites as his source for this Dublin experience pages 197–98 of *An Only Child*: "Corkery's idea was that since I could never get into a university, I should become an art teacher, and he even arranged a scholarship in London for me. But I was in a frenzy to earn a little money, and, instead, like a fool, I applied for a scholarship to a Gaelic League Summer School in Dublin that had been formed to train teachers of Irish, who would later cycle about the country from village to village, teaching in schools and parish halls. It sounded exactly the sort of life for an aspiring young writer who wanted to know Ireland as Gorky had known Russia." In short, Corkery *didn't* hand him the opportunity to go to Dublin; he made it for himself. With the facts lying on the page in front of him, Mr. Matthews hasn't bothered to be accurate. Also he has invented feelings that O'Connor couldn't in the circumstances have had. (How could he have jumped at an opportunity that Corkery hadn't offered him?) It isn't the only instance in the book of a fact that is, in a significant way, untrustworthy.

O'Connor continues, "The Summer School was held in the Gaelic League headquarters in Parnell Square, and the head of it was a sly, fat rogue of a West Cork man called Hurley, who was later Quarter-Master-General of the Free State Army. I did not like Dublin, probably because most of the time I was light-headed with hunger. I lodged in a Georgian house on the Pembroke Road, and having rarely eaten in any house other than my own, I contented myself with a cup of tea and a slice of bread for breakfast. I decided that the chamber pot in my bedroom was for ornament rather than use. I was even more scared of restaurants than of strange houses. I had never eaten in one except when Mother took me to Thompson's café in Patrick Street for a cup of coffee—her notion of high life—so I lived entirely on coffee and buns in Bewley's. It was to be years before I worked up the courage to go into a real restaurant. Besides, the scholarship did not amount to more than the price of modest lodgings, and I needed every penny I could spare for the books I could pick up cheap at the stalls on the quays. I could not keep away from them. There were books there the like of which one never saw in a Cork bookstore. It was there that I picked up for a few pence the little *Selected Poems of Browning* published by Smith, Elder, which for me has always been one of the great books of the world, and when the hunger got too much for me I would recite to myself: 'Heap Cassia, sandal-buds and stripes of labdanum and aloeballs' as though it were a spell.

"Far from being recognized as a genius at the school, I was obviously regarded as a complete dud. The reason for this did not dawn on me till years had gone by. All the other students had had a good general education, some a university education. I talked Irish copiously, but nobody had explained to me the difference between a masculine and feminine noun, or a nominative and dative case. Nobody explained to me then, either, probably because the problem of a completely uneducated boy masquerading as a well-educated one was outside everyone's experience."

In compressing all this to four sentences, Mr. Matthews has passed over, as of no importance, material that is deeply revealing both of O'Connor's circumstances and of his character.

When the author of a literary biography is himself insensitive to language, the results are bound to be unsatisfactory. Mr. Matthews' misuse or misunderstanding of words and idioms is remarkable. Viz.: "Insecure to a fault he . . ." and "like any unpedigreed provincial, he drove himself to achieve excellence." O'Connor was a provincial in the same sense that Flaubert and Chekhov were, and in no other. As for being unpedigreed, a dog, yes, but a *writer?* Sometimes Mr. Matthews' syntax turns and bites him: "At the funeral [of his father] Michael mourned honestly, not so much in public display as in bitter confusion over the loss of someone both dear and dreadful." Sometimes it is hard to tell what is literary ineptitude and what is muddle. What, for example, is one to make of this: "Other stories may reveal what he thought about War, or Love, or Justice, but 'Michael's Wife' reveals what he felt. It is as autobiographical as anything O'Connor wrote—not because it is about his personal experience but because it is a personal experience"?

Mr. Matthews has a natural talent for casting aspersions, the way some people have a talent for pitching horseshoes or finding four-leaf clovers.

Item: "He held no competitive grudges against them"—that is to say, against AE's scholar friends—"as he so often showed toward other writers." (No evidence offered in support of the latter part of this statement.)

Item: ". . . the tired couple escaped to a guest house on the Tralee Road conveniently near the Aghadoe Church, 'the main interest of which,' O'Connor confidently claims in *Irish Miles,* 'is that its peculiar capitals enable you to trace the mason who did it from Holy Island in Lough Derg, through Clonkeen in Co. Limerick.' That sort of brash assumption probably made thoroughly trained specialists in Romanesque architecture quiver, but it gave an otherwise obvious travel book an entertaining petulance." (The specialists in this case are an invention of the biographer, like the petulance.)

Item, in a footnote: "Michael O'Donovan strove to be a good man; indeed he had to see himself and present himself as a good man. Frank O'Connor strove to be an artist, and in his art there

is little posing." (The idea advanced in the first sentence is left
hanging. Is Mr. Matthews saying that as a man O'Connor somewhat deceived himself about his own nature and was at some
pains to deceive others? To suggest possibilities of this kind and
not deal with them is dirty pool.)

Item: "Everything was grist to Yeats's mill, every remark,
every poem, every incident. He may have been what O'Connor
called a 'born plagiarist' "—the context of this remark is unfortunately not given—"but was no more or less so than O'Connor
himself who spent a lifetime plundering stories from the casual
anecdotes of friends." (To plunder means, of course, to take
something from someone by force. The friends whose stories
O'Connor made use of were not themselves writers, and it is
extremely hard to believe that they weren't gratified when he
turned their anecdotes into something beautiful and permanent.)

Item: In comparing O'Connor's *The Big Fellow,* which is a
life of the Irish patriot Michael Collins, with Seán O'Faoláin's
biographies of de Valera and the Countess Markievicz, Mr. Matthews says, "O'Faoláin was a professional man of letters, capable
of the most exacting scholarship and objectivity, but O'Connor
was a fumbling, improvising amateur." (A professional man of
letters, I would think, is someone who writes in a number of
literary forms and has his writing published. This was equally
true of both men. I have not read O'Faoláin's biographies, but
I have read *The Big Fellow* and it did not strike me as fumbling
or improvisation. And what amateur writer can you think of
who has published ten collections of short stories, two novels, a
biography, an autobiography, four volumes of poetry, six volumes of literary criticism, two travel books, and more than two
hundred and fifty articles and reviews?)

Mr. Matthews is particularly given to the damaging sideswipe
that alters the meaning of the sentence by insinuation rather
than by direct statement: "In *Towards an Appreciation of Literature* O'Connor had written: 'Swift, Wilde, Yeats, and Joyce

have certain characteristics like insolence, introspection, and a tendency to wear a mask which are not uncommon among writers brought up in Ireland.' Not only could O'Connor diagnose mental disorder with relative ease, but he was also quick to spot phoniness—*in other people*" (my italics).

Praise is either grudging ("In all fairness, Michael deserved the attention he was getting") or followed more often than not by some injurious statement that will, so to speak, take the curse off it. Even when pointing out that O'Connor's enemies among the directors of the Abbey Theatre were unfair, Mr. Matthews manages to find excuses for them. His judiciousness is that of the hanging judge.

Had O'Connor lived he would now be eighty-five. There are several of his contemporaries still living in Ireland whose close friendship with him goes all the way back to their youth. Mr. Matthews took the trouble to consult them, uses their testimony to make a point here and there, but withholds from the reader their understanding of O'Connor's character, which must surely be different from his.

I find very little resemblance between the Frank O'Connor Mr. Matthews has presented in this book and the person I knew. In the memorial volume *Michael/Frank*, edited by Maurice Sheehy and often referred to by Mr. Matthews, there are eighteen essays by men and women who knew and worked with O'Connor—among them Wallace Stegner, Honor Tracy, and Richard Ellmann—and the composite portrait of him that emerges from this collection I *do* recognize.

O'Connor, being dead, cannot defend himself against Mr. Matthews' charges. Possibly he would have considered them too small and mean-spirited to deserve an answer. In a letter to a friend he wrote, ". . . there are occasions when we all feel guilt and remorse; we all want to turn back time. But even if we were able, things would go in precisely the same way, because the mistakes we make are not in our judgments but in our natures. It is only when we do violence to our natures that we are justified in our regrets. . . . We are what we are, and within our limitations we have made our own efforts. They seem puny in the light of eternity, but they didn't at the time, and they weren't."

The Bohemian Girl

Edith Nesbit and the journalist Hubert Bland shared a plate of strawberries at a picnic, and apparently that did it. She was seven months pregnant when she was married, and not a single member of her upper-middle-class family was present at the civil ceremony—in all probability because none of them was invited; she does not seem ever to have been estranged from them. Two disasters occurred almost immediately—Bland lost all his capital in a commercial venture, and he nearly died of smallpox. With public recitations and hand-painted Christmas cards and writing stories for *Sylvia's Home Journal* and other Victorian periodicals, she kept the wolf a few yards from the door. Fortunately, she had enough energy for six women, and she was deeply in love with her husband. He had no talent for making money, but he was strong and athletic, he was intelligent, he talked extremely well, and he was interested in social questions, particularly the welfare of the working classes. Through him, she also became interested. They helped to found and were active in the affairs of the Fabian Society. More and more she wrote. She wrote poetry for public recitation, for the nursery, and what she hoped was the genuine article. She wrote novels. She wrote horror stories, sentimental love stories, and stories in dialect; she wrote birthday books, book reviews, Socialist propaganda, and reminiscences of her youth; she retold the plays of Shakespeare in language that a child could understand; she wrote an instructive book on dogs. She could have written an instructive book on what it is like to be married to an inveterate skirt chaser. She discovered Bland's infidelities in the third year of her marriage. They went right on, and were so numerous as to remind one of Leporello's aria. To add the finishing touch, he strongly disapproved of all forms of sexual license. E. Nesbit's biographer,* Doris Langley Moore, tends to take a broad-minded view of things when she might, instead, have been wickedly amused. But at least she dug out the facts while it was still possible to get at them. No one else was interested in doing this at the time, and it was far from easy. Two or three years after that first painful discovery, Alice Hoatson, the Blands' unmarried housekeeper, had a child, which Edith Bland out of compassion adopted, only to discover that the child's father was Bland. For various reasons, including love for him, she put up with a permanent *ménage à trois* and raised as, and with, her own children his illegitimate daughter and son—for of course he did it again. In that period—the eighteen-eighties—it was not considered that he had given his wife grounds for a divorce, which perhaps she did not want anyway. The barometer of the household frequently registered stormy weather.

If she was energetic, so was he. He took over the editorship of a paper called *To-Day*, with a small circulation but with many distinguished contributors. Two of Shaw's novels appeared in it, and the first English translation of Ibsen's *Ghosts*. Her writing brought in more and more in the way of royalties, and he also began to do well financially. They moved into larger and more comfortable houses, which were always full of house guests, who thoroughly enjoyed themselves. H. G. Wells was so taken with the Blands that instead of waiting for an invitation to stay with

*E. Nesbit. Chilton Books, 1966.

them he simply turned up one day on their doorstep, with his valise, and was welcomed with open arms. No more hospitable couple than the Blands ever lived, and their kind of hospitality is expensive. Neither of them knew what to do with money except spend it, and they always spent much more than they had. But consider the charmed life they led: a big red-brick, badly run-down, eighteenth-century house in Kent—the Moat House of the Bastable stories—and a house by the sea. The Blands both had work that interested them, and time left over for the Fabian Society, the Browning Society, a debating society; for sailing, bathing, and walking trips; for informal dances, *tableaux vivants*, and charades; for charitable work on a grand scale (what began as a Christmas party for twenty poor children ended up, in a few years' time, as a party for a thousand); for a wide variety of stimulating friendships. He was a conservative about everything but politics. Many people found him irritating, but not so much so that they didn't go and stay with him, and he was a friend to all promising and ambitious young men. The one picture of him in Mrs. Moore's biography shows an absurd-looking Englishman with a monocle, but it probably fails to do him justice. Her pictures are enchanting. Havelock Ellis saw her only once, on the occasion of the founding of the Fabian Society, and remembered her beauty all the rest of his life. She was a genuine bohemian, and there was very little that she could have done to shock the neighbors that she didn't do. Her clothes were Pre-Raphaelite and all wool, which was avant-garde in those days. She cut off her hair and left off wearing corsets. In the right mood, she would demonstrate the high kick. She leaned backward over a gate and touched the ground with her head. She smoked cigarettes in public. There was always some promising young man sitting at her feet, more often than not in love with her, and once or twice she paid her husband back in his own coin. As a mother she was fond but capricious and neglectful. Barefoot, hatless, gloveless, her children ran where they pleased, and had holes in their underwear. She was not as understanding of them as her books would lead one to expect. When she made a mistake—she could be both harsh and dictatorial—she apologized for it handsomely. Her character had many faults, but they were all of the forgivable kind, and it is too much to ask that people who spend very much time in a world of their own, as all writers do, should immediately and invariably grasp what is going on in this one.

As a writer, E. Nesbit was wildly prolific, but her talent lay in one direction only. *The Railway Children, Harding's Luck, Nine Unlikely Tales, The House of Arden, Five Children and It, The Wouldbegoods*, and the others of that remarkable series of juvenile classics appear to have been a natural flowering that took place when she was in her forties. The events of her life throw very little light on it and could have been dealt with adequately in a biographical essay. What gives Mrs. Langley Moore's book half its interest is the frieze of literary figures whose acquaintance she and her husband sought out or who sought out theirs. On the extreme left you have the young George Bernard Shaw: an impartial flatterer of men, women, and children, horribly untrustworthy (he repeated things), untruthful, and very plain—dead-white face, sandy sleek hair, and a loathsome small, straggly beard. Everyone rather affected to despise him ("Oh, it's only Shaw"), but everyone admired him all the same. Walking arm and arm with him in Regent's Park, and conversing in a particularly ladylike manner, Edith Bland startled him by exclaiming, "Shaw, I do believe it's going to rain like hell!" After a time, she fell in love with him. When Mrs. Langley Moore approached Shaw for help with her biography, she received this communication, signed by his secretary:

> Mr. Bernard Shaw desires me to say that as Edith was an audaciously unconventional lady and Hubert an exceedingly unfaithful husband he does not see how a presentable biography is

possible as yet; and he has nothing to contribute to a mere whitewashing operation.

In the end she got through to him, and he proved to be both kind and immensely helpful. The information he gave her—he was then seventy-five—was the most exact she received from anybody. When she asked him if he had been in love with Edith Bland, he replied, smiling, "No, I have never been in love with anybody—much." With his usual sleight of hand he turned her inconvenient passion for him into a lifelong friendship. He was responsible for getting Hubert Bland his first journalistic work. On the far right, the frieze ends with the young Noël Coward. As a child he had not been able to afford bound copies of her books, but on his way to school he passed a second-hand shop where for a penny one could get back numbers of *The Strand Magazine*, and when he had saved up a shilling he bought all twelve installments of the book he wanted. He was the last of the promising young men, and his friendship was a great pleasure to her. By that time she was in her middle sixties and her name was Mrs. Tucker. The charmed life had long since come to an end. Along about 1910, one thing after another began to go seriously wrong. Hubert Bland's health failed, and he lost his eyesight. In 1912, for the first time in many years, there was no series by E. Nesbit running in *The Strand*; her agent had queered the arrangement. She all but stopped writing in order to prove, by ciphers and by the Napierian system of logarithms, which she did not in the least understand, that Bacon wrote the plays of Shakespeare. Also *The Faerie Queene* and *The Anatomy of Melancholy*. She drove her friends half out of their minds with all this. In 1914, Bland died suddenly, of a heart attack. And the First World War changed a great many things for her, as it did for everybody else. Her books did not sell as they had, and as the royalty checks grew smaller and smaller she supplemented her income by taking paying guests. This is never very lucrative, and in her establishment they were far outnumbered by the non-paying kind. By the time she had been a widow for three years, the muddle of her life was so great that a sensible old man, a ship's engineer who had given up seafaring and was running the Woolwich ferry, took pity on her and asked her to marry him. He was everything that Hubert Bland was not, and they were very happy together. Though he could not make good all the losses, he did a great deal to make her life less burdensome. He moved her into a smaller and more manageable house, weeded out the undesirable guests, and got her to writing again. In 1921, three years before she died, E. Nesbit received a letter from Clemence Dane asking when she was going to gratify her admirers with a new fairy tale, and she replied, "Publishers tell me that children don't want my sort of book any more." It is a fact I wish I hadn't learned. Since she expressed the intention of returning to this life after quitting it, one might as well be fanciful and hope she has discovered that publishers can be mistaken. For they were, quite. In the current *Books in Print*, fourteen titles are listed beside her name.

The Whites

Though by no means an ordinary man, through literary prestidigitation E. B. White managed to make his inner self seem
much like anyone else's—an act that is in itself endearing, even
though in his case it was not intended to be. In the foreword to
his collected essays he said, "I have always been aware that I
am by nature self-absorbed and egoistical; to write of myself to
the extent I have done indicates a too great attention to my
own life, not enough to the lives of others. I have worn many
shirts, and not all of them have been a good fit. But when I am
discouraged or downcast I need only fling open the door of
my closet, and there, hidden behind everything else, hangs the
mantle of Michel de Montaigne, smelling slightly of camphor."

In *Letters of E. B. White* there is an introductory section of
ten pages, again written by him, and intended to orient the
reader in the correspondence that follows. It begins, "If an unhappy childhood is indispensable for a writer, I am ill-equipped:
I missed out on all that and was neither deprived nor unloved.
It would be inaccurate, however, to say that my childhood was
untroubled. The normal fears and worries of every child were
in me developed to a high degree; every day was an awesome
prospect. I was uneasy about practically everything: the uncer-
tainty of the future, the dark of the attic, the panoply and dis-

cipline of school, the transitoriness of life, the mystery of the church and of God, the frailty of the body, the sadness of afternoon, the shadow of sex, the distant challenge of love and marriage, the far-off problem of a livelihood. I brooded about them all, lived with them day by day. Being the youngest in a large family, I was usually in a crowd but often felt lonely and removed. I took to writing early, to assuage my uneasiness and collect my thoughts, and I was a busy writer long before I went into long pants.''

In the face of *that*, not to mention the very considerable amount of autobiographical writing in the essays, it might have seemed the better part of wisdom for a biographer simply to back away and go write about someone else, whose prose style didn't outclass that of virtually every expository writer in sight and who hadn't so thoroughly anticipated his efforts. Furthermore White had not yet gone to join the ranks of the illustrious dead, and his snicker was unimpaired. Scott Elledge, who is a professor of English at Cornell, was not deterred.

White, when approached by him, was courteous: "As a man who has frittered away the best years of his life writing about E. B. White, sometimes with affection, sometimes with distaste, always with charity aforethought, I can sympathize with your project without envying your labors. But whether I sympathize or not, the Constitution empowers you to write about anything that comes along, and although being written about is not my favorite diversion (I prefer sailing) I deem it my civic duty to meet you half way. . . .'' What this amounted to was making his papers at Cornell available to Professor Elledge but retaining absolute censorship as to the use of this material, and putting up with a fair number of visits and phone calls. In his introduction Professor Elledge says White "never failed to be friendly and prompt in his responses to my requests for facts that only he could supply. Beyond that, however, he has left me completely on my own. Early on, he answered one of my questions by saying in effect that he couldn't remember the answer, that I could look it up, and that after all *I* was the biographer. From the start he viewed my activities with mild interest, slight skepticism, and some amusement, but he gave no sign of wishing to get in the game or to coach from the sideline." When White read the finished manuscript, he offered "a dozen pages of editorial notes, most of them made in the interest of accuracy of fact and clarity of expression; none concerned the substance of what I had said about him." The right of censorship was exercised to protect others. White expressed neither approval nor disapproval of the biography* itself, apart from saying that it was too long. Most biographies are.

Professor Elledge produced a straightforward, orderly account of White's life. To the extent that in his writing White viewed disorder with an affectionate eye, and found it illuminating, it could be said that the biographer and his subject were at cross-purposes with one another.

White was born into about as pleasant circumstances as the year 1899 could provide. Both his parents loved children. He had three older sisters and two older brothers. His father was general manager of Horace Waters & Company, which manufactured pianos and player pianos. They lived in Mount Vernon, New York, in a large late-Victorian frame house with an octagonal corner tower, porches on two sides, and a barn where—I am quoting White—"everything smelled wonderfully ripe: the horses, the hay, the harness dressing, the axle grease, the liniment, the coachman." There were other barns that he had access to and other children his age all up and down the street. The town still had woods, a pond, and unbuilt-on land, and there was nowhere that it wasn't safe for a boy on a bicycle to

*E. B. White. Norton, 1984.

go. He suffered from severe attacks of hay fever, and from the time he was six the family spent the month of August on a lake in Maine that was, so far as he was concerned, the Earthly Paradise. "He seems not to have been babied or spoiled by his family, but as the last of their children he must have seemed especially precious to Jessie and Samuel, and he may have learned to be anxious by observing the anxieties of his parents," Professor Elledge says, and, wonder of wonders, lets it go at that. A rather startling incident—"White's earliest recorded memory is of finding his mother one day stretched out on the settee, recovering from an accident with a runaway horse. He thought she was dead"—is passed over without comment.

He was much happier out of school than in, and "suffered tortures every day of the school year" thinking about the moment when he would have to go up onto the assembly platform, as all the pupils were eventually required to do, and speak in public—a thing that in his adult life he never did, no matter how great the provocation. He was physically slight but not frail, and, unlike most introverted youngsters, competent at sports. He was an avid reader of and contributor to *St. Nicholas* magazine.

In the fall of 1917, having won two scholarships that added up to a thousand dollars, he entered Cornell, where his brothers had preceded him. Along toward Thanksgiving he wrote in his journal, "I've been feeling sick for the past week and I think I must have consumption. If I have, I will leave college and travel for my health." Instead, he became a freshman reporter on the Cornell *Daily Sun*, and pledged a fraternity. In his junior year he took an advanced course in writing under Professor William Strunk, and learned to avoid the tame, the vague, the colorless in favor of the clear, the brief, and the bold. He was also invited to join the Manuscript Club, composed of students and faculty who met on Saturday nights at the house of a member of the English Department, Martin Sampson, and read their work aloud. Sampson defined their creed as "To be frank, to use one's brains, to write what is in one to write, and never to take oneself too damned seriously or too damned lightly." The members were encouraged to avoid the expression of excessive emotion and to understate their feelings in witty and comic statements. In short, very few writers come from nowhere, uninfluenced by anybody, and the young Andy White was in part shaped by these men and this literary experience. According to his own account he was profoundly affected by a course in European history. "My chance encounter with George Lincoln Burr was the greatest single thing that ever happened in my life, for he introduced me to a part of myself that I hadn't discovered. I saw, with blinding clarity, how vital it is for Man to live in a free society. The experience enabled me to grow up almost overnight; it gave my thoughts and ambitions a focus. It caused me indirectly to pursue the kind of work which eventually enabled me to earn my living. But far more important than that, it gave me a principle of thought and of action for which I have tried to fight, and for which I shall gladly continue to fight the remainder of my life."

In the spring that same school year he became editor-in-chief of the *Daily Sun*, one of the two daily college newspapers published in America at that time and Ithaca's only morning paper. It subscribed to the Associated Press wire service and carried national and international news. During the winter of his senior year, White, through the editorial columns of the *Sun*, waged a successful campaign for the establishment of the Honor System. And when spring came he sat in the bleachers of an empty athletic field with a girl who had played the part of Columbine in the campus production of Edna St. Vincent Millay's *Aria da Capo* and watched the falling stars.

After Commencement he went home and landed a job as a reporter with the United Press. Assigned to cover the funeral of Senator Philander C. Knox in Valley Forge, he took the wrong train, and got there just in time to see the coffin being lowered into the grave. At the end of his second week, feeling unable to cope with the requirements of the job, he quit. His application was turned down by various papers, including the *Times,* and he was hired by a public-relations man to write press releases and edit the house organ of a silk mill. That, too, lasted only a short time. In January he got a job with the American Legion News Service, and in February he decided to quit and drive to the West Coast with a college friend, in a Model T Ford roadster. It was a matter, really, of his approaching his destiny by going as far as he could in the opposite direction.

I doubt if anyone could read about this journey and not be reminded of what it is like to be young. They had next to no money, and their plan to pay for their expenses by selling accounts of their travels failed to work out as they had hoped. The friend, Howard Cushman, didn't know how to drive a car. What with one hesitation and another, including a side trip to Ithaca, it took them five weeks to get out of the state of New York. In Kentucky, White heard his first whippoorwill and won twenty-two dollars on a horse race, only to lose it a week later at the Derby. They slept in fraternity houses, and picked up a little cash by selling a poem or a feature story to some local newspaper, or by working at odd jobs, such as selling roach powder from door to door and "signing the name 'Horace C. Klein' on a thousand direct-mail advertising letters, for forty cents an hour." From Minneapolis west, they frequently were on unpaved roads, in North Dakota and Montana sometimes no more than a couple of ruts extending ahead of them across the plains. Angels were watching over them the whole way. In Yellowstone Park, with only three dollars between them, they were accused of not putting out a campfire and threatened with a five-hundred-dollar fine. White had dislocated his right elbow, and was all but blinded by hay fever. On the banks of the Columbia River, as they were trying to drive up a steep incline onto the ferry, the rear end gave way. They had a blowout and White walked thirty-two miles to the nearest town, carrying Cushman's typewriter—his own he had already parted with— which he sold in order to get money for a new tire.

White found a job on the Seattle *Times*, first as a reporter, then writing feature articles and a daily column. After nine months he was fired, and bought a ticket on a cruise ship that went from San Francisco through the Bering Strait to the east-ernmost tip of Siberia. His ticket ran out at Skagway, Alaska, where he signed on as saloon boy (but soon found himself car-rying iron stewpots as big as a bushel basket down a swaying, vertical, steel ladder to the firemen's mess room in the bowels of the ship) and so worked his way back to Seattle. From there he took the train home—a place that, until now, he had consid-ered it unsuitable at his age to be.

His brothers and sisters had all gone, and he was alone in the house with his mother and father. He found a job as a layout man with a New York advertising agency, and on the side wrote poems and squibs that were published in Christopher Morley's column, "The Bowling Green," in the *Evening Post*, or in F.P.A.'s "The Conning Tower," in the *World*.

In February, 1925, on his way to catch the train to Mount Vernon, he stopped at a newsstand and bought a copy of the very first issue of *The New Yorker*. Nine weeks later, *The New Yorker* published his first contribution—a two-hundred-word piece on the coming of spring.

In writing about that magazine people have sometimes suggested that Harold Ross, its first editor, was illiterate and a boor. He was neither. His hair was unruly, his lower lip stuck out, his remarks often began "Jesus Christ, that's the most . . ." but he had a wonderful light in his eye of amusement and intelligence, and the blind trust that he placed in newly hired employees often turned them into dedicated editors overnight. Where others hid their ignorance, he wrote on the margin of a galley proof, "Ariel, who he?" The men and women he worked with directly loved and respected him and found him as mysterious as a force of nature. He may not have read *The Tempest* but he knew Fowler's *Modern English Usage* backwards and forwards and inside out.

In the summer of 1925, six months after its first issue, *The New Yorker* was struggling to stay alive. Katharine Angell was taken on as a part-time manuscript reader at a weekly salary of twenty-five dollars. Two weeks later she was working full time and within three months she was doing a good many other things besides reading manuscripts. She was thirty-one years old, she was well read, she had an eye for literary talent in its first stages, she recognized genuine humor (as distinct from the forced, unfunny kind) when she saw it. For a time she edited both factual pieces and fiction, and dealt with problems of makeup and scheduling. She was one of the four editors who in the weekly Art Meeting decided on covers and drawings. Ross did not like to be personally involved with writers and artists and she did.

Writing that was confused or pretentious had no chance of getting by him. Anything tending toward overstatement was certain to be queried. In a letter of introduction Ross wrote "This is to introduce Mrs. Angell, who is not unattractive." She was, actually, a beautiful woman. Because of her manner and New England accent she was sometimes taken for a Proper Bostonian but the background of her family was western Massachusetts and Maine. She, too, has been the subject of a biography* that leaves a good deal to be desired. She was born Katharine Shepley Sergeant and descended on her father's side

---

Onward and Upward: A Biography of Katharine S. White, by Linda H. Davis. Harper & Row, 1987.

from a Congregationalist minister who helped found the town of Stockbridge, Massachusetts, and devoted his life to educating the local Indians. Her father, Charles Sergeant, was orphaned at the age of seventeen. Like a character out of Horatio Alger he went to work for a bank, then for a railroad, taught himself engineering and ended up vice-president of the Boston Elevated Railway Company.

Katharine's maternal grandfather left his law practice in a small town in Maine to take up sheep ranching in California and was murdered. His widow moved to Boston and opened a boarding house, which did not prosper, partly because she had very bad servants and partly because she thought it unprincipled to buy any but the best cuts of meat. Charles Sergeant became a boarder and, in 1880, married her daughter Elizabeth. Elizabeth was a timid mother, cried over the household accounts, and died of a ruptured appendix when Katharine was six years old. Elizabeth's place in the household was taken by her husband's sister Caroline, who had been headmistress of a girls' school and was articulate to the point of eccentricity.

Charles Sergeant had been subjected as a boy to such a thorough dose of Congregationalist puritanism that he limited his adult churchgoing to Christmas and Easter. Even so, the inherited rigidity persisted; though he was in general an affectionate father he forbade his eldest daughter, Elsie, to cry at her mother's funeral. Katharine had almost no memory of her mother and no conscious sense of loss. By her own account her childhood was happy. When she was eight her father bought a handsome brick house on three acres of ground in the socially more than acceptable Boston suburb of Brookline. The move must have been made for the sake of the children. He did not take easily to the outdoors. He was afraid of anything that buzzed. The sight of a dandelion on his lawn inflamed him.

Katharine was a prim little girl, educated at home until the seventh grade when, five days a week, she boarded a streetcar that carried her into Boston and the Winsor School. Like her two older sisters she was then enrolled in Bryn Mawr, which was small, the most bluestocking of the American colleges for women, and ardently feminist. Its requirements for admission were matched only by those of Harvard. The president of the college, M. Carey Thomas, said, "It is undesirable to have the problems of love and marriage presented for decision to a young girl during the four years when she ought to devote her energies to profiting by the only systematic intellectual training she is likely to receive during her life." Dancing was forbidden. At the Junior Prom the girls walked around the room with their male partners. In her senior year Katharine was editor of the school magazine and the literary annual, and managed to wheedle a contribution out of Marianne Moore, who was an alumna. Katharine graduated fourth in a class of seventy-nine.

A year out of college she married Ernest Angell. She had known him since childhood. While still an undergraduate at Harvard he spent two winters with the Grenfell medical mission in Labrador. Much later in his life he was for a very long time chairman of the board of the American Civil Liberties Union. Their first home was in Cleveland, Ohio, where he had been taken into his father's law firm. From the very beginning she had a job of one sort or another—reading scripts for the Cleveland Play House; conducting in the worst slums of Cleveland a door-to-door survey of the crippled and handicapped, with a view to finding work for them; representing the Consumer's League at legislative hearings on working conditions in factories. When she and her husband moved to New York they lived pleasantly and somewhat beyond their means, with a house in town staffed by a cook, housemaid, and nurse for their two children, and a place up the Hudson. He was appointed to represent Haiti and the Dominican Republic in the Senate investigation of the American occupation of those two countries, and she went to the islands with him and wrote articles, which

The New Republic printed, on political and social conditions there. She also did reviewing for *The Atlantic Monthly* and *The Saturday Review of Literature.* As an Army Intelligence officer during the First World War, Angell discovered that he had a taste for philandering. His infidelity could not be kept secret and the happiness of their first years together gave way to furious quarrelling.

White continued to publish light verse and short prose pieces in *The New Yorker,* and toward the end of 1926 Mrs. Angell suggested to Ross that he be hired as a part-time staff writer. White somewhat reluctantly accepted the offer. He edited newsbreaks, rewrote Talk of the Town pieces, and captioned drawings—his best-known caption probably being " 'It's broccoli, dear.' 'I say it's spinach and I say the hell with it.' " It was quoted so often that it became a watchword and passed into the language. White's presence on the staff was a kind of anonymous blessing. The unsigned paragraphs that he wrote for Notes and Comment set the prevailing tone of the magazine, insofar as it has had one, and gradually broadened its concerns; the parodies and other divertissements that appeared over his three initials made its humor more civilized. One day, after reading something of White's in the magazine, Ross left a note on his desk that said simply, "I am encouraged to go on."

On meeting Katharine Angell for the first time, White was left with the impression "that she had a lot of back hair and the knack of making a young contributor feel at ease." Working together day after day they fell in love. They met in Europe in the summer of 1928, had a brief affair in the South of France and Corsica, and agreed not to continue it. She went to Reno to get a divorce. White was seven years younger than she was, and afraid of all binding arrangements, including marriage. She was never in any doubt about her feelings for him. In the end, taking his Scottish terrier, they drove to a suburb of Manhattan and were married in a church that was decorated with autumn foliage left over from a funeral. White recalled that "it was a very nice wedding—nobody thew anything, and there was a dog fight."

Mrs. White was in part responsible for turning *The New Yorker* from what was originally a funny magazine advertising itself as "not for the old lady from Dubuque" into something more original, more ambitious, more literary, with a point of view that was immediately recognizable and that became widely shared. She went to considerable pains to train young editors who would otherwise have been left to sink or swim. Though it appears that she was awkward in mothering her son by White and her two children by Ernest Angell, "maternal" is the word that best describes her concern for the work and lives of writers and artists. They found themselves confiding to her. When they turned work in, they felt she was on their side, and in fact she was. Of the two kinds of editors, the no-sayers and the yes-sayers, she was a yes-sayer and if possible would find a way to save a manuscript that was almost but not quite right. She did not take kindly to some of the things Brendan Gill wrote about her in *Here at The New Yorker* but his summing-up of her qualities as an editor is entirely accurate: ". . . militantly proud (as the Bryn Mawr graduates of those days especially were) of her fitness to take part in matters of importance in the world, she . . . had not only a superb confidence in herself and in her eye for quality; she was as stubborn . . . in pushing for the acceptance of her opinion as some weighty glacier working its way down a narrow Alpine pass. She must often have intimidated Ross . . . she certainly gave him what amounted to an intellectual conscience. . . . Always a resourceful opponent, when she was not the glacier, she was the narrow Alpine pass."

For White, living in New York City and working for *The New Yorker* was not a complete life. They bought, in Maine, an eighteenth-century farmhouse with its back to pine woods and a cove of shining salt water, and then more and more he wanted to live there. In 1938 he gave up writing Notes and Comment for the opening pages of *The New Yorker* in favor of a monthly column for *Harper's Magazine*. Janet Flanner said crossly, "I just can't forgive Mrs. White for deserting the office. She is the best woman editor in the world, had the best editor's job in the world, and what does she do, leave it all and retire to a farm in Maine."

Neither of them left entirely: he continued to write captions for newsbreaks, Ross asked her to keep an eye on the magazine and occasionally sent her manuscripts to read, and for a while, until this too became irksome to White, they spent the winter months in New York. It was not easy for her to break herself of the habit of authority, and her relationship with G. S. Lo-brano, whom she picked to succeed her as fiction editor, became increasingly tense. When his death, of cancer, created an emergency, she came back on full time briefly, but had to give this up because of ill health.

The Whites' preoccupation with illness went far beyond the garden variety of hypochondriasis. White did die of Alzheimer's at the end of a very long life but more often than not it turned out that he didn't have the disease he was sure he was suffering from. Even a partial list of her afflictions is appalling. A spinal-fusion operation. Infectious hepatitis. Mumps. An emergency appendectomy. Diabetes. A blocked carotid artery that required surgery, after which she went into shock and nearly died in the operating room. As they went from doctor to doctor her condition was aggravated by misdiagnosis and the side effects of dangerous medication. She developed what was diagnosed as "subcorneal pustular dermatosis," blistered all over, and shed her entire skin. The huge doses of a cortisone derivative she was treated with produced osteoporosis. All this she endured with patience and fortitude.

Confined to a wheelchair or the living-room sofa, she refused to give in to old age, and was a gallant and touching figure—

arranging and annotating her books and papers for the Bryn Mawr library, answering her mail and even some of White's, writing letters to her senator and congressman when failing eyesight obliged her to use a magnifying glass and glasses with special magnification in order to read and she found it impossible to hold the magnifying glass and a pen in her hand at the same time. After her death White wandered disconsolately about the place, seeing what needed to be done but, without her, lacking the will to do it.

Many people become writers because of their love of reading. White was an exception. It took him fourteen months to get through *Anna Karenina*—a novel that most readers do not find hard going. Writing to his brother in 1947, he says, "I'm glad to report that even now, at this late day, a blank sheet of paper holds the greatest excitement there is for me—more promising than a silver cloud, prettier than a little red wagon. It holds all the hope there is, all fears. I can remember, really quite distinctly, looking a sheet of paper square in the eyes when I was seven or eight years old and thinking, 'This is where I belong, this is it.' "

Few mature writers have been as fortunate in the way their work was received. White could probably have counted on the fingers of one hand the number of times something he wrote did not please the editor it was intended for. Ross, in his efforts to keep White on as a staff writer, told him to make out his own ticket. White wanted his freedom instead. He wanted to write what he felt like writing.

The familiar essay is not generally considered to be a popular literary form. *Harper's,* during the three weeks after the publication of the first of the monthly columns White wrote for it, picked up eleven thousand new subscribers and its newsstand sales increased by twenty per cent. When the columns were published as a book, it sold over thirty thousand copies. A hundred and fifty thousand copies were printed for the American Armed Services, and further editions of fifty thousand copies in French and German. As for his children's books, Professor Elledge says that for the previous twenty years in America *Charlotte's Web* had outsold *Winnie-the-Pooh*, any single Mary Poppins book, *The Wind in the Willows*, *The Little Prince*, and *Alice in Wonderland*.

Honorary degrees and literary honors (the Presidential Medal of Freedom, the National Medal for Literature, the American Academy of Arts and Letters' Gold Medal for Essays and Criticism) showered down on White like autumn leaves.

Some degree of self-doubt is essential to a writer's equilibrium. The rejection of a manuscript, though painful, is also proof that his work is being subjected to serious consideration, and that the writing that was not rejected must therefore be successful. Where there is nothing but rejections, then the writer can only conclude that he is a misunderstood genius or should be in another line of work. But what is the writer to think whose work never meets with an unsympathetic or an unfavorable reception? Does it mean that the standards that hold for the work of other people do not hold for him? And that no acceptance is really to be trusted? Does it mean that anything he writes, whether he puts very little or a great deal of effort and thought into it, is good? Of all things inimical, the enemy within—complacency—is the most frightening. White was extremely fortunate in that the child for whom every day was an awesome prospect and who was uneasy about everything never let go of his hand. To say that the two of them were the greatest worriers who have ever lived would be an exaggeration, but they must be fairly high up on the list. Suspecting the worst, having nervous indigestion, having palpitations, feeling the ground come up and hit their shoe, they reminded one another that they had made it this far. On those occasions when their life's work was being held up for public admiration, they usually managed to be elsewhere. To the siren voice of complacency they presented a deaf ear.

In his eighties White looked and acted considerably younger than his age. It was no doubt because of the company he kept.

One Creature

Maurice Goudeket discovered Colette through her books when he was fifteen or sixteen years old, and announced to his parents, "I am going to marry that woman. She is the only one who will be able to understand me." In his account of their life together he dismisses the incident as simply the incredible pride and fancifulness of adolescence. Nevertheless he did marry her. In his book* about their life together he tells how she put salt and garlic on her bread and how she liked her morning coffee, what houses they lived in, who her friends were, what sort of books she read, how they came to America on the maiden voyage of the Normandie, how the Queen of Belgium came to lunch, how Colette tried unsuccessfully to put M. Gide at his ease, how she got Goudeket released from a German concentration camp, how they survived the war, how, bedridden with arthritis, she accommodated herself to immobility and old age. The reader is allowed to see her and know her informally—to know her preferences in music (she did not care for Mozart and called Bach "a sublime sewing machine"), to know her faithful servant, Pauline, to be present at her waking in the morning, to

*Close to Colette. Farrar, Straus and Cudahy, 1957.

watch her put kohl on her eyelids, to go walking with her in the Forest of Rambouillet. The reader is free to follow her around like a child following its mother, indoors, outdoors, happy, unhappy: with her dog and her cat; with friends, with her daughter, Colette de Jouvenel; now worried about money, now unable to sleep because every sound all night is the Germans coming to take her husband away again; with Cocteau, with Segonzac, with her brother Léo, the little boy in *My Mother's House* who said, "Don't you think it looks sad, a garden without graves?" and who as a grown man was a living ghost; with the Princesse Edmond de Polignac, who was an American, immensely rich, and the patron of all the best musicians of the last fifty years, and who complained to Colette, "My dear, I have no luck. I buy a little hut in the country, tell my architect to add a tiny little wing to it while I am in Venice. I return and what do I find? The Louvre." And, finally, one sees her writing: "The word inspiration seemed to her one of the most suspect in the French language. . . . But when she was writing Colette used sometimes to concentrate so hard that she would gradually get colder and colder. She put rug after rug on her knees and shawl after shawl on her back. When she was finishing a book her application became such that one had the impression she was really giving of her substance, as a bee gives its honey. Capable at such times of working eight or ten hours at a stretch, she used in the end to look like a cocoon."

For a reader who stood day after day looking up at the windows of that row of houses on the north end of the garden of the Palais-Royal, wondering which window was hers, feeling a pull like that of the moon on the ocean, but unable to persuade himself that, unarmed with a letter of introduction and not speaking French, he could or should knock on her door, all this is no small present.

*   *   *

Maurice Goudeket made Colette's acquaintance in 1925, at the house of friends. He was thirty-five and she was fifty-two. He had not been told she would be there, and when he walked into the room, she was lying flat on her stomach on a sofa and looked like a large cat stretching herself. "Why it was I do not know," he says, "but I observed her without charity. At table I found I was placed on her right. . . . Hardly had she sat down when Colette seized an apple from a basket of fruit placed in front of her and bit hungrily into it. I thought that she was playing the part of herself, and my suspicion increased. But I could not take my eyes off that most individual profile of hers, with the eye set so expressively in the shadow of a lock of ash-blonde hair." He filled her wineglass, and she appeared astonished by this and shot him a look blue as night, ironical, and searching. He was aware of something countrified and healthy emanating from her. But she did not take part in the conversation. The evening dragged. She did not enjoy herself much. Neither did he. The whole little scene is a lesson to novelists—to English novelists, that is; no French novelist would need it. "What used to disconcert visitors to Colette," he says elsewhere in the book, "was a simplicity which did not seem to them natural, and a naturalness which seemed to them a snare." It took a persistent series of meetings, all accidental, a long, unavoidable automobile trip, an inscribed copy of *La Vagabonde,* and an invitation to lunch before he could overcome his suspicion of her. He does not mention, strangely, her suspicion of him. Perhaps in that one look she saw everything there was to see.

As a young man, Goudeket says, he was reserved and cautious with everyone, anxiously concealing his real nature, which was romantic. He was city-bred, and his parents were extravagantly citified. "My father would say to my mother, 'You do not look well today. I bet you've been to the Bois de Boulogne again.' His theory was that trees absorb all the available oxygen from the air, leaving us not enough to keep us alive." Though Maurice Goudeket was a well-to-do businessman until the depression, and later became a journalist, all that he really asked of life was to be near Colette.

They lived together for ten years before they decided, for reasons of domestic convenience, to get married. Wanting not to stir up the press, he asked to be excused from publishing the banns, and the official at the prefecture whom he approached said to him, like a character out of a French movie, "Your desire for discretion is not a sufficient reason. The only motive that you could put forward is the fear of scandal. So just tell me that, since your district has thought you were married for a long time, it would create a scandal if they were to learn, precisely through your marriage, that you were not. Then I can give you the necessary permission." And so, after two marriages that were impermanent and unhappy, Colette was lured into a third that was serene and happy and companionable, and lasted her straight through to the end.

As husband and wife, they continued to practice certain forms of politeness with each other. He did not see her in the morning until her face was made up. Except in moments of the greatest stress, they did not ask, "What are you thinking of?" They did not permit themselves displays of ill temper or try to impose on each other all their own ways of seeing and feeling. Different though they were in temperament and background, it appears that on the most important matters they were in agreement. For example: "We were agreed that suffering is not in itself an honorable state and that there is no need to bear any of it that you can avoid." When they were separated, it sometimes happened that her letters answered questions he had not yet put to her in his. "The fact is," he says, "that she and I lived together in the most natural way. That was what made our happiness."

Though Colette spent most of her life in Paris, she remained a countrywoman. "Her way of making contact with things was through all her senses," Goudeket says. "It was not enough for her to look at them, she had to sniff and taste them. When she went into a garden she did not know, I would say to her, 'I suppose you are going to eat it, as usual.' And it was extraordinary to see her setting to work, full of haste and eagerness, as if there were no more urgent task than getting to know this garden. She separated the sepals of flowers, examined them, smelled them for a long time, crumpled the leaves, chewed them, licked the poisonous berries and the deadly mushrooms, pondering intensely over everything she had smelt and tasted. Insects received almost the same treatment: they were felt and listened to and questioned. She attracted bees and wasps, letting them alight on her hands and scratching their backs. . . . When at last she left the garden, she would pick up her scarf, slippers, stockings, dog, and husband, which she had shed one after the other. With her nose and her forehead covered with yellow pollen, her hair in disorder and full of twigs, a bump here and a scratch there, her face innocent of powder and her neck moist, stumbling along out of breath, she was just like a bacchante after libations."

She did not distinguish, insofar as her feelings were concerned, between plants and animals, any more than she distinguished between animals and people. Once, when she and Goudeket were watching a speeded-up movie short about germination, growth, and flowering, she gripped his arm in her intense excitement and said, "There is only one creature! Do you hear me, Maurice, there is only *one* creature."

When, brought down like any other wild animal ("First one stick, then two, then a wheel chair for out of doors, and finally a wheel chair for moving about the house"), she had to renounce her inheritance, she made a kind of substitute world indoors, in a room that was entirely red—walls, ceiling, velvet curtains, armchair, and bedspread—and with her bed pushed against the window, so she could observe what went on in the Palais-Royal garden, and books within reach. Travel books, books on natural history. (She read Proust all the way through about every two years.) Little by little, the bookshelves became masked by boxes of South American butterflies, sea shells, objects of emblematic meaning. Beside the bed, her table, into which had been incorporated a desk with an adjustable rack that straddled the bed. Within reach, a brown morocco-leather box, designed to hold a rare copy of Pascal's *Les Provinciales* but actually containing her lipstick, mirror, etc. All around her, glass paperweights, exotic seeds, photographs, compasses, a handyman's tool kit, her spectacle case, her scissors, the telephone, a miniature of Sido, Colette's mother, which had turned up miraculously in the Flea Market. On the wall just above her head, the barometer. Outside but within view, the thermometer. A wood fire burning. On the mantelpiece, more glass paperweights, Chinese glass balls. Here and there and everywhere, glass walking sticks, trumpets, pipes, necklaces, more butterflies, paintings of fruit and flowers. And during the last summer of her life, as her strength began to leave her, always the magnifying glass—not because her sight was failing but because she wanted to look more closely.

If the secretive person cannot afford to be curious, because to ask questions is to lay oneself open to questioning, the reverse is also true. The really curious person has no secrets; they would interfere with his pursuit of knowledge. More curious than Colette was it probably isn't possible to be. And who she was, what she was, at all times lies open to you like a landscape when you read her. She never describes anything she has not observed. Every important thing about her is there. Nothing is held back from the reader who may be curious about *her*. And yet when all curiosity about Colette has been satisfied, she continues to exert a pull, an attraction. She was a great writer, and that is partly the source of it, but there is something else, which seems to belong in the same category with certain ordinary human desires; for example, the desire to live in the one house that you know your way around in in the dark, to be within calling distance of the person from whose identity your identity derives, to be able to raise your eyes and see, every day of your life, not a different place but the same place, the same familiar arrangement of foreground and background, of ground and sky. All these varieties of the desire for nearness to someone or something have this in common—they are proof of the presence of love. That's really all it is, and was, with Colette.

Let us begin with the animals: "When Colette worked in the afternoon, the Cat used to sleep against her side. She would wake from time to time, pull Colette by the sleeve, give her a long look of love and ecstasy, and fall asleep again." Colette never left any animals indifferent, though sometimes they were hostile to her. "What is normally referred to as 'love of animals,' " her husband remarks, "has certainly nothing in common with the veritable connivance that existed between them and Colette. And one might almost say as much for the vegetable world. When she busied herself over flowers it was not, as with the rest of us, merely to keep them beautiful as long as possible. The important thing was to save and sustain life; it was a question of pity and love."

Now for people: A purse-snatcher in Nice, learning from the newspapers that it was her purse he had taken, returned the three thousand francs that were in it, with a note: "I didn't know it was you." Her old friend the Queen of Belgium climbed the steep stairs to Colette's apartment, her arms loaded with flowers, and with honey from her own bees, and would not let Goudeket take them from her, and sat down at the foot of Colette's bed. The natives of the Palais-Royal approached her "with that mixture of respect and niceness [*"gentillesse"* it is in the French text] which is compounded in the heart. They kept away the tactless from her, and those who did not 'belong.' In return, Colette's door was never closed for Mademoiselle Mauduit, who sold lampshades and canvas for tapestries, for Rose Cohen, the little antique dealer, for Madame Groves, the bookseller, for Madame Albert, for the baker's children or those of the concierge next door. When they passed through the garden they waved to her and from her window she replied with ample gestures." One of the prostitutes of the Palais-Royal, who was secretly bringing up a younger brother on the proceeds of her soliciting and who sometimes wrote to Colette, asked for one of her books. "Which one?" Colette wanted to know. "The saddest," the prostitute said. Because she was no longer able to attend the luncheons of the Académie Goncourt, the members sometimes came in a body to her flat and gathered around her. "Closer, closer," she said. "Sit on my feet."

"From the four corners of the earth," Goudeket says, "they [her readers] sent their messages, too numerous soon for her to answer them all, a fact which distressed her. I can only give a feeble idea of this movement of love which went on growing right up to Colette's death." Celebrity, which is a movement of a different kind, also reached out at her. "One receives it at first without distrust, and when one wants to curb it it is too late. Very soon there was no longer an investigation in which Colette was not invited to take part, no jury on which she was not invited to sit. A hundred projects were submitted to her, her post began to grow out of all measure, strangers, professional or just idle, knocked at her door, the pile of books and photographs to be autographed grew higher." Even so, Goudeket never ventured to praise her without precaution, because it made her ill at ease. "Once I said to her that she was one of the greatest writers of all time. She looked at me out of the corner of a blue and sceptical eye, and said, 'That would be known.' . . . She was set on being just like everybody else. If a stranger or an interviewer tried to entice her onto what they considered heights of thought, she eluded them adroitly." She never refused to inscribe copies of her books, since she could see no way of discriminating, and piles of them were dumped on her. Sometimes, yielding to irritation, she wrote, "To Monsieur X, whom I do not know." During her last public appearances, people would pick up dirty scraps of paper from the ground and get her to sign them. They would stop her in the road and bar her passage. Before her state funeral, out-of-doors, in the garden of the Palais-Royal, the people of Paris filed past her coffin, thousands and thousands.

Now for the schoolboy who foretold his destiny. "Oh, how sorry I am for you," she would say, "having a wife so much older than yourself." He had various answers to this, and the final answer is here: "In the room where I am writing, nothing has changed. On the chimney-piece there are the Chinese crystal balls. The armchairs are there, adorned with strips of tapestry which she worked with her own hands. Behind me, above the books and surmounting a niche, there is a head in plaster by the sculptor Saint-Marceaux, which followed her in all her removals. . . . Nothing has changed except that I shall never get over the impulse which draws me into the next room."

Well, none of this is really surprising. Love was her subject.

She was never at any moment or in any way ill, Goudeket says, speaking of the end of her life. "All that happened was an imperceptible drooping. . . . Little by little she became more silent." He took her for a drive in the car. "She bent forward so as to see better. The few people who were near her then will remember how she held her two hands before her, at shoulder level, palms forward, in a gesture of wonder. But she returned tired out.

"It was toward the end of June that that lowering vitality, that slow withdrawal became marked. I noticed that she no longer touched the newspapers which were brought to her in the morning and hardly opened her letters. . . . She began to sleep a great deal. When she awoke from those deep sleeps, she would first lift to her ear a big repeater-watch, which struck the hours, the quarters, and the minutes in a silvery voice. Then she consulted the weather, the position of the sun. . . . Then came the day when she was too weak to raise herself. It was toward the twentieth of July. Colette de Jouvenel, Pauline, and I started a vigil whose duration we could not guess, although we knew how it must end. . . . I went out one morning to find a book for her and brought her back a beautiful album of colored lithographs representing butterflies, insects, and birds, which enchanted her. She read the descriptions aloud, following them with her finger. One of the butterflies was called *blaps, portent of death.*

"Two days before the end, she emerged from a great weariness into an hour of great lucidity. We looked at the album together. I was sitting on the floor in the space between the bed and the window. It was a hot August day with a veiled sky. The swallows were passing level with the open window, with sharp whirrings. Colette bent toward me and I put my head against her side. She pointed to the boxes of butterflies on their shelf, the book, and the birds in the garden. 'Ah!' she said. So near to death and knowing it, everything appeared to her more beautiful, more astonishing than ever. Her hands fluttered about her like wings. She leaned closer to me. Her arm described a spiral which embraced everything she had shown me. 'Look!' she said to me. 'Maurice! Look!' "

Eighty-one she was, and one of the wonders of the world.

Your Affectionate Son

Samuel Butler's *The Way of All Flesh* is read mostly by the young, bent on making out a case against their elders, but Butler was fifty when he stopped working on it, and no reader much under that age is likely to appreciate the full beauty of its horrors, which are the horrors not of the Gothic novel but of family life. Every contemporary novelist with a developed sense of irony is probably in some measure, directly or indirectly, through Shaw and Arnold Bennett and E. M. Forster and D. H. Lawrence, indebted to Butler, who had the misfortune to be a twentieth-century man born in the year 1835.

At the end of his life he gathered his correspondence together, annotated it, and had it bound into sixteen manuscript volumes, which are now in the British Museum. It was his hope that these volumes would prove helpful to his biographers, and they of course have. Professor Arnold Silver, of the University of Massachusetts, has published a selection from the correspondence of Butler and his father, who was the rector of a small village in Nottinghamshire, canon of Lincoln Cathedral, and the most important figure in Butler's life. The book* contains also a number of letters to and from Butler's mother and sisters, and

* *The Family Letters of Samuel Butler.* Stanford University Press, 1962.

one or two other relatives. Butler's very interesting annotations are printed in full. Two-thirds of the hundred and ninety letters in this volume have never been printed before, and many others were until now not available in their entirety. They are melancholy reading. Butler's letters to his mother and father were signed "Your affectionate Son" and to his sisters "Your affectionate Brother," and there is every reason to believe that they none of them felt the slightest affection for him.

In a letter to his sister-in-law, Butler says, "I cannot go down to Wilderhope [a village near Shrewsbury, where his father lived after his retirement] much. For years past they have never once asked me to come, or said when I went away that they had been glad to see me, and hoped I would come again as soon as I could. I have always had to write and say I should be glad to come: then I am allowed to do so—in the coldest terms that can be used with decency, and am let to go again without, as I said, any of those little civilities which people expect, even though they know they do not mean much. . . . If I was not most anxious to avoid giving my father any reasonable ground of complaint I should not go near him."

Without going near his father, simply by taking his pen in hand, Butler gave the Canon some reasonable and many unreasonable grounds of complaint. Butler was expected to follow in the footsteps of his father and grandfather and become a clergyman, and he was well on the way to this when he discovered that he had doubts of so grave a nature as to make him unfit for ordination. The Canon was, quite naturally, disappointed. Butler wrote home that he was thinking of emigrating to Liberia to raise cotton. He then considered becoming a homeopathic doctor, a painter, a tutor, a farmer. No sooner did he pick up one possible career than he dropped it for another, defending them all on grounds of congeniality with his temperament. The Canon urged his son to take up the study of law, or if he didn't want to become a barrister, what about being a schoolmaster?

The law and teaching, Butler wrote, were deeply uncongenial with his temperament. He then thought of emigrating to New Zealand, and the Canon offered, as a last resort, diplomacy. Butler's indecisiveness lasted only five months, which is not very long for such post-adolescent shilly-shallying, but it is, of course, a situation calculated to strike terror to the heart of any father, loving or otherwise. The Canon's replies are, on the surface, patient and reasonable, if you allow him an occasional outburst of the irritability that was a conspicuous part of *his* temperament, and don't mind the fact that now and again, when the old fox had written something outrageous and totally unjust, he then, in the spirit of reason and self-control, crossed it out lightly *in pencil.* But even reading the letters quickly one after another in a book, which is not how poor Butler read them, you soon become aware of something that is not reasonable but in fact very queer indeed:

> I take it you know less of farming than even I do. Couldn't buy a cow, horse, sheep, or estimate its value or know what a labourer ought to do in a day. . . .
>
> By writing you might pick a poor and scanty subsistence. School books are the only ones that pay, and it may be you won't be read. . . .
>
> Your mother conjectures that you look to bookselling. To this I should have no objection if I thought you fit for it but you have not the mercantile element in your character necessary to insure success and I can't advance capital to be sunk in some overwhelming breakdown. . . .
>
> You speak about . . . the army. . . . But the risk not only of your not liking it but of your getting into difficulties with your superior officers is too great. . . .
>
> I judged that it was wisest for your good that I should not encourage you in your artist's career. This is my sole motive for refusing to assist you in it. You have shown no decided genius for drawing. You are as yet just at the commencing point. To

all except men of a decided professional talent it is a very uphill and hopeless task and I think still I should do wrong to afford you the slightest possible encouragement to a course for which for aught I know you may be just as unfitted as for a soldier, lawyer, schoolmaster or tutor.

One would almost have thought that the Canon was anxious lest his son succeed at something—as in fact he did. Within a year after he arrived in New Zealand, Butler was "working a run of about eight thousand acres"—I am quoting Professor Silver—"and had stocked it with over three thousand sheep. Directing a force of seven hired men, he built a homestead, transported supplies over treacherous rivers, and proved himself extremely adept in business matters."

The Canon advanced his son two thousand pounds for his sheep-raising venture and promised him three thousand more. This was not a loan but a gift outright, with which his son was to establish himself in life. When Butler had committed himself to expenditures roughly equal to the whole amount, the Canon wrote that two thousand pounds was to be reserved in his keeping until the affair had been tried. Later, he sent a thousand pounds of the reserve and kept back the other thousand, to meet a crisis of an unspecified nature. When Butler protested, the Canon wrote:

> It is I have no doubt, as you state, that this time twelve months you received a letter from me offering to capitalize the whole of your remaining £3000. You happily declined it at the moment [this was news to Butler, who had understood that the money was to be forthcoming on three months' notice] and I have since felt that it was a foolish offer—do not feel aggrieved that it is withdrawn. I feel more and more that some reserve is most desirable.
>
> I promised however in my last letter to borrow £600 for you which I gather to be the amount of your incumbrances. . . .

The remaining £400 I do not think it right to advance.

You have gone out with advantages far greater than you will find most of your neighbours have enjoyed and must be content to let time be one of the elements of success.

Butler never did get the thousand pounds, but managed without it; there was really no stopping him. At the end of four and a half years, he sold his sheep farm at a hundred-per-cent profit, invested the eight thousand pounds that it brought him in New Zealand land mortgages at the current rate of ten per cent, and came home with an income more than adequate to his needs. This happy turn of events the Canon no doubt met with Christian fortitude. He was not through skirmishing, in any case. When Butler became, briefly, an important London literary figure as the result of the publication of *Erewhon*, the Canon wrote:

Dear Sam:

I shall take your advice and not read your book. It would probably pain me and not benefit you. I do not the least object to your putting your name to it tho' I may not value the éclat. The grief is that our views should be so wide asunder.

Perhaps the book might pain me less than your letter leads me to infer. I gladly give it the benefit of the doubt.

Your affectionate father,
T. Butler.

At home, they didn't any of them read his book, or the books and articles that followed, and they took pleasure in reminding him of the fact. This even extended to the fringes of the family. His uncle Philip Worseley was fond of telling him that *Erewhon* owed its success in great measure to its having been published anonymously. But nobody could touch the Canon when it came to disagreeable insinuations and false or damaging statements. A

year and a half after the publication of *Erewhon,* Butler's mother
died, while the family was abroad. It appears that she had cancer. The Canon informed Butler that his book, which she had
not read, caused her death.

When all other subjects failed them, Butler and his father
always had money to correspond about. The Canon was not, it
appears, entirely honest or entirely dishonest. He bamboozled—
the word is Butler's—his son by getting him to agree to the sale
of a part of what is referred to as "the Whitehall property,"
which Butler had an interest in, by entail, and for which he
received no compensation. But then in time, under pressure
from Butler, he made some restitution. He often threatened to
cut off Butler's allowance ("But I think it right to tell you that
not one sixpence will you receive from me after your Michael-
mas payment till you come to your senses") and held back sums
that he had promised Butler or that actually belonged to him.
(Butler to his father: "Thank you for your note in re the legacy
due to me—I am sure that you will as you say pay it in good
time and am in no hurry.") When Butler was forty-three, he
found himself in serious financial straits, partly as the result of
following the advice of a friend, a banker who proved to be a
swindler, partly because he had for many years been supporting
another friend, who—though Butler did not learn this until after
the man's death—had more money than Butler had and made a
career of sponging on his acquaintance. Butler had no one to
turn to but his father, who was receptive but insisted on expla-
nations. Butler's letter, marked "Private and Confidential" and
going on for eleven printed pages, is almost too painful to read.
The Canon bailed him out and then announced that Butler was
to have only a life interest in the greater part of what he intended to leave him, which meant that Butler could not borrow
against it. In the end, the Canon was persuaded to lay this
particular whip aside because it could have resulted in the mon-

ey's going to Butler's brother Tom, who was the real black sheep of the family; he was an alcoholic, and abandoned his wife and children and lived with prostitutes, who blackmailed him.

Butler was never so infuriated at his father that he did not end his letters with the words "Your affectionate Son," and with each truce in the quarrelling he promptly returned to a tone that was filial and kind. Even when the Canon wrote indignantly, "I have kept your letter a day to wonder over it! . . . I have never had a sign of gratitude for all I have done for you and you talk magnificently of what is due to yourself as if you were treating me with the greatest generosity in not using hard language. This is simply absurd," he nevertheless signed himself "Your affectionate Father." Possibly it was unthinkable in the Victorian era for a father and son of the upper middle class to sign their letters any other way. Or it may have been a matter of good manners, of custom—as we sign our letters "Yours sincerely" when no special sincerity is called for.

The Way of All Flesh did not appear until both the Canon and Butler were dead, and so the Canon did not know that he was sitting for the portrait of Theobald Pontifex, who is, it is probably safe to say, the most unpleasant father in all English literature. It seems also safe to assume that if the book had been published during the Canon's lifetime, he wouldn't have read it, or have thought any worse of it than he already thought of *Erewhon* and the others. If you like, you can hold it against Butler as a man that during the years 1873–85, when he was writing the novel, he was applying to his father for financial help. It is not something that can be held against him as a writer that he took his material so directly from life, because if he had done otherwise he would not have produced a great work of art, or, in fact, any novel at all, and in the end the problem resolves itself into a question of how truthful the autobiographical novelist has been. Butler was more truthful than most writers would have been in his circumstances. He did not, these letters show, make his father out to be worse than he was, and neither did he painstakingly present his own actions in a favorable light.

The Canon lived to be eighty-one, and during the last five years of his life, like most old men, he softened. The accusations and recriminations fade out of the correspondence altogether. It becomes, instead, ordinary and amiable. Butler is assiduous in collecting specimens for his father's botanical collection, and he goes to considerable trouble to procure for him a jar of the very finest Swiss honey. When he brings out a new book, though the Canon doesn't go so far as to read it, he does allow himself to look at one or two of the reviews. He even encourages and supports Butler in his efforts to be appointed to the Slade Professorship of Fine Arts at Cambridge. Butler writes:

Did I tell you that I came across a lady with four parrots? She said to me, "I tell them *everything.*" I said, "But parrots don't keep secrets do they?" She said, "Mine can." They won't allow her to read the newspapers aloud to her husband, but make a tremendous chatter, until she introduces their names—then they think it is something about them, and listen most attentively. If they do not hear their names mentioned again presently, they say to themselves, "This is poor stuff—it is not about us at all—come, come, we can't have this" and begin to make a noise again.

The Canon writes:

I am very glad you are going to poor Uncle John's funeral. It is quite out of the question for me to do so or I would. I had much regard for John [Mrs. Butler's younger brother] as an upright honest man in spite of all his little peculiarities and I think he was generally respected.

I would have inclosed a little cheque for the cost of the journey which I feel you are taking on my behalf but think you
may have set off before this reaches you so will send it by the
next day on to reach you on Tuesday evening as you may not
improbably sleep in Bristol.

We have a keen East wind still so don't catch cold if you can
help it.

This is as far as either of them could go, and it is quite far,
certainly. The amiability is constructed on a framework of caution, but it is not false; it is what they both would have liked
the relationship to be. That the relationship fell something short
of this can be deduced from the fact that in one of the Canon's
letters Butler underlined all the places where his father had
shown hesitation in writing or traced over individual letters.

In Butler's notebooks there is this entry about his father:

> He never liked me, nor I him; from my earliest recollections
> I can call to mind no time when I did not fear him and dislike
> him. Over and over again I have relented towards him and said
> to myself that he was a good fellow after all; but I had hardly
> done so when he would go for me in some way or other which
> soured me again.
>
> I have no doubt I have made myself very disagreeable; cer-
> tainly I have done many very silly and very wrong things; I am
> not at all sure the fault is more his than mine. But no matter
> whose it is, the fact remains that for years and years I have
> never passed a day without thinking of him many times over as
> the man who was sure to be against me, and who would see
> the bad side rather than the good of everything I said and did.

The Canon's death was widely mentioned in the press, and it
was nowhere said that Butler was his son. An obituary in the
Shrewsbury newspaper that has been used to show that Butler's
view of his father was distorted and not shared by his contem-

poraries turns out to have been written by Butler himself. It could have been written by the angels.

Beside the words "He never liked me, nor I him" should be placed, as a kind of corrective footnote, this memorandum: "My father died on the evening—about half past five—of Wednesday, Dec. 29, 1886. I and Rogers and the nurse were alone present. I was supporting his head between my hands as he died. . . ." That is to say, it is not all that easy to hate your father.

The Element of Lavishness

Sylvia Townsend Warner was born on December 6, 1893, at Harrow-on-the-Hill. Her father, George Townsend Warner, was a Harrow housemaster. Her mother, Nora Hudleston, as a child lived in India. According to some notes that were taken down from Miss Townsend Warner's dictation in 1966, her mother fell into labor at the sound of a knell—a Harrow governor had just died—and she was born with a caul, which the midwife claimed and probably sold to a sailor as a protection against death by drowning. The ghost of her maternal grandmother visited her cradle. Who saw this apparition the notes do not say. She herself as a grown woman not only believed in ghosts but described how she saw them, on two different occasions—the daughter of the house, who had died a year or two before her visit, and an old man who had taken his own life.

One of her earliest memories was of a sudden storm in June. Hailstones shattered the window in her nursery, glass fell across the tea table, and her father rushed in with an eiderdown and wrapped her in it and carried her to safety.

She grew up in two societies, School and Town. Her father lived by the school rhythm—up by bell at 6:45. On hot summer evenings the sound from the cricket fields of the bat striking the ball, in winter the "melancholy mooing" of the crowd watching a football match. She was an only child.

Her mother taught her to read, partly from the Bible. When she was about seven she was sent to kindergarten. Without any malicious intentions she mimicked the mistresses and disrupted discipline and her parents were asked to remove her from the school. Foreseeing that this would happen again and again, her father decided that she should be educated at home. Her mother gave her lessons for two hours every morning in her workroom at the top of the house. At the bottom of the house there was another room that survives in *A Spirit Rises*. The framework of this story is a conversation, at a party, between the middle-aged daughter of a dead schoolmaster and one of his favorite pupils. "She saw once again the long room, running the whole width of the house. At one end was the fireplace, with St Jerome above it, his bald, studious head eternally bent, his small lion for ever waiting for a word of recognition. At the other end of the room was the carpenter's bench, with its array of tools, and near by it the rocking horse. The rocking horse was ten hands high and a dapple grey, with tail and flowing mane of silvery horse-hair. The saddle and harness, scuffed with usage, were of crimson leather, and it was mounted on rockers, painted green. . . . The room was a half basement . . . dusky, shabby, smelling of books, wood shavings, tobacco, and sometimes glue. Its windows looked out on a steeply rising bank where ferns and irises grew and autumn scattered fallen leaves from a Virginia creeper. The bookshelves lining the walls gave it an additional sombreness, and as there were heaps of books on the floor . . . one had to pick one's steps. . . . She had no consciousness of those pupils arriving to supplant her. Perhaps they had not even begun to arrive, for at that time her father was a young man, a junior master at the foot of the ladder. Certainly at that time he had more leisure. The sounds of carpentering ascended through the house; he fitted new limbs to her wooden dolls and showed her how to bore holes with a gimlet. He strolled into the garden, snuffing the sweetbriar or hunting for slugs among the auriculas; he was chief mourner at many tadpole funerals. When her mother was out for the afternoon, he would fetch her down to have tea with him—in summer under the hawthorn where you could hear people walking and talking in the road behind the tall wooden paling, in winter below St Jerome, where the fire and the reading lamp changed the rest of the room into a cave. After tea, she would stay on till her bedtime, pulling out from the lower shelves books she couldn't read and methodically replacing them while he wrote at his desk, a cat dripping from his knee, or sat on the dapple-grey horse, reading and gently rocking."

When she was eight she went with her parents to Ireland to stay with her grandmother's younger sister, who was married to Ponsonby Moore, later Earl of Drogheda. Her great-aunt drank water from a jewelled chalice and was a friend of Hugh Lane and Lady Gregory. The house, Moore Abbey in County Kildare, had a splendid avenue of yews, a wonderful Georgian doll's house, and a sedan chair that the child spent hours sitting in. It also had a notorious poltergeist that on occasion made such an uproar no one in the place could sleep. "It was eventually let,"— I am quoting from the notes—"or sold, to Count John McCormack, the singer, who had it exorcised—but for all that it was burnt to the ground."

Like Virginia Woolf, she had the run of her father's library; she found and read halfway through *Vanity Fair* before she was ten. Also Mackay's *Popular Delusions.* And she remembered sitting on the stairs repeating the spells for raising the devil, from the chapter on witchcraft, to her black cat and "feeling a black hope that they would work."

The nursemaids of her childhood were succeeded by a French governess, whom she did not like very much, and her father taught her history informally on holidays in Cornwall or on the Continent. He was an inspiring teacher, and in time, like the woman in the story, she was all too aware of "those special pupils who came thronging between her and her birthright, whose voices rose and fell behind the study door, who learned, who profited, who demanded, who endeared themselves by their demands, who were arrayed for the ball while she, her father's Cinderella, went barefoot like the cobbler's child in the adage."

She came of age thinking she was committed to music, and would have gone to Vienna to study composing with Arnold Schönberg if the outbreak of the First World War had not prevented it. Instead she went to work in a munitions factory. Her first published writing was an article about this experience.

Her father died in 1916, at the age of fifty-one—partly of a broken heart, she believed; one after another of the pupils he had had such high hopes for had fallen on the battlefields of Flanders. Her mother was an immensely capable, witty, autocratic woman and not easy to live with. Both were strongminded. Rather than stay in Devonshire and quarrel with her mother she went to live in London, on an extremely small allowance.

Through her friendship with the music master at Harrow, Dr. Percy Buck (knighted in 1936), she was drawn into the field of musicology. In a letter that was intended to be used as source material for a publisher's blurb, she wrote: "For the last six years I have been romantically engaged in tracing scoring and collating Masses, Motets and so on by the Henrician and Elizabethan composers, which only exist in contemporary Mss part-books. It is the rediscovery of a lost epoch: for in the XVI cent. England was more celebrated for its music than even for literature or piracy, and it (the music) was completely forgotten. Names of composers, if required: John Taverner, Thomas Tallis, William Byrd, Orlando Gibbons." Fifty years later she recalled this experience. "The discrepancies between the earlier (Elfin) stories and those which I wrote later are like nothing but *The Gospels*, or Taverner's *Missa Salve Intemerata* which bore four conscientious scholarly Tudor Church Music Editors into regular nervous breakdowns once a week. There we sat round a table, saying But if; or with a gleam of hope, But why not? And the tugs on the river hooted, clearer & clearer, as the traffic quieted, till the Almoner's house in the Charterhouse (where we sat) became almost as hushed as when it was part of the real Charterhouse, in the clayey Moorish fields.''* The fruit of their combined labors, *Tudor Church Music,* is a monumental effort of English musical scholarship that ranks with the *Paléographie Musicale* and the *Bach-Gesellschaft.*

She was as steeped in poetry as she was in music. In 1953 she wrote to an American acquaintance, "Do you remember the quack doctor in Crabbe, who treated the young man for syphilis, and said so consolingly

> 'Just take the boluses from time to time,
> And hold but moderate intercourse with crime.'

Crabbe is a poet I delight in. No one has such a repertory of aunts, no one has a better control of humdrum, nor a bleaker gaunter way of ascending to his high spots. Long ago, when I was first living in London, poor, hungry and sensual, I walked out on a late summer morning to buy a loaf at the bread-shop, and paused twice on the way back, first to buy half a pound of those very small tomatoes that are clipped off the vines to encourage the growth of large tomatoes, and then to buy, from the sixpenny tray outside the second-hand bookshop, a battered volume of Crabbe's poems in an embossed Victorian binding. And I can still remember the intense happiness of that morning, reading more and more Crabbe, and eating more and more

*Letters of Sylvia Townsend Warner, edited by William Maxwell. Viking, 1982.

bread, and all the tomatoes—with everything that I should have been doing, and even the things I ought not to have done and which would have been my natural occupation, all forgotten and amnestied. I read him *as though I were writing him;* there is no comparable excitement to that. And never again have there been such tomatoes, or such heavenly dry bread."

Among her friends in London were a certain number of bright young men whom she had known as little boys at Harrow. One of them, the sculptor Stephen Tomlin, carried her off to David Garnett's literary bookshop at 19 Taviston Street and introduced them. In *The Familiar Faces* Garnett has left a vivid portrait of her as a young woman. "Sylvia is dark, lean and eager with rather frizzy hair. She wears spectacles and her face is constantly lighting up with amusement and intelligence and the desire to interrupt what I am saying and to cap it with something much wittier of her own. I sometimes speak slowly, waiting for the right word to come to me and when I am talking to Sylvia it very rarely does come, for she cannot restrain herself from snatching my uncompleted sentence out of my mouth and giving it a much better ending. She quivers with eagerness as though I were really going to say something good and then dashes in and transforms my sentence and my meaning into a brilliance that I should have been the last person to have thought of. In her company I soon come to think I am witty, though vicariously witty, it is true.

"The first time that we met Sylvia spoke of the beauty of the Essex marshes and I suggested that we should visit them together on the following Sunday. It was a grey wintry morning and we spent most of it in the unwarmed carriage of a very slow train and later splashing through the mud while I listened, and Sylvia gave an extraordinary display of verbal fireworks. Ideas, epigrams and paradoxes raced through her mind and poured from her mouth as though she were delirious. Meanwhile we plodded under a grey sky across grey fields toward an invisible grey horizon. Finally we reached a bank of *zostera* and mud and the limits of the Thames estuary at high tide. Sylvia was right, the grey marshes had a melancholy eerie beauty that was all their own." In the late afternoon, after a long day's tramp through the mud, they climbed half-frozen into another empty badly lit railway carriage and were carried back to London. Too exhausted to talk, she was "the quiet intimate companion who sat beside me in the cold train with her clothes and even her face spattered with mud from the Dengie Flats."

She gave him one of her poems to read and he sent it on immediately to Charles Prentice at Chatto & Windus, who asked to see more, and published them. He then asked if she had ever thought of writing a novel and she showed him *Lolly Willowes*, which he also published, with considerable success.

Stephen Tomlin saw to it that she met Theodore and Violet Powys, whose acquaintance he had made on a walking trip in Dorset, and they became her friends as well. The Powyses lived in the village of East Chaldon, about a mile from the sea between Lulworth and Weymouth. On her visits to them she kept hearing of a young woman in the village who lived alone and who exchanged books with Theodore. She had been married at twenty and the marriage had been annulled. She wore trousers, which were not commonly found on women at that period. Not in Dorset, anyway. And she wrote poetry. Sylvia Townsend Warner's first meeting with Valentine Ackland was not a success. She felt afterwards that she had seemed aggressively witty and overtalkative, and she noticed that the younger woman was avoiding her. A year or so later Valentine Ackland wrote to her, asking if she would like to borrow her cottage for the summer, an offer she was unable to accept, but word of it got round, and the farmer who owned the cottage, assuming it was being sublet and probably for a vast sum, turned his tenant out of it at a week's notice. Feeling responsible, Miss Townsend Warner bought another cottage, with the idea that Valentine Ackland would live there. Shyness prevented her from being altogether clear about her intention. In the course of making this rather cramped and neglected place habitable they uncovered a depth of feeling for each other that bound them together for the rest of their lives. They lived in one place and another and finally settled permanently in a house by the River Frome, a short walk from the village of Maiden Newton, in Dorset.

Profoundly affected by what was going on in Germany at the time and believing that there was a very real danger of the madness spreading to England, they concluded that the only adequate defense against Fascism was Communism. In 1935 they applied for membership in the Communist Party of Great Britain and were accepted. Miss Townsend Warner's letters of this period sometimes have the irritating tone of the newly converted. In at least two of her novels, *Summer Will Show* (1936) and *After the Death of Don Juan* (1938), a political element is obvious. It doesn't take the form of propaganda.

In 1937 the two women went illegally—that is to say, the British Foreign Office refused to grant them a permit because they were not accredited journalists, so they went anyway—to Spain to take part, as guests of the Loyalist government, in a writers' conference. To a cousin Miss Townsend Warner wrote, "And think, dear Oliver, of hearing these words, *los intelectuales*, spoken, and never dreading them, never feeling the usual awkwardness and confusion of being a representative of culture. Think of hearing soldiers and people in small country towns, and peasants harvesting, speaking those words with genuine enthusiasm and understanding and kindness. Think, in fact, of being able to be, at last, genuinely glad, genuinely unembarrassed at being a representative of culture—not, as in England, a mock and scorning, not, as in USA, a sort of circus animal, but something that is really a credit to the human race."

In the summer of 1939 she and Valentine Ackland went to
New York to attend the Third American Writers' Conference,
called to consider the loss of democracy in Europe—an affair
invented and run by the Party, though many important writers
attended it who were not Communists. They came home in
October to an England at war, and took part, as fire wardens
and in other war-related jobs, in the defense of Britain. It is,
needless to say, a matter of chance which letters survive to fall
into the hands of an editor, but I have been struck by the fact
that the letters written after Miss Townsend Warner's return
from America no longer have the same political fervor. Or indeed mention the Party at all. The fact that they were living
deep in the country, with no petrol and with restrictions on
travel, does not seem, in itself, to account for this. There was
no counterpart in the British Isles of Senator McCarthy, and in
any case she was not an easily intimidated woman. On the other
hand, during the nineteen-forties she was writing for Edgell
Rickword's *Left Review* and *Our Time,* and for *Theatre Today*—
all Party-oriented publications. And there is a further piece of
evidence; at the New York conference she had admired a speech
by a young American Communist named Hope Hale about
writing for a working-class audience, and had entered into a
correspondence with her. In a letter written in 1962 she said
again how useful the methods outlined in the speech were "for
our purpose. I say, our purpose, for I hope you are still of the
same mind—as I am." Perhaps what she forswore, if she forswore anything, was activism. After Valentine Ackland's death,
in going through her things, she came upon and subsequently
offered to the poet Arnold Rattenbury a motor-horn which they
had used to take with them when they went to public demonstrations, to honk at policemen with.

*   *   *

An American friend, the poet Jean Starr Untermeyer, said again and again that she ought to submit something to *The New Yorker.*

At last, in order to prove that *The New Yorker* would not publish her—for she was somewhat irritated by this nagging—she did submit something, a hilarious piece called "My Mother Won the War." The battleground in question was local, a Red Cross committee where two equally high-handed women could not agree as to whether the soldiers' pajama trousers should have a button on them. It appeared in the issue of May 30, 1936. Over the next four decades *The New Yorker* published a hundred and forty-four stories by her, and nine poems. (If this isn't a record it is close to it.)

When Mrs. E. B. White, her first editor, left New York to live in Maine, I inherited Miss Townsend Warner. I had been reading her with delight since I was in college. I met her for the first time when she came to the *New Yorker* office in the fall of 1939. She was dressed in black. Her voice had a slightly husky intimate quality. Her conversation was so enchanting it made my head swim. I did not want to let her out of my sight. Ever. The dimensions of the Second World War were not yet clear, but there wasn't much to be optimistic about, even so. The Embassy was encouraging British citizens who happened to be abroad at that moment to stay there, rather than return home and become another mouth to feed. I begged her to remain in the United States, where bombs were unlikely to fall and we could continue our conversation. I didn't persuade her, but the conversation did continue, in letters back and forth and on the margins of galley proofs. Viz.: ". . . On galley seven I have substituted clattered for *flounced* for the noise that Rosalind made with the bucket. If you have a bucket handy, and some nice echoing floor, and snatch the bucket up and put it down again rather violently in much the same place that you took it from, that will be what I choose to call flouncing with a bucket; and

anyone who has taken part in church decorations, especially
at Easter when tempers are at their worst, will recognize the
action."

If storytelling had not appealed to her more, Sylvia Townsend
Warner might have been a formidable historian. She had a secure sense of what it was like to live in other times than her
own. Chaucer's England, France during the Revolution of 1848,
seventeenth-century Spain, Polynesia during the reign of Queen
Victoria. She also knew—and not merely from her reading—
what it was like outside the comfortable and cultivated social
class she was born into. She had a connoisseur's eye for the
bogus, and a hatred of the assumptions of privilege. Her heart
was with the hunted, always. An American woman who was
being shown around her garden, unfamiliar with *Bellis perennis*,
asked if it hurt English daisies if you walked on them, and her
reply was "It doesn't do anything good to be stepped on."
Along with an extraordinary fancy she had a deep understanding
of human behavior, so that nothing, no feeling, seemed to lie
beyond the reach of her imagination. Her finest short story is
about a love affair between a brother and sister. She considered
the innocent and the guilty with the same judicial and ironic
detachment. Her literary style is rather formal but not Manda-
rin. She had the true novelist's awareness of the wheel (the image
is hers) turning and turning in "the bright implacable river" of
life.

  Among her seven novels, I have a particular fondness for *Mr.
Fortune's Maggot, Summer Will Show,* and *After the Death of
Don Juan.* In a note on the composition of *Summer Will Show*
she said, "It must have been 1920 or 21, for I was still in my
gaunt flat over the furrier in the Bayswater Road and totally
engaged in *Tudor Church Music,* that I said to a young man
called Robert Firebrace that I had invented a person: an early

Victorian young lady of means with a secret passion for pugilism: she attended prize-fights dressed as a man and kept a punching-ball under lock and key in her dressing-room. He asked me what she looked like and I replied without hesitation: Smooth fair hair, tall, reserved, very ladylike. She's called Sophia Willoughby.

"And there she was and there she stayed. I had no thought of doing anything with her. A year or so later and equally out of the blue I saw Minna telling about the pogrom in a Paris drawing-room and Lamartine leaning against the doorway. And there she stayed. I had written my first three novels and *Opus 7* and *The Salutation* and was living at Frankfort Manor in Norfolk with Valentine when we went to Paris (1932, I think) and in the rue Mouffetard, outside a grocer's shop, I found that I wanted to write a novel about 1848. And Sophia and Minna started up and rushed into it.

"When we got back I went to the London Library for histories and memoirs, as close to the date as I could find. This was a lesson in history. Legitimists, Orleanists, Republicans all told incompatible versions of the same events, and several times didn't even agree on dates. But their prejudices made them what I needed. It was from one of these that I read how Marie-Amélie urged poor Louis-Philippe to go out and confront the mobs, adding, '*Je vous bénirai du haut du balcon.*' I reflected that this nonsense coincided with the Communist Manifesto, and this shaped the argument of the book. I read several guidebooks of that date, too, and discovered Columbin, who sold English buns, and the Dames Réunies, and I reread Berlioz's *Mémoires*, and with an effort put the French novelists out of my mind.

"Caspar came out of the Scotch branch of my own family tree. My grandmother remembered his black hand beside her white one when he arrived in Edinburgh as the little boy Uncle Alexander was interested in. She remembered, too, being held over a lime-kiln for whooping cough.

"The character I most enjoyed creating was Léocadie; she was so detestable and so estimable. In the end, I found she was the only person on her side of the fence who had enough stuffing to be set opposite Engels.

"I drafted the book in Norfolk, continued it in Dorset, ended it at Lavenham in Suffolk, where I had gone to be alone with it. Once it was begun, I wrote it with great impetus—too much impetus, for there are some howlers. The Sabbath candle should have been lit by Minna's mother, for instance. But mainly I was lucky. If one goes fast enough, one is less likely to trip."

Various accidents and impressions contributed in much the same way to the conception of her other novels, and the effect in every case is of an inevitability that makes assessment seem pointless; there is nothing like them nor, I think, ever will be. She also published eight collections of short fiction and four volumes of poetry. The early poems are compact and narrative, showing an influence of Crabbe and Thomas Hardy, the later ones abstract and philosophical. At the age of seventy she was prevailed upon to do a life of T. H. White. The result stands with the few perfect biographies. In her eighties she had a sudden late flowering and wrote some twenty stories about elfin kingdoms and their heartless inhabitants—stories that are of great beauty and that have such an appearance of authenticity that they suggest, like William Blake's account of a fairy funeral procession, a firsthand knowledge.

In the midst of an active life Miss Townsend Warner managed to keep a private journal, as yet untranscribed, that runs through forty notebooks. And she wrote letters, thousands of them. The letters from the first half of her life are written, more often than not, on a typewriter. After that they were usually by hand, I think because it was late at night when she sat down to them and Valentine Ackland was often unwell and she did not want to disturb her. At the beginning of the Second World War she wrote: "If I had known we would be left so long in Norfolk I would not have left my typewriter behind. My handwriting looks as elegant as a vine, but no one can read it; and the thought of being a lost hieroglyphic in one's own lifetime deters one from writing letters." Her handwriting is not really all that difficult, and nothing deterred her from writing letters for very long. It was not unusual for her to write two or three a day.

When the two women were separated for any reason they usually wrote at the beginning and end of every day, and these letters, love letters, largely through happenstance were preserved. After Valentine Ackland's death Miss Townsend Warner put them in the proper sequence and had them transcribed and wrote an introduction and connecting narratives, all with the idea that they should someday be published. She also put certain restrictions on their publication; they were not to be published during the lifetime of Valentine Ackland's sister and one other person, who is still living.

When the American novelist Anne Parrish died, in 1957, Miss Townsend Warner wrote to the executors, asking that her letters be returned to her. I assume that they were but do not know it to be a fact. They were not found among her papers and it is quite likely that she asked for them in order to destroy them. I do not think it occurred to her that her correspondence might be collected and published until she had finished transcribing and editing the letters to and from Valentine Ackland. In a letter written after I had agreed to be her literary executor, she said, "I will try to clear things away, or mark them for destruction. The people who were attached to me might, however, like a collected volume of my letters. I love reading Letters myself, and I can imagine enjoying my own."

The personal correspondence of writers feeds on leftover energy. There is also the element of lavishness, of enjoying the fact that they are throwing away one of their better efforts, for the chances of any given letter's surviving are fifty-fifty, at most. And there is the element of confidence—of the relaxed backhand stroke that can place the ball anywhere in the court that it pleases the writer to have it go. No critic is looking over his shoulder; the writer's reputation is not at stake—not that Sylvia Townsend Warner was much concerned with either. But consider this: "We were in Sherborne this afternoon, it was raining, and in one of the half-holiday classrooms a boy was practising the trumpet. Other more respectable boys were outside, holding pads and cricketing boots and looking at the sky and waiting for it to clear. Not so he. He was *not* playing cricket, he was enjoying both sacred and profane love, the virtue of practising his trumpet, the pleasure and rapture of playing it. Every note said so. Such flourishes! Such offended blackbird's squawks." And this: "I hope you have had the same moonlight nights there have been here: the downs like sleeping deities and a moonlit badger feeding on the lawn." And this: "I wish you could see the two cats, drowsing side by side in a Victorian nursing chair, their paws, their ears, their tails complementally adjusted, their blue eyes blinking open on a single thought of when I shall remember it's their suppertime. They might have been composed by Bach for two flutes." Though they are characteristic of the way her mind worked, sometimes her comparisons are so unexpected that I think even she herself must have been a little surprised by them.

Mr. Fortune, the missionary hero of her second novel, who went to the South Sea island of Fanua armed with tinned meats, soup-squares, a chest of tea, soap, a toolbox, a second-hand harmonium, an oil lamp, and a sewing machine to make clothes for his converts, found himself at the end of the first year with only one disciple, and by the end of the following year had lost his own faith. As he is on the point of leaving this paradise he remarks to himself sadly, "One does not admire things enough: and worst of all one allows whole days to slip by without once pausing to see an object, any object, exactly as it is." It is possibly the voice of his creator speaking through him, but in its context it is a very sad observation.

Her letters written when she was away from home pick up the place where she is bodily and send it through the mail: "Everything falls into our laps like ripe plums. We managed to arrive at San Lorenzo fuori le Mura at the same moment as a funeral—with such a hearse, gold angels all over its roof and sitting on either side of the coachman in a glistening black cocked hat and black cloak, and a fat priest in his vestments came out of the first coach like an overgrown dahlia, and roared his way through the service with a speed only to be matched by the speed of the organist, who kept on tripping him over with the first chord of the responses, like a rugby tackle. After that a sexton, equally brisk and efficient, tossed us and two stout travellers from Southern Italy into the confessio and left us to contemplate de Gasperi's coffin. After this riveting introduction we all went for an affable walk in the Campo Verano, where the simpler Southern gentleman was absolutely spellbound by the verisimilitude of a marble mattress (with a dead lady on it), and kept on poking his finger into its dimples with sighs of admiration. I thought the lady very fine, too, especially the lace on her nightgown; but he had eyes only for the mattress." The moonlit badger feeding on the lawn, the traveller from Southern Italy serve no larger plan or purpose. The boy with the trumpet exists only for that moment. He, in fact, *is* that moment. The experience rises from the page, unrevised, unimprovable. It resembles the play of fountains. Even when she is giving rein to a fancy, the image is exact, the scene recognizable: "There is a stretch of wooded round-shouldered hills near Leintwardine which seems Arthurian, it is so remote, so solitary, so *forgetful.* You know those landscapes that have forgotten centuries of history and now listen rather inattentively to what the woodpeckers have to say."

Her letters to people she saw frequently and was in very close touch with are, on the whole, less interesting (that is to say, they are like anyone's letters) than the letters to people who lived at a distance from her.

This correspondence with people in faraway places provides a running report on her life—on the weather, the annual arrival of gypsies, flowers blooming in the garden, Rembrandts at the National Gallery, *The Turn of the Screw* as an opera, a drinking old lady, Proust's shortcomings as a literary critic, the fountains of the Villa d'Este, the creatures of the river, often in flood, that flowed past her house, the pleasures of travel, politics, a dream of King Arthur and Merlin, remedies and recipes, Rupert Brooke at the Café Royal, the ingratitude and bad manners of the birds, a séance with the celebrated Screaming Skull, a Victorian merry-go-round signed and dated by the maker, a *crèche animé* in Provence, the physical benefits of singing, Goethe's Conversations with Eckermann, the mysterious being that walks overhead when she is downstairs and on the ground floor when she is upstairs, the Spanish Civil War, Blake's verbs, cold houses, thunderstorms, the Cuban Missile Crisis, swans, the parish magazine, divorce, what Edward Thomas was like, the inequity of the human condition, an impending guest, a bad fall, a sick animal, a perverse moorhen, and so on. To index the letters is pointless; everything is as interesting as everything else and it would be like indexing life itself. Better to think of her as she once described herself—Frau Noah leaning out of a window with a coffee cup in her hand admiring last night's flood and seeing everything exactly as it is.

Giacometti Working

Though there is no reason to disbelieve a word of James Lord's account* of sitting for Giacometti, it is best read as a short comic novel with two characters—an artist at the height of his powers and reputation who sometimes sits hunched over, his head and hands hanging toward the floor, thinking of suicide, and an American, somewhat younger, from a well-to-do family in Englewood, New Jersey. The artist has agreed to do a portrait of him. It has to be a quick portrait sketch on canvas that will take an afternoon at most. They have known each other for a long time and the American has written several articles about the artist, who lives and works in four rooms looking out on an open passageway in what has been described as one of the sadder parts of Paris.

On a Saturday in September, the year unspecified, James Lord arrived at the studio of Alberto Giacometti. He found Giacometti sitting by the telephone staring at the floor. Nearly an hour passed, during which he worked on various pieces of unfinished sculpture. Muttering irritably, he then inspected every single one of the fifteen or twenty paintings stacked against the walls. Finally he put a fresh canvas on the easel, poured turpen-

*A Giacometti Portrait. Farrar, Straus & Giroux, 1980.

tine into a little dish until it overflowed onto the floor, and picked up his palette and a bunch of brushes. As he worked he looked at Lord constantly and also at everything around him. After a couple of hours he said, "That's enough." He had completed the drawing of the figure and sketched in the background—a tall stool on the left, a potbellied stove on the right—and entirely painted in the face in black and gray. He moved away from the canvas to study it and then said, "It's a beginning, at least."

"A beginning?" Lord asked. "But I thought we were going to work only once."

"It's too late for that now," Giacometti said. "It's gone too far and at the same time not far enough. We can't stop now."

So Lord agreed to pose on Monday, and they went to a neighborhood café, where Giacometti ate his ritual lunch: two hard-boiled eggs, two slices of cold ham with a piece of bread, two glasses of Beaujolais, and two large cups of coffee. "If I could just do a head, one head, just once," Giacometti said, "then maybe I'd have a chance to paint a portrait. Ingres could do it. He could finish a portrait. It was a substitute for a photograph and had to be done by hand because there was no other way of doing it then. But now that has no meaning."

Lord said what about Picasso's portraits and Giacometti said, "I hate them. They're vulgar."

"But if you had to say which period of Picasso's you like best, which would it be?"

"None."

Lord remarked that Cézanne had painted some pretty good portraits. "But he never finished them," Giacometti said. "After Vollard had posed a hundred times the most Cézanne could say was that the shirt front wasn't too bad. He was right. It's the best part of the picture. Cézanne never really finished anything. He went as far as he could, then abandoned the job. That's the terrible thing: the more one works on a picture, the more impossible it becomes to finish it."

Giacometti preferred to talk as he painted. They both talked about all sorts of things: about Giacometti's trip to London, about how far away from the model van Eyck was when he painted the portrait in the National Gallery of a man wearing a red turban, about neuroses, about self-destruction. "The terrible thing about dying," Giacometti said, "is that you can only do it once. I've been rather attracted by the idea of being hanged. A beautiful strong rope around the neck."

By the end of the second sitting the head had become more elongated and vaguer than the day before, and was crisscrossed by black and gray lines and surrounded by a halo of undefined space. "There has been some progress," Giacometti said, "but we have to go further. We'll work tomorrow, won't we?"

At the third sitting, as he began to paint he said, "I've noticed that not only do you look like a brute full face but your profile is a little degenerate. Full face you go to jail and in profile you go to the asylum." They both laughed. The afternoon passed slowly. Giacometti said, "I've been wasting my time for thirty years. The root of the nose is more than I can hope to manage." Sometimes he said, "You've moved. Raise your head a little. . . . No, no, you were all right before. Lower it again."

The next day he said, "I'm not as tired today but I'm in a foul humor. I think I'll give up painting for good. . . . I simply can't seem to reproduce what I see." Presently he murmured, "There. The nose is in place now. That's some progress." And a few minutes later: "I know where I'm going now. I see how I can advance things a bit."

Lord, who had to get back to New York and already had changed his reservation twice, agreed to sit for another week. In the evenings, or sometimes on the spot when he was left alone for a minute, he made notes, which became the basis of this book: what Giacometti said, what happened that day in the studio. Each afternoon before the sitting began, Lord would take the canvas out into the passageway and photograph it. Giacometti had been exceedingly generous to him in the past and he had never been able to demonstrate his esteem and affection in a tangible way. Now at last, miraculously, just by sitting still, he was contributing something that was useful to Giacometti in his work. It was an unhoped-for satisfaction. When he tried to tell Giacometti this, he wouldn't listen. Presently he started gasping aloud and stamping his foot. "Your head's going away!" he exclaimed. "It's going away completely."

"It will come back." Lord said.

"Not necessarily. Maybe the canvas will become completely empty. And then what will become of me? I'll die of it!" Giacometti pulled his handkerchief out of his pocket and stared at it and with a moan threw it on the floor. Then he shouted, "I shriek! I scream!"

The next day, when the painting continued to go badly, Lord finally said, "Why don't we stop for the day? Shall I stand up?" and Giacometti said, "Yes, and put me out of my misery. . . . Don't move! I was only joking."

It began to get dark and again Lord suggested that they stop. After a while Giacometti's brother Diego came into the studio and said, "What are you doing?"

"I'm working," Giacometti said.

Diego laughed. "It's dark," he said. "You can't see a damn thing." When the lights were turned on they revealed that half the afternoon's work had disappeared into a gray vagueness.

Two days later, standing in the street with Lord and looking at the acacias, Giacometti remarked, "One should be a tree."

The sittings continued. The face on the canvas came in and out of focus. "Merde!" Giacometti cried. "You don't look at all the way you did before." And then, after a little while, "I'm destroying everything with great bravery." That day the sitting again went on until the light failed and Lord could no longer see the features of Giacometti's face, wreathed in cigarette smoke. "I like working in the dark," Giacometti said. He was not pleased, even so, with what he had done. When Lord was allowed to look he saw that the head seemed to be inside a small cage of lines. He said, "There has been some progress, though, hasn't there?"

"Oh yes. There is always some progress," Giacometti said, "even when things are at their worst, because then you don't have to do over again all the negative things you have already done."

Privately, to Giacometti's wife, Lord said, "But it could go on for months," and she answered, "Sometimes it does."

On the eighteenth day, when the portrait had passed through one transformation after another and had arrived at a state that was suddenly superb, Lord persuaded Giacometti to stop. They stood and looked at the canvas in the studio and then out in the passageway, from a greater distance. "Well," Giacometti said, "we've gone far. We could have gone further still, but we have gone far. It's only the beginning of what it could be. But that's something, anyway." Lord said that *he* thought it was admirable. "That's another matter," Giacometti said.

At the beginning of each chapter there is a photograph of the portrait in its various stages. The other portrait—Lord's of Giacometti—never goes out of focus or collapses into a gray vagueness or is anything but admirable. If there is a more endearing study of the artist as maniac, as child, as intelligence, as driven haunted slave, or selfless master, as who knows which of the nine orders of angels, I have not encountered it.

Bright as a Windblown Lark

Something more in the way of writing is to be hoped for from the autobiography of a poet than from most books of that kind. Laurie Lee's* begins: "I was set down from the carrier's cart at the age of three; and there with a sense of bewilderment and terror my life in the village began. The June grass, amongst which I stood, was taller than I was, and I wept. I had never been so close to grass before."

He was rescued by his three big sisters, who came scrambling and calling up the steep, rough bank and, parting the long grass, found him. "There, there, it's all right, don't you wail anymore," they said. "Come down 'ome and we'll stuff you with currants." It was the summer of the last year of the First World War, and 'ome turned out to be "a cottage that stood in a half-acre of garden on a steep bank above a lake; a cottage with three floors and a cellar and a treasure in the walls, with a pump and apple trees, syringa and strawberries, rooks in the chimneys, frogs in the cellar, mushrooms on the ceiling, and all for three and sixpence a week."

Shortly before this, his father, "a knowing, brisk, evasive man, the son and the grandson of sailors," had decamped, leaving his

*The Edge of Day. Farrar, Straus and Cudahy, 1957.

mother to bring up their four young children and four more by his first marriage—on what it would be an exaggeration to call a shoestring. But at least he didn't abandon them entirely; he sent them a few pounds a year, and though they were always hungry, they never quite starved, for the simple reason that they had neighbors. "See if Granny Trill's got a screw of tea—only ask her nicely, mind," his mother would say. Or "Run up to Miss Turk and try and borrow half-crown; I didn't know I'd got so low." And the child spoken to would say, "Ask our Jack, our Mother! I borrowed the bacon. It's blummin'-well his turn now."

"Our Mother" is larger than life-size. She was descended from a long line of Cotswold farmers, and the village schoolmaster, finding that she had a good mind, lent her books and took considerable pains with her, until her mother fell sick and she was needed at home and her father put a stop to her education. At seventeen, wearing her best straw hat and carrying a rope-tied box, she went into domestic service and worked as a scullery maid, household maid, nursemaid, and parlormaid in the houses of the gentry—an experience that haunted her, because she saw luxuries and refinements she could never forget and to which, her son says, she in some ways naturally belonged. "Real gentry wouldn't hear of it," she would tell the children. "The gentry always do it like this"—with the result that they, too, were haunted by what she passed down to them. She had been more than pretty, and she was still a strong, healthy, vivid, impulsive woman. She was also extravagant and a dreadful manager. They were often six months behind with the rent.

There would be no meat at all from Monday to Saturday, then on Sunday a fabulous goose; no coal or new clothes for the whole of the winter, then she'd take us all to the theatre; Jack, with no boots, would be expensively photographed; a new bedroom suite would arrive; then we'd all be insured for thousands of pounds and the policies would lapse in a month. Suddenly the iron-frost of destitution would clamp down on the house, to be thawed only by another orgy of borrowing, while harsh things were said by our more sensible neighbours and people ran when they saw us coming.

Add to a love of finery unmade beds; add to her anger, which did not last, her gaiety, which was indestructible. To the old newspapers that were knee-deep all over the house add—in bottles, teapots, dishes, and jugs—all manner of leaves and flowers: roses, beach boughs, parsley, garlic, cornstalks. Add to her detailed knowledge of the family trees of all the Royal Houses of Europe her genuinely kind, genuinely compassionate heart. The bus driver is honking his horn and all the passengers are leaning out of the windows and shaking their umbrellas crossly, and a voice, sweet and gay, calls from down the bank, "I'm coming—yo-hoo! Just mislaid my gloves. Wait a second! I'm coming, my dears." She drove her children half crazy; she infected them with the wonder of life.

Here she is getting supper:

Indoors, our Mother was cooking pancakes, her face aglow from the fire. There was a smell of sharp lemon and salty batter, and a burning hiss of oil. The kitchen was dark and convulsive with shadows, no lights had yet been lit. Flames leapt, subsided, corners woke and died, fires burned in a thousand brasses. "Poke round for the matches, dear boy," said Mother. "Damn me if I know where they got to."

Here she is with a sick child:

Then Mother would come carolling upstairs with my breakfast, bright as a windblown lark. "I've boiled you an egg, and made you a nice cup of cocoa. And cut you some lovely thin bread and butter."

And here she is in bed:

> My Mother, freed from her noisy day, would sleep like a happy child, humped in her nightdress, breathing innocently, and making soft drinking sounds in the pillow. In her flights of dream she held me close, like a parachute, to her back; or rolled and enclosed me with her great tired body so that I was snug as a mouse in a hayrick.

Though she bestrides the book, her largeness is not of the kind that results in somebody else's having to be small. The author says that there was no male authority in the house and that he and his brothers were dominated entirely by their mother and sisters, and yet he and the three other boys and every other man he writes about are thoroughly masculine. Somewhere, somehow, it all came out right.

They were not isolated. The stone house they lived in had once been a small manor house and was now divided into three cottages, in two of which lived two immensely old women who referred to each other spitefully as " 'Er-Down-Under" and " 'Er-Up-Atop" and lived only to outlive each other. One spent all her time making wine out of almost everything you can name, including parsnips. The other sat taking snuff and "biding still," and, if pressed, would take down the almanac and read about disasters to come, or tell the children about her father, who was a woodcutter and so strong he could lift a horse and wagon.

Gradually, little by little, the reader gets to know the people in other houses round about. The beautiful English landscape had a sufficient number of figures in it, and under the author's hand, one after another, they come to life. But not statically, not as set pieces or portraits, but as people who are being swept along in the current that flows only one way. Old people give up and die, children are picked up bodily, kicking and bawling, and carried off to school. The boys that were roaming the fields are lured under the hayrick and marry, all in good time, as trees come into leaf or shed their foliage, as plants come into flower. But not all of them, of course. For example, in the author's family there was another sister, who slipped away without warning when she was four years old, and every day of his mother's life she continued to grieve for and talk about that dead daughter, whose name is included, most touchingly, in the dedication of the book, among the living sisters and brothers.

The word I have been avoiding using all this time is "love." It is conveyed on virtually every page of this book. All kinds of love. And also, as might be expected of any place where love is amply present, murder and mayhem, fornication, incest, perversion, rape, suicide, grief, and madness. All of which the village managed in its own private way. Outsiders were not called in to punish or adjudicate, and when they came of their own accord, their questions were met by stares, and the information they sought after was given to every man, woman, and child of the village, in detail, so that they would know what it was they were to hide.

On the brighter side, here is the Parochial Church Tea and Annual Entertainment:

> The stage curtains parted to reveal the Squire, wearing a cloak and a deer-stalking hat. He cast his dim, wet eyes round the crowded room, then sighed and turned to go. Somebody whispered from behind the curtain. "Bless me!" said the Squire and came back.
>
> "The Parochial Church Tea!" he began, then paused. "Is with us again . . . I suggest. And Entertainment. Another year! Another year comes round! . . . When I see you all gathered together here—once more—when I see—when I think . . . And here you all are! When I see you here—as I'm sure you all are— once again . . . It comes to me, friends!—how time—how you—

how all of us here—as it were . . ." His mustache was quivering, tears ran down his face, he groped for the curtains and left.

His place was taken by the snow-haired vicar, who beamed weakly upon us all.

"What is the smallest room in the world?" he asked.

"A mushroom!" we bawled, without hesitation.

"And the largest, may I ask?"

"ROOM FOR IMPROVEMENT!"

"You know it," he muttered crossly. Recovering himself, he folded his hands. "And now O bountiful Father . . ."

The motorcar brought all this to an end. The last days of the author's childhood were also the last days of the village, the end of a thousand years' life, in that remote valley:

> Myself, my family, my generation were born in a world of silence; a world of hard work and necessary patience, of backs bent to the ground, hands massaging crops, of waiting on weather and growth; of villages like ships in the empty landscapes and the long walking distances between them; of white narrow roads, rutted by hooves and cart wheels, innocent of oil or petrol, down which people passed rarely, and almost never for pleasure, and the horse was the fastest thing moving. Man and the horse were all the power we had—abetted by levers and pulleys. But the horse was king, and almost everything grew round him: fodder, smithies, stables, paddocks, distances and the rhythm of our days.

Granted that one has to live in one's own Age or give up all contact with life; nevertheless, one puts this book aside not with nostalgia but with a kind of horror at what has happened. There was perhaps no stopping it, one thinks, and at the same time as one thinks that, one thinks that it should never have been allowed to happen, that our grandparents would not have put up with it—with the terrible, heartbreaking impoverishment that is not confined to a single village in a remote valley of the Cotswolds, or to any one country. It is all but general, and very few of us know, at first hand, anything else. Like a fatal disease, it has now got into the bloodstream.

Mrs. Woolf

The earliest surviving letter of Virginia Woolf is a note in block letters (she was six years old) to her godfather, James Russell Lowell. "Have you," she inquires, "been to the Adirondacks and have you seen lots of wild beasts and a lot of birds in their nests?" The letter is characteristic only in that it is deeply personal. As a young woman she was much given to cloying pet names and whimsey. This awful cuteness survives in her maturity only in the letters to Leonard Woolf, which are few, since they were seldom separated. For the most part the tone of her letters is affectionate and intimate—to a point where one feels at times that one is in the same room with her. ("I sit over a fireless grate with my head in my hands. Are you happy?") Books and writers are mentioned and commented on briefly, because how will the friends know what her life is like if they do not know what she has been reading? She allows herself to be funny: "We are now more or less settled. Of course, my necklace broke the first thing, but I think necklaces always do on getting into a new house." There are sentences that foreshadow the lyricism of the novels ("When you and Adrian are talking I plunge about in a phantom world, and wonder who the people are in hansoms, and what is going on in a certain place in the New Forest"). She starts to write a sentence about the weather and it turns into a story: "It pours, it pours, it pours; all the roofs from my window are like policemens waterproofs. Yesterday the Thames overflowed; and one poor old gentleman, being caught asleep on a seat, was marooned in midstream; lost his head; ran up and down like a polar bear at the Zoo, while the crowd collected on the Bridge and hooted." She describes the scene that is in front of her with an ease that carries everything before it: "From our garden we look over a dead marsh; flat as the sea, and the simile has the more truth in that the sea was once where the marsh is now. But at night a whole flower bed of fitful lighthouses blooms—O what a sentence!—but irritants are good I am told—along the edge; indeed you can follow the sea all round the cliff on which we stand, till you perceive Rye floating out to meet it, getting stranded halfway on the shingle." Surely this passage is a good deal better than those labored-over pages of italicized descriptions in *The Waves*.

A little more than half of the six hundred and thirty-eight letters in Volume I of her collected letters* are to Violet Dickinson, who was seventeen years older than she was, and on friendly terms with all the young Stephens. This gawky, goodhearted woman lived with a bachelor brother in Hertfordshire and moved in aristocratic and literary circles, with Virginia Stephen at her side. When Virginia Stephen suffered a severe mental breakdown after her father's death, Violet Dickinson took her into her house, under the care of three nurses, for several months. There would not be so many letters to her if Virginia Stephen had been merely fond of her. Like most love letters, they are embarrassing to read: "Is mother wallaby soft and tender

*The Letters of Virginia Woolf, edited by Nigel Nicolson and Joanne Trautmann. Harcourt Brace Jovanovich, 1975.

to her little one?" The impatient reader would do well to read
the first half dozen and then, since they are all pretty much the
same, skip-read, except for the letters written between November 7 and December 18, 1906. On his return from a tour of
Greece with his sisters and younger brother and Violet Dickinson, Thoby Stephen came down with typhoid fever and died of
it. By this time, Violet Dickinson also had typhoid fever, and
was very ill, and Thoby's death was kept from her. The bedside
bulletins continue, only now they are imaginary, and too well
done. It makes your hair stand on end: "Thoby is well as possible. We aren't anxious"; "There isnt much change. His temp.
is up to 104 again this afternoon, but otherwise his pulse is good,
and he takes milk well"; "Thoby is going on splendidly. He is
very cross with his nurses, because they wont give him mutton
chops and beer"; "Thoby sends his love"; and so on, ending
finally with "Do you hate me for telling so many lies? You know
we had to do it"—for Violet Dickinson, by now convalescing,
had picked up the *National Review* and in the midst of a criticism of Maitland's *Life* had read, "This book appeared almost
on the very day of the untimely death of Sir Leslie Stephen's
eldest son, Mr Thoby Stephen, at the age of 25."

Next to Violet Dickinson, the persons she wrote most frequently to are her Vaughan cousins and Lady Robert Cecil.
There is a very strange letter to Emma Vaughan that begins:

> Yes, it is all very well for you to be indiscreet—but what if
> you knew what I know? Have you heard that— No, I won't
> reveal other people's secrets. Still, she shouldn't go to a lecture
> if she can't control herself; or the Committee should put locks
> on the doors. Why she did it then, instead of waiting till—I
> can't make out; but for the last month or two I have suspected—
> from the color and shape and so on—well, she signs her name
> now with a hyphen.
>
> Poor cousin Mia! is it out at last? I was afraid that last meet-

ing at the Jolly Miller would do for her. Can you imagine? She drove up, in the village omnibus (which takes the Coroner about) at 6 o'clock—not more than a shawl over her shoulder, and her right leg bare. She asked if she were a flower bed that they raked her so?, and sang and sang about geraniums and roses. "Monty's in the cupboard!" she cried at last, and fell into the cistern, afishing for black beetles. But that's the beginning— Aunt Mary heard, and set off at once, in a veil with cupid in the border, chasing butterflies, and reached Rickmansworth just as Charlie was talking to the beadle. She sat with him beneath the plum tree in the garden till the sun went down and at night cried, "I'm only a little bag of bones—And the bed is so big!"

The editors suggest, in a footnote, that she was fantasizing on the contents of a letter just received, but to me it conjures up instead those flights of volubility that were a clinical aspect of her illness.

On the other hand, it is hard to imagine anything more sane or more straightforward than the letter she wrote to Leonard Woolf on May 1, 1912, in which she takes up all the reasons she can think of for and against marrying. "As I told you brutally the other day, I feel no physical attraction in you. There are moments—when you kissed me the other day was one—when I feel no more than a rock. And yet your caring for me as you do almost overwhelms me. It is so real, and so strange. Why should you?"

The visual world, exquisitely described, is everywhere present in her letters, the world of thinking almost never; ideas she saved for her diary. Leonard Woolf's political and journalistic activity is recorded, and so are the ups and downs of the Hogarth Press. Apart from the two occasions when he was called up before the Army Medical Board (he was excused each time because of the habitual trembling of his hands, which must have made typesetting a heroic task) and her asking Lady Robert Cecil to intercede with her brother-in-law Lord Salisbury on behalf of Duncan Grant, who was a conscientious objector, the First World War hardly figures in her correspondence at all. She did not believe in war, and hated patriotism ("Anyhow, please write occasionally, and for God's sake don't sacrifice anything to your country"), and she breaks off a description of the Armistice Day celebration with "But this must be fearfully dull to read about." Though as a matter of fact it wasn't.

There are not dozens of women writers of the first rank—which is not to say there mightn't have been if women had not everywhere and at all times in history been systematically discouraged from intellectual activity. Even though Virginia Woolf was, I think, a writer of the first rank, she could not rest secure in the knowledge of her talent; the prevailing tone of the letters written in her maturity is disparagement. When it is a game and when she means it one would have to have been acquainted with her to know. She and Leonard are invited to the Webbs', and the Bernard Shaws are there. "Shaw went fast asleep apparently, in the midst of all the talk and then woke up and rambled on into interminable stories about himself, and his backbone which is crooked, and his uncle who tried to commit suicide by shutting his head in a carpet bag, and his father who played on the ophicleide and died insane as they all do, and so on and so on."

If that could be merely an accurate description, here is a passage that is not: "I saw Forster, who is timid as a mouse, but when he creeps out of his hole very charming. He spends his time in rowing old ladies upon the river, and is not able to get on with his novel." One recognizes that it has a kind of truth but that it is also a deliberate distortion. It wasn't *because* he rowed old ladies upon the river that he couldn't get on with his novel. And neither was he timid. He might appear to be, if you didn't understand that he was fanatically considerate of the rights and feelings of other people. The truth is, she both liked and respected him.

The work of certain key figures in the Bloomsbury group tends to be overvalued, and almost everybody else is cut down not merely to size but to something considerably less than that: "Please tell me what merit you find in Henry James"; "Now I wish you'd tell me what is the point of Veronese"; "Delacroix I saw no point in"; "I went to see the Rodins at the Albert Museum. I didn't think at all highly of them"; "old decayed Cobden-Sanderson, wearing a red ribbon round his neck, and a workman's blue shirt—but not very inspiring all the same." Her dislike of *Ulysses* was such that it caused her to write in what amounts to personal hatred of Joyce, whom she had not met. It is a relief when she finds something that she has to admire unreservedly: "My great adventure is really Proust. Well—what remains to be written after that? I'm only in the first volume, and there are, I suppose, faults to be found, but I am in a state of amazement. . . . How, at last, has someone solidified what has always escaped—and made it too into this beautiful and perfectly enduring substance? One has to put the book down and gasp. The pleasure becomes physical. . . ." Four years after she had been asked to deal with James in a critical way, she read *The Wings of the Dove* for the first time and stopped being merely dismissive ("the laborious striking of whole boxfulls of damp matches") and confessed, "I have never read his great works; but merely pretended. Certainly this is very remarkable." But then habit asserts itself: "At the same time I am vaguely annoyed by the feeling that—well, that I am in a museum. It is all deserted. Only you and I and Melian Stawell and some wretched little pimpled spectacled undergraduate, and say Gilbert Murray, are to be seen. It is vast and silent and infinitely orderly and profoundly gloomy and every knob shines and so on. But—I am too feeble minded to finish—besides, little though you believe it—they are actually burying the white horse in the field; a man has arrived with two pick axes."

Sometimes one winces because the objects of her ridicule are such easy game:

> Then there was the theosophist, Mr Watt in the cottage which I once hired; and he lives on nuts from Selfridges, and a few vegetables, and has visions, and wears boots with soles like slabs of beef and an orange tie; and then his wife crept out of her hole, all blue, with orange hair, and cryptic ornaments, serpents, you know, swallowing their tails in token of eternity, round her neck. The rain, they said, often comes through the walls on a wet day, so I'm glad I didn't settle there. But can you [the letter is addressed to Lytton Strachey] explain the human race at all—I mean these queer fragments of it which are so terribly like ourselves, and so like Chimpanzees at the same time, and so lofty and high minded, with their little shelves of classics and clean china and nice check curtains and purity that I can't see why its all wrong. We tried to imagine you there, snipping their heads off with something very witty.

On the whole, strangers get off lightly compared to what happens when she is writing about friends:

> Lady Cromer is an old battered beauty wearing such a hat as you see on Bank holiday in the gutter. We talk about the revolution, and how it's high time that the daughters of Longleat (her father's house) stepped onto the scaffold. She buys herrings for her dinner, and as we walked along Cromwell Road in the moonlight, she had out her purse and turned the coppers, with which it was bursting, to bring her luck. Seeing an apple stall, where the apples were a penny less than in St John's Wood, she darted off, and there I left her, cheapening apples, while from her neck swung a dozen large cupboard keys, attached to a bootlace, for as she told me, one can't trust charwomen. Now all this, though written quickly, is quite true.

It may all be true (though I doubt it; it is too much a work of art), but the coldness of the eye that is recording that walk along the Cromwell Road in the moonlight! One might almost think she had been kissed by the Snow Queen. And consider this: "Rupert and Bryn came to tea the other day; she has a glass eye—one can imagine her wiping it bright in the morning with a duster." If it isn't pleasure in being cruel, what is it?

When she was young, she felt the sorrows of other people. Maitland died, of pneumonia, on a voyage to Tenerife, and she wrote, "I dont know that he would have minded dying, he was already so refined away that the body seems to be a small part of him. But he was very human and loveable—and everything to her and the children. I hate to think that they should begin to suffer. I was thinking that I should see him often, and perhaps he would come and dine with us—and anyhow he would be there always." Ten years later, speaking of Leonard's sister, she wrote, "Bella is dressed all in black silk, with long widow streamers. She . . . talks incessantly, and is always making jokes, though I gather she is really much depressed by the loss of her husband, who was practically the same thing as a cauliflower (he was a botanist) and he died in his bath." And, in another letter, "The other day we went to tea with Nelly Cecil, and met old Beatrice Thynne, who is more like a sunburnt tinker who has just had a mug of beer than ever, notwithstanding the death of her mother and nephew." A footnote reads, "Beatrice's nephew, John Alexander, Viscount Weymouth, was killed in action, 13 February 1916, aged 20." The letter continues, "She is going to live in lodgings over St Johns Wood post office, in order to economize; she uses margarine instead of butter; and wears no underclothes. She spends all her time reading family letters, and tying them up in bundles, as they are too many to burn, and all perfectly dull. Nelly"—here Lady Robert Cecil comes in for a few whacks—"is going to economize by living in Henry James' flat. It is wonderful how entirely detached from sanity the aristocracy are; one feels like a fly on a ceiling when one talks to them." These were both women she had been on affectionate terms with for fifteen or twenty years. People do, of course, make wicked remarks about their friends, and have days when they are uncharitable. With Mrs. Woolf it had become a game she could not stop playing. In another letter she says, "I dont like aristocrats when they write . . . they're all so rich and distinguished, and their writing is so much admired, and it is so pretty and smart compared with middle class writing. But I have no room to develop this very important argument." That "important" *is* ironical, isn't it? In either case, beside this railing against the privileged put "I dont like the children of the poor," and one begins to feel a lack of oxygen in the air. In fairness, one must put beside that still another remark—"Why the poor dont take knives and chase us out of our houses, I can't think"— and also Leonard Woolf's statement that there was something about her appearance and manner that made her stared at in the street, and sometimes even jeered at. "I am more charitable about them," she wrote mournfully, "than they are about me."

The letters to Violet Dickinson taper off after her marriage, and the person she then writes most often and most intimately to is Vanessa Bell. Because they lived near each other when they were in the country, her letters to her sister tend to be about practical arrangements—trains and taxis, outings with Vanessa's children, clothes ("Do you think you have any small Chinese coat or wrapper which I could wear in the evening while the Webbs are here?"), shortages of milk and sugar, and crises involving servants, whom they passed back and forth. The servants were given to making scenes and carrying tales and in one way and another making their presence felt. They came down with German measles. In the middle of the night they mistook the aurora borealis for a zeppelin and traipsed down to the kitchen with their bedding. Or they threatened to leave, and other servants were looked into. Mrs. Bell being housebound and also, one suspects, indolent, this is done by her sister: "Dearest, I've just been round to see N.F., as I thought it best to arrange that she should see you here, and find that she has already left 1 Gloucester Gdns and Mrs Parry tells me that she decided not to go as nurse, and also that she wanted to stay in Richmond. It seems hopeless therefore. Three other people have been after her, as parlourmaid and Mrs Parry said it was useless. I have the address of her rooms, and will try to see her tomorrow, but she was out today. I don't suppose its any good—though Great haste V.W. Let me know what you decide as soon as you can about Nelly and coming up. I'll write tomorrow." Letters such as this there is very little point in our reading more than half a century later. It was also necessary for the sisters to keep one another informed about who is coming for the weekend, since there was a certain amount of bicycling back and forth. And who is staying at Garsington and Tidmarsh, the country houses of Lady Ottoline Morrell and Lytton Strachey, figures a good deal in their correspondence. At that time, in that circle, visiting seems to have been a kind of secondary career, and laid one wide open to malicious detraction.

The letters to her sister often employ the language of court-ship, and I don't suppose Mrs. Woolf would have gone to such lengths in ridiculing their acquaintances if she hadn't thought it would give her sister pleasure. The same thing is true of her letters to Lytton Strachey, except that in writing to him she is not as easy and trusting, and one feels she is having trouble striking the right note about his sudden fame. The gossip is even more stonyhearted. The effect is unpleasantly like a performing dog or an overstimulated child. It is unreasonable to make moral judgments while reading a volume of letters. Mrs. Woolf wrote in the expectation of privacy. *"You ought to burn my letters always,"* she wrote to Vanessa, who didn't.

"Kindness don't flourish in our corner of Sussex," Mrs. Woolf wrote blithely. Prejudices did flourish. "But I admit its horrible to be rejected even by the coffee colored"; and, of T. S. Eliot's embarrassment when his friends tried to collect a fund for him so he could give up his job in a bank and devote himself to writing:

> Tom's psychology fascinates and astounds. There he has let us all go on writing and appealing for the past 6 months, and at last steps out and says he will take nothing less than £500 a year—very sensible, but why not say so at first; and why twist and anguish and almost suffocate with humiliation at the mere mention of money? . . . Very American, I expect; and the more I see of that race the more I thank God for my British blood, which does at any rate preserve one from wearing 3 waistcoats; enamel buttons on one's overcoat, and keeping one's eyes perpetually shut—like Ezra Pound.

We read other people's mail at our peril.

But where all this time was the writer? Tending to business. Writing *The Voyage Out* and *Night and Day* and the stories in *Monday or Tuesday* and *Jacob's Room* and innumerable unsigned essays and reviews for the *Times Literary Supplement,* and this letter to Gerald Brenan, in 1922:

> You said you were . . . wretched, and tore up all you wrote, and felt you could never, never write—and compared this state of yours with mine, which you imagine to be secure, rooted, benevolent, industrious—you did not say dull—but somehow unattainable, and I daresay, unreal. But you must reflect that I am 40: further, every ten years, at 20, again at 30, such agony of different sorts possessed me that not content with rambling and reading I did most emphatically attempt to end it all; and

should have been often thankful, if by stepping on one flagstone
rather than another I could have been annihilated where I stood.
I say this partly in vanity that you may not think me insipid;
partly as a token (one of those flying signals out of the night
and so on) that so we live, all of us who feel and reflect, with
recurring cataclysms of horror: starting up in the night in agony:
Every ten years brings, I suppose, one of those private orienta-
tions which match the vast one which is, to my mind, general
now in the race. I mean, life has to be sloughed: has to be faced:
to be rejected: then accepted on new terms with rapture. And
so on, and so on; till you are 40; when the only problem is
how to grasp it tighter and tighter to you, so quick it seems to
slip, and so infinitely desirable is it.

In 1922 Gerald Brenan had not published anything. He was a
forlorn young man living in a mountain village in Spain. She
hardly knew him. The letter is as much to us as it is to him.

2 — HER DIARY

The five volumes of Virginia Woolf's diary* add up to more than
seventeen hundred pages. The last entry is for March 24, 1941—
four days before she drowned herself. Not counting the introduction and index, the one-volume selection that Leonard Woolf
published in 1953 is only three hundred and sixty-five pages. In
the preface he remarks, "It is, I think, nearly always a mistake
to publish extracts from diaries or letters, particularly if the
omissions have to be made in order to protect the feelings or
reputations of the living." Among the passages that he cut for
this reason was a sentence about the bibliophile, bibliographer,
and editor John Hayward, who suffered from muscular dystro-

*The Diary of Virginia Woolf, edited by Anne Olivier Bell and Andrew
McNeillie. Harcourt Brace Jovanovich, 1977.

phy: "Has a great thick soft red lip: frozen green eyes; & angular attitudes like a monkey on a string." No doubt Hayward's feelings would have been hurt by Mrs. Woolf's description of him if it had been published during his lifetime. But there he is, preserved without particular malice but with no sympathy either, as he must have appeared. And here is another: "Willie Maugham came in: like a dead man whose beard or moustache has grown a little grisly bristle after death. And his lips are drawn back like a dead mans. He has small ferret eyes. A look of suffering & malignity & meanness & suspicion. . . . Sat like an animal in a trap: or like a steel trap. And I could not say anything that loosed his dead man's jaw." It would have been a great pity if, for any reason, the diary had never been published in its entirety. Mrs. Bell's ten-year labor of editing has provided a text that is trustworthy, and her crisp footnotes have left no question unanswered that could be answered.

"At the best and even unexpurgated," Leonard Woolf continues, "diaries give a distorted or one-sided portrait of the writer, because, as Virginia Woolf herself remarks somewhere in these diaries, one gets into the habit of recording one particular kind of mood—irritation or misery, say—and of not writing one's diary when one is feeling the opposite." Probably. But it seems to me that the image of Mrs. Woolf that emerges from her uncut diary is less distorted than the impression of her character that one has from reading her letters. If that impression is not entirely likable, it is perhaps because her letters tended to be a performance, and it is more entertaining to be savage about one's friends than to do them justice. But if it is for her own eyes only, her judgments are noticeably more rounded out, and more charitable. When she writes, after the death of Lady Ottoline Morrell, "To Philip to choose a ring & emotionalise," it is not Philip Morrell's grief that she is being sardonic about but the element of falseness in her own relations with that generous but also very odd and sometimes tiresome woman. Having read in a newspaper that Katherine Cox, who was devoted to her in her youth and helped nurse her during an earlier period of madness, had died of a heart attack, she wrote, "And what do I feel? Oh that one could feel more for the deaths of ones friends! But it comes & goes, feeling." After a neatly balanced list of the dead woman's virtues and exasperating qualities, she concludes, "I wonder, did she know she was dying? & what did she think of it all? And why? As usual, I regret: that she sent me cream at Christmas, & in the flurry of L.'s illness I never wrote & thanked; that she suggested coming, & absorbed in Nessa last autumn, I did not arrange it." But when her nephew Julian Bell was killed driving an ambulance in Spain, she grieved sincerely, without self-examination, and for a long time.

In general she was more candid about her feelings than most people manage to be: "Owing to my impulsive idiocy—saying I hoped to see him—Eddy Sackville has imposed his petulance upon us for this week end. Shall I tell him so? or must impulsiveness be punished? But remember another time how people grasp at straws. And how I hate being a straw." But she is also given to—the novelist in her is given to flights of understanding of the emotional situation of others. In writing about the death and funeral of her mother-in-law, for whom she had only a very moderate liking, she remarks, "I always notice the weather in which people die, as if the soul would notice if its wet or windy. . . . The truth was, age had taken everything away that was real, I think: only age left the pathetic animal, which was very real; the body that wanted to live."

"One cant dislike people in the flesh" is something that the letter writer would have hesitated to confess.

Through habit and so many years of practice her journal style attained a kind of nervous perfection of density and expressiveness. It was written at odd moments—usually before lunch, when she had finished working for the day—and in haste. When she does stop and consider something carefully, for example Elizabeth Bowen's stammer ("her whirr of voice as she cant alight on a word—a whirr of sound that makes the word quiver & seem blurred"), it is like an intense white light being focussed on the subject. There are items dealing with the Hogarth Press; with her literary jealousy (less as she grew older) and vulnerability to criticism; relatives and friends; her walks in London or in the country; plays; politics; public events ("The marriage stretches from one end of the paper to another. Pictures of the D. of York & the Princesses fill every cranny. Mrs. Simpson is snapped by lime light at midnight as she gets out of her car. Her luggage is also photographed. Parties are forming. The different interests are queueing up behind Baldwin, or Churchill'').

There are wonderful set pieces, as is only to be expected from the diary of a novelist. They spring from the page, almost without the help of words. The sounds of an English village on Sunday. The crowd gathered outside Buckingham Palace at midnight waiting for bulletins on the condition of George V, who was dying at Sandringham. A visit to Penshurst Place, the Elizabethan house of the impoverished Algernon Sidney, fourth Baron De L'Isle and Dudley. The offstage appearance and character of the actress Viola Tree. What is surprising when one goes back and rereads these set pieces is how little space they take.

The journal that has no bizarre or small domestic details is not likely to be very readable. One enjoys knowing that when Leonard Woolf found a drowned hedgehog in the lily pool he tried to resuscitate it. And, remembering how irritable that saintly man could be, smiles when the clumsy maid of all work trod on his spectacles. And is charmed by this entry for October 22, 1937: "Waking at 3 I decided I would spend the week end at Paris. Got so far as looking up trains, consulting Nessa about hotel. Then L. said he wd. rather not. Then I was overcome

with happiness. Then we walked round the square love making—after 25 years cant bear to be separate. Then I walked
round the Lake in Regents Park. Then . . . you see it is an
enormous pleasure, being wanted: a wife. And our marriage so
complete."

A conversation overheard in the ladies' lavatory of the Sussex
Grill at Brighton is preserved from oblivion. Likewise, tea with
Lady Colefax. There are entries dealing with writing and writers
("A[uden]. wants innumerable blankets on his bed; innumerable
cups of tea; then shuts the shutters & draws the blinds & writes");
with the books she is reading ("Home, & dine alone, & sleep
over Mr Clarkson's memoirs. He had a sexual kink, & a passion
for fish—ran Sarah Bernhardt's errands; & I suppose—but all
details are lacking, made 40,000 wigs for one show"); with her
fear that a loan of a hundred and fifty pounds to an improvident
friend will not be repaid; with improvements at Monks House,
their weekend place in Sussex. Abnormal mental states are studied as if they were a slide under a microscope ("I wish I could
write out my sensations at this moment. They are so peculiar
& so unpleasant. Partly T[ime] of L[ife]? I wonder. A physical
feeling as if I were drumming slightly in the veins: very cold:
impotent: & terrified. As if I were exposed on a high ledge in
full light. Very lonely. L. out to lunch. Nessa has Quentin &
dont want me. Very useless. No atmosphere round me. No
words. Very apprehensive. As if something cold & horrible—a
roar of laughter at my expense were about to happen").

Changes in the weather are noted, as they are in most diaries,
though of what interest it will be to the diarist to read at some
much later time that there was "a great gale all yesterday & a
dusk over everything & rain" it is difficult to see. However, it
offers a way of getting started. Motoring to Scotland, she sits
by the side of the road, under the Roman Wall, while Leonard
cleans the spark plugs. She tries to imagine what it will be like
to be old, to lose the power of sequence, be unable to prolong

an emotion. She remembers her parents: "How beautiful they were, those old people—I mean father & mother—how simple, how clear, how untroubled. I have been dipping into old letters & fathers memoirs. He loved her—oh & was so candid & reasonable & transparent. . . . How serene & gay even their life reads to me: no mud; no whirlpools."

The Woolfs have weekend visitors. Servants give trouble, and leave, and are later rehired. And leave again. And there are, of course, a great many entries about her work. Her refusal to believe that *Between the Acts* was as good as her husband and John Lehmann, the only two people who had seen the manuscript, said it was either brought about or coincided with a return of her madness and she chose not to go on living.

Though to judge by the diary alone she was not morbidly preoccupied with the thought of suicide, external events obliged her to dwell on it. There was every reason to believe that when the fighting in France ended, the invasion of the British Isles would follow. Leonard Woolf was Jewish, and she did not wish to live if he died. He kept a can of gasoline in the garage of their Sussex house for suicide, and it is obvious that this haunted her mind. On May 15, 1940, she wrote, "This morning we discussed suicide if Hitler lands. Jews beaten up. What point in waiting? Better shut the garage doors. This a sensible, rather matter of fact talk." And later on in the same entry added, "Mr Pritchard (the old one) dead at last. No, I dont want the garage to see the end of me. I've a wish for 10 years more, & to write my book wh. as usual darts into my brain." And on June 9th: "I dont want to go to bed at midday: this refers to the garage." But before any of this the reader is brought up short by the entry for August 17, 1938: "The old woman who lived up at Mt Misery drowned herself 3 days ago. The body was found near Piddinghoe—my usual walk. Her son died; she turned queer; had been a midwife in Brighton; lived in the broken windowed half of Mr Bradfield's house. She used to moon over the downs

with a dog. Once she came to the shop late on Sunday to beg
2d of paraffin—she was alone in the dark. They threatened to
turn her out—farm wanted. She had killed her dog. So at last
off she goes, on Monday perhaps when the tide was high in the
afternoon, & jumps in. Louie [the cook] says her brother found
a drowned woman the other day at Barcombe Mills—a horrid
sight." It seems possible that these two incidents were stored
away in the back of her mind and were reënacted in her own
drowning.

Throughout the final volume, the war comes nearer and nearer
until the German planes are flying over Monks House. "We lay
down under the tree. The sound was like someone sawing in
the air just above us. We lay flat on our faces, hands behind
head. Dont close yr teeth said L. They seemed to be sawing at
something stationary. . . . Will it drop I asked? If so, we shall
be broken together. . . . Then another came from Newhaven.
Hum & saw & buzz all round us. A horse neighed on the marsh.
Very sultry. Is it thunder? I said. No guns, said L."
    Her concentration is destroyed by a bomb dropping so close
that she curses, thinking it is Leonard slamming a window. They
become accustomed to the sinister sawing noise, which occurs
generally about eight-thirty in the evening, grows louder and
fades. Then begins once more. "Now & then theres a thud. The
windows shake. So we know London is raided again." While
they are outside watching a dogfight, the cook joins them, looks
at the sky, and then inquires if the fish is to be boiled or fried.
    They drive up to London, having been informed that their
house in Mecklenburgh Square has been severely damaged. At
eleven-thirty in the morning there is already a queue, mostly
children with suitcases, outside the Warren Street Underground
station. Their old house, at 52 Tavistock Square, is gone. "One
glass door in the next door house hanging. I cd just see a piece

of my studio wall standing: otherwise rubble where I wrote so many books. Open air where we sat so many nights, gave so many parties." In the Mecklenburgh Square house they find windows shattered, ceilings down, and most of their china smashed. "All again litter, glass, black soft dust, plaster powder. . . . Books all over dining room floor. In my sitting room glass all over Mrs Hunter's cabinet—& so on. Only the drawing room with windows almost whole. A wind blowing through. I began to hunt out diaries." At three o'clock, on their way back to the country, the line outside the Warren Street tube station has grown very much longer, with men and women now, carrying bags and blankets, queueing up for shelter during that night's raid.

Characteristically, Leonard Woolf figures how much it will cost to repair the damage, and she remarks in the diary, "But its odd—the relief at losing possessions. I shd like to start life, in peace, almost bare—free to go anywhere." The Hogarth Press was moved to Letchworth, in Hertfordshire, and the furniture and books from Mecklenburgh Square were stored at Monks House or in the village. After heavy rains, the River Ouse, nearby, overflowed its banks and the marsh became a sea with gulls on it. She read Michelet, cooked dinner, and listened to music. The butter disappeared while they were outdoors playing bowls; suspicion pointed to a voluntary collector for St. Dunstan's, whose card they found tucked in the door. And the bombs continued to fall on their part of Sussex. "Yesterday a raider came popping over the hill: L saw a smoke rise. In fact it was shot down at Tarring Neville. Louie says the country people 'stomped' the heads of the 4 dead Germans into the earth."

She tries to imagine what it would be like to be killed by a bomb. "I've got it fairly vivid—the sensation: but cant see anything but suffocating nonentity following after. I shall think— oh I wanted another 10 years—not this—& shant, for once, be able to describe it."

*　*　*

Years later, Elizabeth Bowen went to see Leonard Woolf at
Monks House and they had tea in the upstairs sitting room,
which was exactly as she remembered. He had gone on living
into his old age in the midst of her things.

ABOUT THE AUTHOR

WILLIAM MAXWELL was born in 1908, in Lincoln, Illinois. When he was fifteen his family moved to Chicago and he continued his education there and at the University of Illinois. After a year of graduate work at Harvard he went back to Urbana and taught freshman composition, and then turned to writing. He has published six novels, two collections of short fiction, an autobiographical memoir, and a book for children. For forty years he was a fiction editor at *The New Yorker.* From 1969 to 1972 he was president of the National Institute of Arts and Letters. He has received the Brandeis Creative Arts Award Medal and, for his novel *So Long, See You Tomorrow,* the American Book Award and the Howells Medal of the American Academy of Arts and Letters. He lives with his wife in New York City.

A NOTE ON THE TYPE

This book was set in a digitized version of Janson. The hot-metal version of Janson was a recutting made direct from type cast from matrices long thought to have been made by the Dutchman Anton Janson, who was a practicing type founder in Leipzig during the years 1668–1687. However, it has been conclusively demonstrated that these types are actually the work of Nicholas Kis (1650–1702), a Hungarian, who most probably learned his trade from the master Dutch type founder Dirk Voskens. The type is an excellent example of the influential and sturdy Dutch types that prevailed in England up to the time William Caslon (1692–1766) developed his own incomparable designs from them.